BEYOND TWISTED SORROW

BOOKS AND ARTICLES BY JAY A. GERTZMAN

Books

Pulp, According to David Goodis

Beyond Twisted Sorrow

Samuel Roth, Infamous Modernist

Bookleggers and Smuthounds:
The Trade in Erotica, 1920-1940

Articles

"Ineffable Blackness, but In God's Bosom:
Denis Johnson's Angels," Academia.com

"The Essential Western: The Searchers, Violence,
Rescue, and Family," *Mystery Readers Journal*

"Rural Noir on 'The Dark Fields of the Republic',
Paperback Parade, February 2021

JAY A. GERTZMAN

BEYOND TWISTED SORROW

SORROW

The Promise of Country Noir

DOWN&OUT
BOOKS

Down & Out Books
3959 Van Dyke Road, Suite 265
Lutz, FL 33558
DownAndOutBooks.com

Cover design by Margo Nauert

ISBN: 1-64396-270-1
ISBN-13: 978-1-64396-270-2

To Adele and Karin

And to the memory of my parents

TABLE OF CONTENTS

...And take me disappearing through
the smoke rings of my mind
Down the foggy ruins of time
Far past the frozen leaves
The haunted frightened trees
Out to the windy beach
Far from the twisted reach of crazy sorrow...
—Bob Dylan, "Mr. Tambourine Man"

For a transitory enchanted moment man must have held his
breath in the presence of this continent, compelled into an
aesthetic contemplation he neither understood nor desired...As I
sat there brooding on the old, unknown world, I thought of
Gatsby's wonder...His dream must have seemed so close that he
could hardly fail to grasp it. He did not know that it was
already behind him, somewhere back in that vast obscurity
beyond the city, where the dark fields of the republic
rolled on under the night.
—F. Scott Fitzgerald, *The Great Gatsby*

Now I could see Denver looming ahead of me like the Promised
Land, way out there beneath the stars, across the prairie of
Iowa and the plains of Nebraska, and I could see the greater
vision of San Francisco beyond, like jewels in the night.
—Jack Kerouac, *On the Road*

We're all Americans.
—Jay A Gertzman

PREFACE

"County Noir," a term Daniel Woodrell used but has since disavowed, includes fictions set either in America's desserts, plains, mountain wildernesses or in camps, "hollers," small towns, or declining cities of the Ozarks, Appalachians, rural South, Midwest, or Southwest. The setting varies, from the Civil War period to the present.

I consider to be essential John Cawelti's analysis of the binary contrast in the American character. One ideal is bringing law and order to a group of people congregating in an urban area. The other relishes a struggle with country wilderness . The contrast is between the heroes and heroines of "advancing civilization" and those sustained by the "free and natural life of the wilderness."

Country noir protagonists may have ties to the city and need to visit or live temporarily in an incipient metropolis, fast-developing, law-saturated, and avid for opera houses, elite schools, lecture halls, and centers of government and industry. But the western hero is a "man of the wilderness who comes out of the old 'lawless' way of life." "The most significant aspect of the Western," Cawelti concludes, is the relationship between the hero and the contending forces of civilization and wilderness.

Harry Crews is not exclusively a western or country noir writer, but the following statements are those of a person who needs contention with the wild: "So far as I can see, nothing good in the world has ever been done by well-rounded people. The good work is done by people with jagged, broken edges, because those edges cut things and leave an imprint, a design." He also wrote, "The world is wanting to take the teeth off us so we will be smoothly round. I prefer to keep the jagged edges."

The world of country noir is inhabited by native Americans, Mountain Men, ridgerunners, west Texans, cowboys, ranchers, hunters, homesteaders, rustlers, frontier marshals, social isolates, or most recently, by van dwellers travelling western highways. Its chroniclers have intimate knowledge of its "habitus," which includes language, temperaments, tastes in entertainment and lodging, clothing, food preferences, weaponry, and treatment of animals.

CHAPTER 1

Beasts of the Southern Wild, Country Noir, and 'The Old, Weird America'

Hushpuppy, a dynamic six-year-old, has the power to bring animals back to life. She hears their heartbeats "talkin' in codes." She lives in an abandoned trailer ("the shacko in the backo") in marshy water outside a levee which protects New Orleans. It's called The Bathtub, a small self-reliant community soon to become a ramshackle one. A monster storm is about to hit, which apparently does little damage to well-fortified New Orleans but engulfs outlying places. Hushpuppy's birthplace has little connection to modern culture, indeed subsisting off the discarded, recycled detritus of civilization—a rusted-out bus here, an engine miraculously brought back to life there, repaired fishing nets, oil drums, and cranky hardware. Referring to the clean, well-organized city protected by levees, "Wink" Doucet, Hushpuppy's fiercely aggressive, hard drinking father, sneers, "Ain't that ugly?" Hushpuppy chimes in, "They're afraid of the water like a bunch of babies."

The film *Beasts of the Southern Wild* is a display of the experience of the diverse, still-emerging genre of Country (or Redneck, Ridgerunner, or Ozark) noir: its reluctance to engage with the intrusive technologies that define people by surveilling their emails, financial records, voting patterns, demographics, and entertainment preferences. This genre's protagonists resent being forced to adapt to the lockstep regime of mass production. They have an instinct for community as a coherent territory and recreate the possibly self-destructive but stubbornly self-assertive traits that characterized what Greil Marcus called "the old, weird America."

The film's depictions of New Orleans' citizens—doctors, nurses, babysitters in the evacuation center—are not negative. These city folk offer bodily survival. But the evacuators get rough with Wink, and with three students from their teacher Bathsheba's class, when they resist being taken to safety. The "monolithic community center surrounded by a cement parking lot" (filmscript stage direction) is ironically named "open arms processing center." The kids are taken to school where a teacher dresses Hushpuppy up and lectures her about good manners. Modern science, technology, and medicine are anathema to her. Her father and her Bathtub neighbors taught her that. Although Wink is very ill, the prospect of dying while "plugged into a wall" enrages him. His friends risk their own freedom to liberate him from the New Orleans hospital.

The necessity of such an act is epitomized by Ozark novelist Daniel Woodrell, in an interview following the success of his novel *Winter's Bone* (also about father-daughter loyalty): "It's better to be poor than be beholdin'; wealth is not the object of life…personal honor yet means a great deal, so be polite as long as you can and don't run when you can't be." Or, as Harry Crews stated in an interview, "The world is wanting to take the teeth off us so we will be smoothly round. I prefer to keep the jagged edges." So does Hushpuppy, after she is lectured about politeness, "decent" clothing for a child her age, and respectable vocabulary.

After the storm lays waste to The Bathtub (Figure 1-1), self-help and community cohesion sort things out. They gather at Lady Jo's bar, refurbish the shacko into a kind of boat, stockpile shrimp, crab, and land animals, and continue to celebrate more holidays "than the whole rest of the world." But another invasion of nature is coming, one which is leveling human habitation everywhere. It is the eponymous Beasts, a horde of prehistoric cattle known as Aurochs. These are the pitiless, blank-eyed "rough beasts" of Yeats's "The Second Coming:"

Mere anarchy is loosed upon the world,
The blood-dimmed tide is loosed, and everywhere
The ceremony of innocence is drowned...
Surely some revelation is at hand;
Surely the Second Coming is at hand.

It's possible that the monsters are in Hushpuppy's imagination. The impending death of her rough-edged powerhouse father means the end of her childhood world. The Aurochs have broken free from ancient icebergs and cannibalize each other as they march through the world, on their way to the Delta. Uncannily and prophetically, Bathsheba, Hushpuppy's teacher, sports on one thigh a tattoo of an Auroch. "Ain't gonna be no Bathtub, just a whole bunch of water. Y'all better learn how to survive."

Critics loved Lucy Alibar and Behn Zeitlin's film because above and beyond depicting impending catastrophe, it is aflame with joy (it is adapted from Alibar's play, *Juicy and Delicious*). The film dramatizes the ways by which a six-year old becomes capable of absorbing the strength of a dying father. The most blissful scene, a vivid "ceremony of innocence," is set in the Elysian Fields, a floating fleshpot, dance hall, and jazz parlor. There, Hushpuppy, having absorbed in a final embrace her father's spirit, completes her education. Hushpuppy's resourcefulness in confronting—not opposing or walling out—nemesis is embodied in the performance of Quvenzhané Wallis, whom Zeitlin discovered in a swampy Delta community eighty miles south of—and much more remote, in spirit and culture—from New Orleans. Its inhabitants sense how much more fun it is than the Big Easy. At the end, an Auroch at least ten times the size of

Hushpuppy stops directly in front of the determined, unafraid girl as if waiting for her orders (Figure 1-2). This event resonates with a story the Buddha's followers told: a mad elephant rampaged through the streets. Everyone fled. The Buddha remained tranquil. The beast stopped; the Buddha patted its leathery trunk. It's an act of intuitive communication. Hushpuppy, like the Buddha, is without anxiety, suspicion, or jealousy.

The film was post-Katrina. That made its display of harmony and balance a return to an American ideal long quiescent, because it had been venally exploited by the bad faith of promoters of "priceless" consumerism. That abeyant ideal promotes an optimism that merges radical individuality, pride, and earthly common sense with the humane. Perhaps that is why *Beasts'* admirers praised it as "the film of 2012."

Storm and pitiless rampage may win. In the film's last scene, the Auroch may be relishing in the staunch little Hushpuppy blocking its path a juicy and delicious snack. It does not happen. Hushpuppy, her dying father, and her prophetic teacher Miss Bathsheba, have made her "an orphan in a heaven of mothers." They are joined by a mother-substitute Miss Frankie ("c'mon, smile. Awww"). The isolated, close-knit community and its irrepressible survival instincts lead viewers to imagine *Beasts* as a resplendent victory over sinister flood and rampage. It's a victory only active adventurers, who can stare back at slobbering fire-breathers, can conceive, and achieve. Of course, it may cost such people their lives, as it did in the case of Hushpuppy's teacher.

Beasts' ending is an idiosyncratic closure for a country noir story, where there is little of the juicy and delicious. Rural fiction's protagonists struggle to replace a set of convictions which no longer sustain community or family. Often enough, their struggles produce a generational survival of perseverance, family and clan mutuality, the need for passing tough tests, and spirituality. Add to that an implicit turning away from the culture beyond the militant, surveilled wall, where the power of guilty nightmare governs, taking the form today of "immigrant terrorists," "basket of deplorables," or "tyrants [even if duly elected] who kill their own people." The message is "be very afraid." Wink has bequeathed to his child what she needs to face and face down the implacable, and escape "twisted sorrow."

Below are some themes from *Beasts of the Southern Wild* that are fundamental to country noir.

Bone-deep Resourcefulness

Chris Offutt's story collection *Kentucky Straight* begins with a map of the hillside where the stories take place (it is on no state map). In "Sawdust," a young man walks a considerable distance to sign up for a GED equivalency exam. His father wanted to be a veterinarian but had no clothes suitable to wear. The son passes the GED; his folks think just to take it is "getting above my raisings." But he's not going anywhere, despite a resourcefulness his father, hampered by pride in his own raisings, could not touch. He starts collecting empty bottles to pay back the exam fee. Another Offutt set of short stories, *Out of the Woods*, features "High Water Everywhere," in which a truck driver is jailed on suspicion of blowing up a dike after being seduced by a woman who was, she confesses, the culprit. Cleared of the crime, he decides he wants to go home, because his home is similar to the place he now finds himself. "He needed a heavy load to keep him stable." That sounds like Wink and Hushpuppy—both of whom are part of a community that, under stress, brings out its citizens' unique individual strengths. They are those scrutinized distrustfully by outsiders. Both, like Offutt's characters, will leave a loving legacy where it counts.

Bonnie Jo Campbell's "King Cole's American Salvage" is about an ex-con, Slocum, who desperately needed money to help his girlfriend keep her house and feed her kids. They are his informal family. He nearly kills a junkyard dealer to steal what he needs. He loses everything by being careful to take all the blame on himself. His drinking buddy, nephew of the dealer, who told Slocum that his uncle carried a lot of cash, lied about that on the stand. He envied his friend's bravery, even though Slocum's girlfriend, who gladly took the stolen money and washed the blood off the bills, had abandoned him. The difference between Slocum and the friend and lover, both of whom had betrayed him, has little to do with guilt and more to do with fear of the law and acceptance of being "beaten down." As the accomplice returns to his menial job at the salvage shop, which now includes caring for the brain-damaged dealer, he envies Slocum because he will have fellow prisoners to talk to. His own prison is inside his head, and his sentence will be life. In the accomplice's own words, the biggest difference between Slocum and his betrayers is that the latter will always be "beaten down," no match for an Auroch, while Slocum, who, despite his being a convicted felon, has a close bond with a set of comrades like those Miss Bathsheba, Wink, Miss Frankie, or Hushpuppy enjoy, could believe himself to be a match for one.

A Heavy Load for Rural America

What if the feral Aurochs come disguised as a nationwide necessity—as inexorable progress? How does one strike out at an all-encompassing set of events producing financial and social changes that cast aside habitual ways of working, seeking sustenance, raising families, joining communal institutions, keeping healthy, and being rooted? In 1976, Labor Secretary Earl Butz declared that farmers must "adapt" to the need to produce more crops and sell them abroad, or "die." The survivors would be farmers who had resources to buy high-end equipment and contract with foreign markets. The remainder would face decreased governmental help.[1] That policy has had effective critics, and wealthy corporate-related supporters. One echo of this at present is that skilled and unskilled workers, having lost union protection during the 1980s, are increasingly being replaced by automation. Once self-sufficient rural areas were reliant mainly on local farmer's crops. They are no longer needed when agribusiness can provide genetically engineered food, transported daily straight to supermarkets and kitchens. A town's long-established suppliers to small farms are no longer needed as well.[2]

In the hill country of Southern Indiana, dollar stores and their substandard items have no competition. Abandoned cars and houses, shuttered main street businesses, decaying roads and bridges, and minimum wage jobs are all signs of worsening poverty. Employees serving in fast food restaurants, doing custodial work in malls or gambling venues, and laboring in meat-packing plants cannot expect any financial security. If mining coal is one's occupation, one can expect lung diseases and a short working life. In Alabama, miners working at reduced pay under threat of company closure endured a month-long strike for adequate health care and pensions. They had been forced to work excessive hours in a deep mine leaking methane gas. The corporations responsible know they will find less organized resistance in areas where distances between folks are greater,

---

[1] James Rissner and George Anthan, "Why They Love Earl Butz," *The New York Times*, June 13, 1976, p.195. https://www.nytimes.com/1976/06/13/archives/why-they-love-earl-butz-prosperous-farmers-see-him-as-the-greatest.html.

[2] See Marc Steiner, *From Appalachia to Wall Street, How the US Created an Oligarchic Dystopia*, The Real News Network, May 18, 2021. Jeffrey St Clair's essay, "The Dollar General Theory of Money and Employment (https://www.counterpunch.org/2021/08/29/the-dollar-general-theory-of-money-and-employment/), describes the lack of competition for dollar stores. The article is subtitled "The Retail Carrion Feeders of Rural America." See also Nick Shaxson, "Rural America Doesn't Have To Starve To Death," *The Nation*, March 2/9, 2020, pp.13-17.

means of transportation more problematical, working hours longer, and lawyers' fees unaffordable. Pride of place and kin is replaced with a drug-and-alcohol-driven desperation.

People without cars have trouble getting to work. Credit from banks is harder to get. With diminished resources, they share out-of-date prescriptions and drive long distances over decaying roads. Fracking operations and strip mining provide infusions of cash but contaminate the farmland and wells. Toxic fires burning for years in West Virginia or Pennsylvania coal mines further damage health and property values. On March 31, 2022, CBS Evening News aired a segment on "food deserts": "A growing problem is leaving…vast rural populations without enough grocery stores."

It is rural areas where these disasters occur and persist. If there is one event that outlines in bold relief the vast and alienating injustice that resulted in the blighting of rural towns, it is the OxyContin racket. Over 130,000 victims of Purdue Pharma's painkiller filed suit for addiction or severely damaged health due to overdose. The company's marketing tactics made users—and doctors—believe there was no addictive effect. A "serious and complex public health crisis" resulted. Perdue was run by the Sackler family, who made billions from the operation. In September 2021, a bankruptcy court filed its papers. The Sacklers will pay over four billion dollars; the complete final settlement was for 10 billion. But much of this money will go to municipalities, corporations, and lawyers. Only $750 million will reach the victims. The Sacklers agreed to the settlement because it exempted them from any further legal actions. It was a get out of jail free card, and a free pass for them to increase their fortune to further obscene levels. The former chair of Purdue, Richard Sackler, denied any responsibility for the crisis. The family's only reason for agreeing to the decision, he opined, was to help complainants. But when OxyContin first appeared, he bragged of a "blizzard of prescriptions that would bury the competition."[3] Two New York museums, on the boards of which a member of the Sackler family sat, are no longer accepting donations from them. You can imagine the sneers with which that news was greeted by victims of the Sacklers' Purdue Pharma in areas throughout the country where a visit to New York was even less possible, or desirable, than before.

When OxyContin was banned, meth and cocaine became drugs of choice. As of 2021, fentanyl use had pushed overdose deaths to a new high. The largest "year-over-year increases—exceeding 50 percent—[have been] in California, Tennessee, Louisiana, Mississippi, West Virginia, and Kentucky."[4] Naloxone can prevent overdose fatalities, but states have been recalcitrant in making the drug available. What Big Agriculture started with its steamrolling of small farmers, Perdue Pharma made semi-permanent.

Opioid Addiction means a small-town economy falls into the grasp of drug distributors. Sheldon Compton's *Brown Bottle*, discussed in Chapter 6, dramatizes this development. Law enforcement must form symbiotic relationships with the criminals. Young adults turn from their birthplaces and from parents whose sources of comfort have atrophied. Folks from the hollows, mountains, and villages of Appalachia or the Ozarks find themselves leaving home to seek work in the information society's offices, entertainment centers, salesrooms, or service centers. Young married couples must live close to schools and hospitals, learn

---

[3] Ryan Hampton, "Betraying the Victims of the Opioid Crisis, *New York Times*, Sept 12, 2021, p.2, Sunday Review Section; Brian Mann, "The Sacklers, Who Made Millions from OxyContin, Win Immunity from Opioid Lawsuits," *All Things Considered*, Sept 1, 2021. See Patrick R Keefe, *Empire of Pain: The Secret History of the Sackler Dynasty* (NY: Doubleday, 2021).

[4] Roni Rabin, "Overdose Deaths Reach New High as the Pandemic Spread," hpps://www:/nyimes/2021/11/17/health/drug-overdoses-fentanyl-deaths.html

computer skills, and even place aging parents in institutions, a betrayal unthinkable to a previous generation. Some must brave curses of loved ones who are fighting to keep alive independent means of support inherited by parents and grandparents. Confronting the loss of one's home ground, his/her territory, is a bewildering burden. That's how powerful de-territorialization can be.[5] It's a heavy load which, in these circumstances, keeps no one stable. "The fabric of the universe is coming all undone," Miss Bathsheba says in Alibar's play. I discuss in forthcoming chapters stories that embody such psychic pain, for example Compton's *Brown Bottle*, Woodrell's *Winter's Bone*, Rash's *Something Rich and Strange*, Offutt's *Kentucky Straight*, and Post's *Lightwood*. If Breece Pancake had lived to complete the novel *Ottie*, we would have a first-rate depiction of a man restrained through guilt from forming attachments with others. His foster father blames him for his own son's brain injury. Ottie knows the accusation is false, but it, combined with lack of education and job opportunity, inhibit him from fighting it, and thus establishing respect in his home town. He becomes a replacement worker for striking employees, a "scab."

Ridgerunners are more likely to die from car crashes, drugs, cancer, stroke, and heart disease than urban flatlanders. As the small-town population thins, federal and state divestment from relief funds make recovery increasingly difficult. A 2018 report from the UN's Human Rights Council found a sharp decline in jobs due to factory automation. That report explains why rural women find work harder to find, and suffer from lack of adequate transportation, child care, and health care. The closing of rural hospitals and health care centers (nineteen in 2019) in the last

---

[5] The term usually refers to the cultural adaptations immigrants go through as they conform to the habitus of a location disorientating to them. I use it to refer to the agonizing anticipation of breaking bonds to family, friends, and institutions when bewildering socioeconomic forces make such disruptions necessary. Pancake's stories are exemplary.

decade makes treatment problematic.[6] People who live near or below the poverty line have to economize on medicines, vegetables, warm clothing, or fuel to hold on to their homes, especially renters, as rental assistance is sparse. As Nick Reding[7] puts it, lawmakers and employers pay far more attention to "government lobbyists, long-term trends in the agricultural and pharmaceutical industries, and the effects of globalization and free trade."

As a result of improvements in the safety net in 2020 and 2021, poverty in America has been reduced. But more than half may fall into poverty as some point. Social class is a great determiner: the offspring of a father on or near poverty level stand a much higher than average chance of being poor. With the ever-growing concentration of money among the richest individuals, upward mobility becomes harder. Food stamps force recipients to buy canned instead of increasingly expensive fresh meat and vegetables. "Red State America is suffering what used to be described as inner-city ills: drug use, family breakdown, and joblessness."[8] And all this despite the Republican administration in power from 2016 to 2020, and the advantage of states with rural populations over urban ones in the Senate, and perhaps in the House of Representatives.[9] Organizing lobbies takes donations and agenda-shaping that is all the more difficult when citizens

---

[6] Editor's note, "The Conversation," 13 April 2020 (us.newsletter@theconversation.com), discussing the increased risk of Covid infections in rural areas, where 30% of Americans live. Becca Andrews," A Far Cry: Another Way Trump Hurts Trump Country" (stress on rural hospitals: higher disease and death rates). *Mother Jones*, July/August 2018, 68-71.

[7] Methland: The Death and Life of an American Small Town (NY: Bloomsbury, 2009), 16 (also see Epilogue).

[8] Jason DeParle, "A Historic Decrease in Poverty," *New York Review of Books*, Nov. 18, 2012, pp.17-19.

[9] Elizabeth Kolbert, "Poles Apart: Can American Politics survive an Era of Hyperpartisanship? *The New Yorker*, Jan 3 and 10, 2022, pp.68-72.

with little time and money to spare struggle to find everyday necessities for their families.

Rural noir novelist S A Cosby describes his fictional town of Red Hill, Virginia (in his *Blacktop Wasteland*): Most of the jobs have left town "on the first thing smoking". There is an unenforced social segregation. There is a black part of town and a white part. A wealthy part and a poor part...Miles and miles of cornfields separate you from your neighbors. Single lane gravel roads that connect you to the main part of town like arteries where the light dies quick after the sun goes down. Red Hill is a dying town bleeding people. " But he also says,

> I love my hometown. I love the magnolia trees that line my mamma's driveway. I love going fishing down on the river. I love walking through the woods behind my house, seeing a fawn and its mother in my backyard. I refuse to let that be taken from me, and I refuse to let it be erased.[10]

A fine social document is Sarah Smarsh's memoir of her growing up poor in Kansas.[11] To her struggling but hardworking extended family, contempt for and shaming of people like them seemed to originate in legislatures, suburbs, university centers, and health care administrative centers. The Smarsh family found the social service system inaccessible and patronizing, as

---

[10] "David Joy in Conversation with S A Cosby," August 20th, 2020. https://www.murderbooks.com/Joy-Cosby. Available on YouTube.

[11] *Heartland: A Daughter of the Working Class Reconciles an American Divide* (NY: Scribner, 2018). A book with a very different point of view is J D Vance's *Hillbilly Elegy*. Vance grew up in Middletown, Ohio. He describes middle class prejudices regarding his family and friends, and analyses the behavior patterns of rural underclass culture that prevent people from adopting middle class values and ambitions. Vance was a leading Republican candidate for Senate as of May 2022.

Hushpuppy and her father did when they were brought to a New Orleans hospital while escaping from a flood. Integral to that kind of impersonally regulated culture was a class-based core identity group of well-off professionals. This attitude had first become ascendant in newly-expanding, Gilded Age cities of the West at a time when the frontier was closing. White-shirted "paper collars, "nabobs," "swelled-up men and high-toned ladies" downrated people working in farms, fields, mines, or in service jobs.[12] For prosperous citizens, "decency" and "respectability" became watchwords. These folks would have patronized people like the Smarshs or the Cosbys, Natty Bumppo, Hugh Glass, Wild Bill Hickok, Judge Roy Bean, Calamity Jane, Jesse James, Wyatt Earp, and Doc Holliday were persona non grata once there was a right side of the tracks, and a wrong side, where the young had to develop toughness, wanderlust, physical assertiveness, belligerent suspicion, and home-grown pride.

Endless Wars, Resentment, and the Heartland

Country noir writers often confront our endless-war culture from the point of view of veterans from the Heartland (Joseph Haske's *North Dixie Highway*; Larry Brown's *Dirty Work*; Breece Pancake's "The Honored Dead"; Rusty Barnes's "O Saddam!"). Their protagonists take their traumas back to the upper Midwest, the Rural South, the Ozarks, and Appalachia, where the natives they grew up with express their loss of hope in a viable future by picking fights with bar owners, police, or rivals for jobs; hurting loved ones; beating on other drunks; or drowning bad memories in alcohol or meth. The daring, possibly self-destructive behavior of the Southwestern cowboys, Great Plains and northern Michigan outdoorsmen, and Appalachian and

---

[12] A B Guthrie, Jr., *These Thousand Hills* (NY: Houghton Mifflin, 1956), pp.109-10.

Ozark ridgerunners, all facing desultory futures in "distressed" areas, is fully described by Rusty Barnes, Chris Offutt, Joseph Haske, David Joy, Leah Hampton, Bonnie Campbell, Frank Bill, Eryk Pruitt, and Annie Proulx, among others.

Despite our endless wars, the nation depends on citizens to consume (as George W. Bush, standing alongside a box store attendant in a TV commercial, encouraged them to). Products need to be manufactured, but there is no obligation to evenly distribute them. The standard of living of the "less educated" stagnates, while the urban bureaucratic class, with skills in technology, merchandising, advertising, and distribution of goods, increase their salaries and resources. For these citizens, especially if they have exemptions from service and benefit from regressive tax law, war may be said to be peace. However, farmers and small-town merchants, regardless of their level of formal schooling and income, are much less able to pay increased taxes for combatants' injuries, training of replacements, and new military and surveillance equipment. Improvements they desperately need in education, infrastructure, and heath and child care are "postponed," media jargon for "scrapped." People who do find jobs have little in the way of financial security, especially if they have to sign contracts stipulating they will not leave their present employment if a similar job becomes available.

If there is any bureaucratic operation in which war is efficient, it is in keeping an enervating status quo in place. War does create new jobs, but others are lost. For vets lacking a GED or high school education, taking advantage of the GI Bill requires additional study. Even with adequate qualifications, they are stymied by the problem of not being able to compete with college prepped students, who are far ahead in this game. In Chris Offutt's "Sawdust," a young man earns a GED. "It struck me funny that I had to take a test to learn that I was living in poverty. I'd say the knowing of it is what drove Dad off his feeding for good." The VISTA employee gives him a job application, but he doesn't want it. She opines, "Sometimes I don't know what I'm doing here." He counters that residents of his hollow don't know either, "but what's funny is, everybody gets up awful early anyhow."

The VISTA employee does her best to repair the sociological fracturing of our nation. Country vs. city, along with North vs. South, coast vs. heartland, rich vs. poor, and upper vs. lower class, are all part of America's DNA. An early example is the enclosure of frontier land bought by the wealthy. Thus, it could not be used by free-ranging hunters. This likely is one reason why Boone was always on the move westward, seeking freedom and the excitements of hunting. He is sometimes compared to Natty Bumppo in Fennimore Cooper's *Leatherstocking Tales*. The two men are figures of mythic proportions. The aristocratic Marmaduke Temple, in Cooper's *The Pioneers*, had Natty put in the stocks for his insistence on the new law restricting hunting was undemocratic. Daniel Boone felt the same when he founded Boonesborough in 1775, where, he averred, democracy and brotherhood (except for "savages"), not high reputation and wealth, were supposed to be lovingly prioritized. The landowners' commercial ambition had bred resentment and revolt. [13]

Those with the most capital, and the most efficient methods of using it, end up in control. In John Keeble's novel about Kit Carson and his daughter, *The Appointment*, he notes that the gold and silver strikes after the Civil War produced a few wealthy miners, but most "arriv[ed] and depart[ed] like ghosts...In accordance with patterns everywhere in the West, the monied mining corporations began taking over the region." The fortune in the fur trade that the brilliant middleman Jacob Astor amassed from the labor of Mountain Men whom he never saw is another landmark for resentment. Astor never went west,

---

[13] Richard Slotkin, Regeneration Through Violence: The Mythology of the American Frontier, 1600-1860 (1973; Middletown CT: Harper Perennials, 1996), pp.331, 423; Henry Nash Smith, Virgin Land: The American West in Symbol and Myth (Cambridge: Harvard U. Press, 1950), pp.51-64.

although Astoria, Oregon is named after him. Slotkin explains that Washington Irving identified Astor with agrarian financial progress, since he made it possible for hunters to raise the money they needed to become farmers or tradesmen. I doubt that this *Sleepy Hollow* writer's sentiment would be accepted with anything but curses from rough-calloused Mountain Men of the Rockies. The yearly rendezvous that fur distributers sponsored facilitated payment to trappers, but the gambling, drinking, whoring, and fighting at such events made clear-minded negotiations tenuous. Robert Coover (*Huck Out West*) and Rudolph Wurlitzer (*The Drop Edge of Yonder*) have passages on the drunken chaos of the Rendezvous.

Resentment of urban companies and politicians had additional sources as well. The Civil War left so much of the Confederacy incapacitated that land grants for willing settlers in the Great Plains and Mountain West were a must. Many Southern pioneers hated the federal government, which it blamed for Reconstruction. They had come west to escape what they thought was the Yankee goal for ending slavery: destruction of the South's economy and its culture. After the war, vigilante groups such as Quantrill's Raiders terrorized locations where Reconstruction was under way. Jesse James rode with them, reinforcing his reputation as a role model. Another source of these pioneers' resentment was the price of goods sold from urban warehouses, which pioneers needed for the trip west but could hardly afford. In addition, Christian fundamentalism contrasted with the scholarly revisionist theology of the east coast denominations.[14] It is interesting to note that fear and hate for a dark-skinned enemy provided a shield for another nemesis of the white working-class Southerners: the region's own power structure.

[14] Jeff Guinn, The Last Gunfight: The Real Story of the Shootout at the OK Corral and How It Changed the West. NY: Simon and Schuster, 2011, pp.15-16; Richard Slotkin, Gunfighter Nation: The Myth of the Frontier in 20th Century America. NY: Atheneum, 1992, p.129.

Sociologist Frank Tannenbaum, writing in the 1920s, documented that idleness among poor whites in the South due to paucity of job opportunities was a deliberate political strategy.[15] It made for direct competition with Blacks for jobs. The obvious enemy to fight was the racial outsider.

Binary Oppositions Between City and Country, East and West

Present-day binary oppositions as wide as Hell's Canyon and as tall as the Empire State Building exist between rural and urban regions on issues such as vaccination, the 2020 election, LGBQ demands, "identity politics" from the left (Me Too, Black Lives Matter) and the right (Stop the Steal, The Tea Party, National White People's Party), immigration from Central America, bans on Muslims from entering the country, removal of Confederate-era symbols from public places, police tactics for subduing suspects, climate change, and citizen ownership of assault weapons.[16] Add to that the federal bankruptcy court resolution of the OxyContin crisis, and the release of the aforementioned Sackler family, owner of the distributing company Purdue Pharma, from any criminal responsibility for the addictions and ruined families.

Naturally, the Covid 19 pandemic has brought these oppositions to an impasse which may produce the point of no return from a cold civil war. Federal, state, and local governments' demands for vaccination against the Omicron variant have produced (as of 2021) militant hostility from about 15 percent

---

[15] *Darker Phases of The South.* G.P. Putnam's Sons & Archon Books: New York, 1924

[16] Stephen Holmes, "The Identity Illusion," *The New York Review of Books*, Jan 17, 2019, pp.44-48, reviewing Francis Fukuyama's *The Demand for Dignity and the Politics of Resentment* (NY: Farrar, Straus and Giroux, 2018.)

of the population. The largest number are located in the South and in rural areas. They especially resent the insistence of doctors, CDC officials, President Biden, and Democrats. It strikes them as thought control. They categorize it along with gender reclassification, shaming of slave-owning historical figures, and specification of slavery as the original American sin. Resentment and fear are understandable when people feel the definition of "American" no longer includes them, their brand of patriotism, or the teachings of their fundamentalist churches. Add to that the Auroch of a hovering pandemic, and shifting demands from authorities in Washington as new variants appear. To anti-vaxers, this is proof of a hidden plan to enslave the population. A *New York Times* reporter visited conservative Enid, OK to find examples of insurgency. A student decides not the accept college admission because it is more important to save the country. A devout woman founds a "Freedom Fighters" website because she felt teaching race theory in school means "people are choosing to shame others." A young man travels to Washington on January 6 to hear President Trump speak, although he does not joint join the raid on the Capitol. He returns to work at Chick-fil-A and to teach all who will listen about patriotism. LGBT protests against that restaurant's donations to anti-gay organization occasioned expressions of support for Chick-fil-A by the governor of Arkansas in 2012.[17] Support for venerable religious teachings or hostility to a long-suppressed choice of sexual preference?

The New York *Times*, on the last Sunday of 2021, featured two informative articles about the country's division regarding vaccination. Both were on page one, above the fold. Liberal readers may well have responded with a "basket of deplorables" attitude, a phrase as representative of a radically divided country

---

[17] "A Fight About Masks Reveals a Deep Schism in the Soul of a City," *New York Times*, 26 Dec., 2021, pp.1, 22-23; "Wily Virus Adds Fuel to Defiance of Unvaccinated," *New York Times*, 26 Dec., 2021, pp.1

as any Trump bloviation. Further, Democrats' have been largely silent regarding the pharmaceutical companies' recalcitrance to provide countries in the Global South with instructions on how to prepare inoculations against Covid. This is as regrettable as the conservative equation of teaching racial injustice with a "America-hating" conspiracy. In fact, one of the Enid activists was quite prescient about Big Pharma. She thought it was part of a sinister conspiracy. The practical reason may well have been enthusiasm for protecting its patents.

Words and phrases used to express disdain for perceived enemies (*America hater, egghead, bookworm, corpsuit, pencilneck, Jesus freak, gook, cracker, woke, peckerwood*) all disparage a particular American social group's affections, loyalties and fears. More specifically, these snarl words deride choices in food, clothing, music, hair styles, role models, responses to criticism, voting patterns, job preferences, care giving, end of life and marriage decisions: that is, the "habitus," or tastes, ideals, choices, and emotional dispositions, of the culture of an outlier group. *Beasts of the Southern Wild* dramatizes this succinctly, not only with the men of the Bathtub cavalierly rescuing Wink from the antiseptic hospital where, full of pain suppressants, he lies dying. The film also features festive images of Hushpuppy's habitus: Wink's cooking skills, the gaiety at Lady Jo's bar, and the cakewalking of Miss Frankie at the floating dance hall. Many viewers may, at first, respond with discomfort at behavior they consider irresponsible or inappropriate. The course of events in Zeitlin and Alibar's film allow the audience the space in which to expand their tolerances.

In Appalachia and the Southwest, the habitus includes chicken necks and lima beans, Mustard Fried Crappie, rattlesnake hunting, and keeping a country store open because a few backwoods families shop there for the same items year after year (See Tom Franklin's *Poachers,* discussed in Chapter 7). There's also the happiness of scoring a gift certificate at the Kentucky Fried or the Piggly-Wiggly; sing-alongs in the movie theater starring

John Wayne in *The Green Berets*; doing the tomahawk chop at the Braves' games; rebel caps. It means rebuilding a neighbor's house after a chimney fire; waking up with a hangover with the sheriff apologizing for the rough stuff during the arrest; cookouts with fifteen-year-olds drinking hard liquor; and counting the broken bones in Evil Knievel's body. Outside the home territory, such habits are met with condescension. From the inside, they can be admired as "being sloppy in a mass of tidy people" (Harry Crews).

The history of American responses to racial and ethnic diversity reveals an insularity that breeds the instinct that "beyond this place are tigers." A reporter who went inside the Capitol with the January 6 rioters pointed out the "white nativist entitlement…that leads one invader to pick up a phone in a Capitol corridor in one video and say: 'Can I speak with Pelosi?'"[18] That request for access to the Speaker of the House may not be entitlement, but hatred for a despised political party, or for government itself, the kind that makes people refuse Covid vaccinations because they suspect that congresspeople will use science to manipulate their bodies and minds.

Resentment can be harnessed into a new kind of intransigent extremism when the two opposing cable networks with the largest audiences make "us vs. them" the basis for their respective audience shares. One recent example: in May 2021, the Biden administration set aside four billion dollars to relieve the economic inequities that have reduced the number of Black farmers from 14 to 1.4 percent over the past century. Lack of subsidies had prevented the kind of networking and equipment purchases they needed. Protests from White farmers focused more on reverse discrimination than on insisting that they too face rising fuel costs

---

[18] The *ProPublica* article by Alec MacGillis, "Inside the Capitol Riot: What the Parler Videos Reveal," https://www.propublica.org/article/inside-the-capitol-riot-what-the-parler-videos-reveal, should be required reading.

and land prices.[19] FOX News and CNBC approaches to this story favored ether the charges about letting a minority "jump in line" ahead of them, or the pathological fear of African-Americans for Whites.

Americans are not a "people," at least not since the days when Daniel Boone established his town. The term has been appropriated by too many exclusionary political entities to even try to list. The varied and often belligerent oppositions of Americans to each other might better be understood by thinking of the lands where groups of people live, as Wendell Berry suggests.[20] Perhaps "territory" is an apt synonym for "land."

Apropos of "land," To leave a "ridgerunner," "redneck," or "poor white" culture is perhaps more disorienting than to immigrate to the United States from a country in which one has been schooled in upwardly mobile speech patterns, and customs and techniques of success such as workplace consensus, periodic performance evaluation, or criteria for raises and promotions. One of Breece Pancake's characters, "bound for Germany or China, I don't know yet," feels his fear tumbling from him to join with those of numberless generations of de-territorialized humans. Jim Stegner praised Wendell Berry's conviction about "placed" people. He envied those "who had lived all their lives in the houses they were born in...A place is not a place until people have been born in it, have grown up in it, lived in it, known it, died in it." Only the struggles, the occasional catastrophes, the accommodation to the changing seasons, and the ancestral history of an area produce an appreciation of "who you are."[21]

---

[19] "You Can Feel the Tension': A Windfall for Minority Farmers Divides Rural America." *New York Times*, May 22, 2021 (Updated June 24, 2021). https://www.nytimes.com/2021/05/22/us/black-farmers.html

[20] "You cannot save the land apart from the people, or the people apart from the land."

[21] Wallace Stegner, *Where the Bluebird Sings to the Lemonade Springs* (NY: Penguin, 1992), pp.201-05.

Breece Pancake, Poet of Deterritorialization[22]

The epigraph to Chris Offutt's *Out of the Woods*, by way of Flannery O'Connor, is: "Where you come from is gone, where you thought you were going was never there, and where you are is no good unless you can get away from it." Pancake's stories explore every emotionally fraught insight this sentence suggest. (Figure 1-3). He was one of the best at a theme many country noir writers excel at: the interconnectedness between systemic social decay and betrayals within the home, family, and community. In one instance ("Trilobites") a husband shoots his wife after she runs off with her foreman; then he commits suicide. In the same story, the man about to leave home makes his last night with his girlfriend a brutal rutting. As time passes, and no sustainable future is in sight, the need to leave the area and the emotional trauma of doing so is like casting off part of oneself and leaving it for loved ones to grieve over. Viciousness toward animals becomes a substitute for a loss with which there is no way of coping. In "Hollow" it is fully reptilian, occurring after a miner's girlfriend has run off with another man. He shoots a pregnant doe and watches its fawn breath its last.

In "The Salvation of Me," a feckless youth goes to New York, gets "chewed up and spit out," and comes back telling of his Broadway raves. Naturally, his buds, with no better job than pumping gas, think that if that guy could do it, they could too. Well, at least Andy Griffith did it, as Lonesome Rhodes in *A Face in the Crowd*. Sorta. And the bullshitter's friends needed escape to achieve solvency and start a family. He has spread a kind of "germ" in a community where there was no training in

---

[22] Thomas E Douglass' *A Room Forever: The Life, Work, and Letters of Breece D'J Pancake* (Knoxville: U. of Tennessee Press, 1998) is a detailed biography, with Pancake's letters.

big-city survival. The first few who left for New York killed them-selves rather than come back. They had met their Aurochs. Their dress, speech, hair style, body language, food and drink, strategies of meeting and impressing, networking, managing money—all were outlandish in the hierarchal class structure of New York. These inexperienced young hopefuls had no empathetic friends as Wink did to rescue him from the disease of helpless isolation. In William Gay's *Provinces of Night*, he writes of the men "gone north for something better, and finding there the trouble they'd fled was somehow augmented, their lives multiplied by themselves."

When Breece Pancake killed himself at twenty-seven, he was a college teacher, a writer of growing reputation, salaried by a bureaucratic institution. He assumed the mask of someone who had "been around." A reclusive person, he felt comfortable with people who, like himself, loved the outdoors, hunted, fished, knew rifles, and drank beer. Therefore, he gave colleagues gifts more suitable for use in the woods than the campus. He thought of his own writing as a gift, to be shared by those who understood the spirit of a community offering. His mother states that "God called him home because he saw too much dishonesty and evil in the world and he couldn't cope." On the cusp of an artistic career of uncharted paths and impersonally imposed expectations, he seems to have paused, for reasons his mother gave. On the outside looking in, and in an institutional setting as well, his own ground was getting smaller, and pushing him into a corner from which he could escape, but only by tippy-toeing awkwardly with people staring. He had traveled through enough of America to be aware of that omnipresent feeling.

In Pancake's "The Honored Dead," one of the characters opines, "Everybody's going to school to be something better. Well, when everybody's going this way, it's time to be going that way, you know. Somebody's got to dig in the damn ground." This is the narrator's father speaking. It is his answer to his son's request to leave the family farm, because he and his wife want college-level employment. He is planning to avoid the Vietnam draft, which his friend Eddie did not. He is haunted by the sight of Eddie in his body bag, but equally by his father's act of generosity in Korea, when he found food for a Russian soldier. The story is a subtle panorama of what obligation means through two generations in a community in the twilight of its wholeness. The notable contrast to *Beasts of the Southern Wild's* Bathtub lies in the self-sufficient isolation of that community in the waters of the Louisiana Delta. They do not feel the inevitability of merging with the financial, educational, technological, and social habitus of upwardly mobile America. However, the Bathtub "ain't gonna be no more," due to a terrible storm and invasion by Aurochs. Hushpuppy has been taught how to cope. Pancake's characters have not been. This is one reason why his narratives are so affecting and create such a powerful empathy.

> When you're growing up in a small town
> You'll know you'll go down in a small town
> There's only one good use for a small town
> You hate it and you know you'll have to leave.

I quote these lines by Brooklyn-born poet-lyricist Lou Reed to show the difference between the derisive superiority Reed's outcast feels for his small town, and the predicaments of troubled protagonists in stories by country noir writers. The latter's attachment to their small towns is a result of those locations being an amalgam of long-time devotion to extended family, friends, main street shopkeepers, teachers, coaches, bartenders, local hellraisers, and police. The realization that one will "go down" unless s/he leaves is the birth of awareness of what personal growth means. It is not freedom, but the beginning of a search for it that one has to force oneself to make.

> "I'm leaving here," he said.
> "But you came back," Everett said.

It ain't the same as it is here."
"I know it."
"You will." (Chris Offutt, "Nine Ball," in *Kentucky Straight*.)

Pancake's "In the Dry" contrasts an exhilarating, long-past time with the protagonist's present isolation. The above-mentioned Ottie, a foster child, remembers wading in the cold clear water of a creek, praying that he could stay on that hill farm forever. Years later, a car accident leaves the son of that farm's owner, Buster Gerlack, a paraplegic; Ottie crawled safely out of the wreckage. Since then, Buster's father has blamed Ottie for his son's condition, on the scant evidence of a rivalry for the affections of a cousin, Sheila. He probably is aware of Buster's brutal killing of Ottie's dog with a sickle blade. "I want to show you something," said Buster as Ottie approached the corpse.

Pancake's title is from a biblical question about primordial evil, the crucifixion (Luke 23.31). Could any greater evil have been possible, if the time and place was dark and evil instead of prosperous? (The latter was the case of Israel under the Romans.) Ottie is about to find out.

Ottie has for years driven a semi, sometimes for employers waiting out a strike. That is, he has been a "scab," subsisting on "truck stop pie and coffee" between long hauls. He may be punishing himself for whatever part he played in what happened to Buster, and for leaving Sheila, to whom he has written many letters. He seems to have condemned himself to loneliness, but the story's conclusion is as indefinite to the reader as it is to Ottie. There's also the simmering resentment of Gerlack toward his foster son. The emotional dryness of Ottie's life, not guilt but a grief he cannot confront, is Pancake's subject.

He arrives back home to find Gerlack is prosperous from growing tobacco. He is having a fried chicken "whoop-de-do," hosting wealthy business colleagues with large cars and expensive clothing. Sheila is there. He notes her dusty blouse, chapped skin, and thinning hair, typical of farm women deprived of their full potential. He goes to his old room and regards his childhood trinkets as "pieces of broken life," unable to cohere into any comforting memory. Before Buster showed Ottie that he had the power to kill his dog, and before the accident, Ottie had cared for Sheila. As a guilty wanderer who does not think he deserves a territory of his own, he sees her as just "an old maid in a little town." Pancake adds, with the saddest of understanding, that "he knew her bitterness." It was his own, projected upon the woman who still loved him, whom he was thinking of sending for and settling down with. She asks him if he ever wanted to love her back. He can only shake his head, and hope, when she turns away, that she does not look back. Ottie's foster father wanted Ottie at the party in order to curse him for making his son a wheelchair-bound cripple. "God forgive my wore out soul, but I hope you burn in hell." Ottie has fully internalized Gerlack's wish. In the middle of the night, and maybe henceforth without the love of people he has grown up with, off he goes, shifting his semi into gear, "an awful noise." He's in the grip of a spiritual dryness.

The Aurochs in this difficult, murky narrative, with its implications of lost innocence, frozen sexuality, and unresolved guilt, are inside the characters' heads. Its protagonist feels unfit for a home, so is always on the move, a constant theme in Pancake's much-praised stories. Ottie has thought of quitting hauling freight and settling down. He had thought of asking Sheila to join him. He literally had not the heart to do so. Pancake was planning a novel about Ottie, who has so much struggle with depression and withdrawal ahead. In this penultimate tale in the Holt collection of his stories, there is faint possibility of a despairing Ottie reaching out for resurrection of his soul from the dry.

The final story contrasts with "In the Dry" by treating the dilemma of generational obligation, which is as loving as it is constricting. It is the "First Day of Winter." Responsibility to aging parents is as full of conflict, pain, and anxiety as it is deeply rooted in love. It's a mystic attachment, mixing mutual respect and obligation, made all the deeper because it is set against the tight limits of rural isolation. The protagonist's blind father and feeble but perseverant mother weep as their youngest son pauses to decide if he wishes to follow his brother in moving out. "The valley closed in quietly with humming, quietly as an hour of prayer." Prayer suggests that supernatural help is needed to move forward in life, alone. Equally, it encapsulates the holiness of being with one's parents when they desperately need it. There may be an ominous foreshadowing of Pancake's own suicide in this.

Facing the Aurochs in 'The Old, Weird America'

Court Merrigan, in an important essay, "New Genres: Country Noir,"[23] cogently states, "The characters of country noir don't look to the wider world—they are inextricably mired in their own personalities, locales, family arrangements, and social classes." That is the case with the Bathtub's folk, and of the country ridgerunners and rednecks. But the world crashes in on the protagonists in stories by Daniel Woodrell, Larry Brown, Joseph Haske, Rusty Barnes, Chris Offutt, and Leah Hampton. "Y'all better learn how to survive," said Bathsheba, Hushpuppy's teacher, as the storm, and by implication the Aurochs, approached the Bathtub. And keep the jagged edges, as Harry Crews advised. Mark Turcotte's "Road Noise" shows how.[24] It's about the American wilderness in the hearts of hobos, Native Americans, and gypsy road kids whose world is the truck stops, missions, sawdust dives, skid rows, and "wide-open west Texas nights"

---

[23] https://electricliterature.com/new-genres-country-noir/

[24] In William Hastings, ed., *Stray Dogs, Writing from the Other America* (Lutz, FL: Down and Out Books, 2014), pp.177-87.

where ancestors' shades are glimpsed, dancing against the song of a falling world.

This is part of what Greil Marcus describes as the experience of "the old, weird America." Denis Johnson, Vicki Hendricks, Harry Crews, and Barry Gifford's characters recreate the anarchistic, amoral energies that cannot stand still for law or hierarchy, and have something of the aggressive fierceness of American icons such as Jesse James, Butch Cassidy, Kit Carson, Calamity Jane, Jim Bridger, or Wyatt Earp. Wink, Hushpuppy's father, is another example. Others include Offutt's feuding Melungeons; Denis Johnson and Daniel Woodrell's thieves, drug dealers, bear hunters, and trigger-happy alcoholics; Joseph Haske's vicious drunks who hunt down a sheriff or bar owner simply because they are protecting people from their mayhem. Here, writers draw upon the traditions of Southern Gothic.

Zeitlin and Alibar think it necessary to have Hushpuppy use the phrase "Horsemen of the Apocalypse." The Aurochs are like those horsemen: hell bent, apocalyptic. In E. L. Doctorow's *Welcome to Hard Times* (Figure 1-4), he shows what can happen to a community that is unprepared. The Auroch in this story is a "Bad Man from Bodie," a monomaniac with pale eyes like "shattered glass," who shoots up and burns down the eponymous Dakota Territory town. The mayor, Blue, stayed because, having travelled widely throughout the frontier West, he realized a place flourished due to its people's ability to feel their need for each other, not simply seeing them as objects to make one's own life more tolerable. Unlike the citizens of The Bathtub, those in Hard Times responded to disaster without learning what her teacher taught Hushpuppy: "how to survive". During a winter that drove the half-rebuilt town's inhabitants into sod dugouts, the grocer would not sell goods that he might himself need to survive. A prostitute is appropriated by a stranger whose desire terrifies her. Instead of freeing her, as Wink's friends did from the hospital where he would otherwise die "plugged into a wall," the prostitute's cohorts told her she had no choice but to keep the stranger happy. The cat house owner will not give his customers credit, as Blue had suggested, in order to spread around the money needed for various merchants to stay solvent. Why should he, he asked, when his customers would just spend their money at the dance hall across the icy street? Most of these men were miners, attracted by the false promise of a company regarding a rail line to Hard Times. "Each of us is alone in himself," sighed Blue.

There is also the obsessive attachment of Molly, a saloon B-girl whom the Bad Man had raped, and the boy Jimmy, whose father the Bad Man had murdered. They clung together, especially as distrustful tension heightened in town. There was an Oedipal tenor in Jimmy's growing hatred of Blue. It was the exact opposite of the child-adult togetherness in the floating fleshpot, dance hall, and jazz parlor, where Hushpuppy learns the connection between love and self-respect after her father's death. The Badman seems to intuit this, and makes a second approach to the fragile town. Blue tried to enlist Jimmy's help. He seriously injured the mayor, then feverously rode away, to become The Bad Man from Hard Times, the only sign it once existed. Blue wants to burn up what little is left. One nagging thought torments him: "Somebody will come by sometime who will want to use the wood."

When destructive forces come, fully human responses—combining toughness, love, and togetherness—can be what is needed. Denis Johnson's stories, and his novel *Angels*, show that violence and thievery can set the perpetrator on a path of both suffering and ultimate inner peace, symbols of which the individual sees in the most mundane places. David Joy's outcasts make journeys from the cages their own families have forced on them to waystations beyond personal security and toward transcendence. Tales of redemption are as notable in Country Noir as tales of stagnation and failure were in pulp mass-market crime.

* * *

Violence as Freedom and Fundamental Rightness, Beyond the Law

Rural noir offers more indeterminacy, more mystery, and a great deal less resigned closure than previous crime or mystery stories. Perhaps the image of Hushpuppy facing the Auroch with her friends and teachers, and the spirit of her father, at her back, is an example of the difference. Country noir writers make readers intimate with violence, cruelty, and criminality. But community, character, and the "heavy load" often keep protagonists "stable," or at least deserving of a future. The sequels and prequels of Barry Gifford and novels by several other accomplished writers are examples. One is Sheldon Compton in his *Brown Bottle*, where a man trying to stop, through violence, the drug distribution in his town is reluctantly shot by the sheriff, in order to short circuit the turmoil the reformer's campaign would cause. But the dead man's effort convinces his nephew to give up his habit.

In Chris Offutt's *Country Dark* (Figure 1-5), his hero, Tucker, has learned in Korea that in war "there are no sides…Everyone was eventually caught in the middle of something." He has supplemented his survival skills with lightning quick moves with guns and knives, and lethal use of his hands. All he wants is a quiet, isolated life with his family deep in the Kentucky woods. When a state official for aid to poor families decides Tucker's kids would be better off in a child care center, Tucker kills him with a knife to the kidney. He works many years running drugs, using driving skills that would make James Sallis's Driver envious. His boss decides to send a biker gang to kill Tucker while he is serving a short prison sentence, to take the heat off the drug gang. Tucker breaks one thug's arm, then slashes another's belly open so the biker can see his gut protruding. After that, Tucker is left alone. He uses a nest of hornets to disable his boss's nephew, patches him up enough to find and kill the boss, then gives the nephew two in the head. The law is as helpless to make a case as it was to refuse the drug boss's bribes. The only witness is blind. Tucker never has cause to use his weapons again, chiefly because he and his wife live in a small, isolated community free from drug addiction. That is due to Tucker's uncannily brutal resourcefulness. Offutt's epigraph, a quote from Daniel Boone, is double edged: for Boone, Kentucky was a "second paradise" in which he wanted to live with his family "at the risk of my life and fortune." *Country Dark* itself is evocative of what Richard Slotkin has specified as the American predisposition for "regeneration through violence."

In *Give Us a Kiss* (Figure 1-6), Daniel Woodrell's Missouri-born narrator, Doyle Redmond, tells of a confederate general who, after the Civil War, took a band to Mexico in hopes of establishing a "new empire of Southerness." It was quixotic to the max, but "anything was preferable to the humiliation of surrender." Not for nothing was Doyle's father, General Joe, named after that no-surrender Confederate general. Doyle's family of Missouri hillbillies fight laws they consider insulting to their bone-deep idea of independence. To preserve that was the reason they settled in the Ozarks several generations ago.

Doyle is a successful writer long gone from home, and thus "narrowed down" or "citified" by Kansas City and university study. But he starts fistfights in which he is not satisfied until he not only wins, but also has inflicted humiliating punishment to the opponent. Panda, his boxer grandfather, had the same trait. Doyle's spurts of violence cost him university grants and teaching jobs. "Being sloppy among a mass of tidy people" is worth the price, if the "tidy" inhabitants of one's state have representatives with the repressive power of Aurochs. Woodrell's own family, he explains, settled In the Ozarks to be free from "sheriffs, taxes, social conformity. They sought isolation." "Not toeing the mark the world has laid down" is the Redmond clan badge of honor. Doyle finds his outlaw brother's fast-cash scheme and girlfriend's nubile daughter too dangerous to resist. His own namesake is one of those family ancestors who died young and violently. That man's memorial is a photo displayed in Panda's house along with other kinfolk. This is done in the same way an aristocrat's forebears would be displayed, in expensive frames, in a Southern plantation mansion.

"Do Not Underestimate the Strangeness of These Cultures"

So warns Greil Marcus, referring to the isolated mountain, farmland, and riverbank cultures. "A bigger, more various, less finished, less fated self" is possible, he concludes. It may include violence, mistakes that cannot be rectified, or vigilantism against one's own kin, as in Offutt's Melungeon stories and his "Old of the Moon," or Woodrell's *The Death of Sweet Mister*, or Pancake's "Time and Again," about a son's discovery of his father's murders of young men to steal their money for his son. Woodrell gives the reader an indelible picture of the "locals" living near a campground:

> Pioneer-lean old men who poached deer whenever hungry and wouldn't pay taxes, their wives wearing gray braids and combat hats, clasp knives sheathed at their belts; men with the beards of prophets who read the bible at a certain slant and could build anything...reluctantly coming in contact with the conventional world for want of baby formula or headache powders...("Twin Forks," in *The Outlaw Album*)

In the writing of Chris Offutt, Barry Gifford, Bonnie Campbell, Breece Pancake, and Denis Johnson, the real protagonists are supposedly failed or criminal individuals. They, however, are humane, self-aware, and able to retain integrity and fundamental obligations. While in twentieth-century crime stories, these traits are masculine ones, in the tales of Steph Post, Bonnie Campbell, Carolyn Chute, or Leah Hampton, they belong to female protagonists. Whatever their gender, they are often social isolates. Critic Robert Warshow wrote, "the Western hero is...a figure of repose"[25]—a stoic, but not resigned to failure, not characterized by a slow, sad smile but rather, by a head held high.

There's an "insistence on mystery as inseparable from any honest understanding of what life is about," as Greil Marcus put it in his liner notes for Dylan's *Basement Tapes*. A hardscrabble, hard-won optimism results from the irrepressible protagonists in Rusty Barnes's *Reckoning*, Gary Phillips's *Accidental Outlaws*, John Williams's *Butcher's Crossing*, Robert Coover's *Huck Out West*, and Sheldon Lee Compton's *Brown Bottle*. There is an appreciation of the anarchic life force therein, the cruel humor, the "demons, dancers, drinkers," and people who speak directly to God. As Jack Kerouac's ecstatic young explorer Sal Paradise declared, "Now I could see Denver looming ahead of me like the Promised Land, way out there beneath the stars, across the prairie of Iowa and the plains of Nebraska..." F. Scott Fitzgerald may have intuited the same in the last pages of *The Great Gatsby*. It was in the mountains, canyons, waters and plains, he wrote, that pioneers "came face to face for the last time in history with something commensurate to his capacity for wonder." He goes on to say Gatsby, born in the west and brought east by a millionaire yachtsman, never imagined his dream of redeeming struggle "was already behind him, somewhere back in that vast obscurity beyond the city." That is the promise many rural noir writers explore.

A Bathtub-like Strangeness at the edge of New Orleans

The Batture consists of a dozen riverbank houses, or camps, at a bend in the Mississippi, near the US Corps of Engineers building.

---

[25] "Movie Chronicle: The Western," in *The Immediate Experience* (1962; Cambridge U. Press, 2002), p.107.

Freed Blacks and stranded northerners built there after the Civil War, living off the land. Today, there are about the same number of residents, living without electricity, indoor plumbing, or running water. The settlement cannot be seen from other parts of the city. It is especially vulnerable to hurricanes, the only feature it shares with the contemporary Big Easy. One resident, Macon Fry, chose to move there the night he heard about it. In 2021 he published a history of The Batture. It was hard to gather information, because isolation from machines, levees, hospitals, and any kind of surveillance media is life and freedom to them. Fry, like his neighbors, cherishes "wildness, beauty, eccentricity, self-reliance. Freedom."[26] They did not want to be quoted or named in his book, but they helped him with keeping his "camp" in order: the necessary uses of motor oil, spark plugs, oil drums, driftwood, and other big-city, and possibly the Corps of Engineers, discards. The Batture has its own ecosystem; a remarkable array of animals provides food, amusement, and affectionate company.

That the strangeness of The Batture's culture equals that of Bathtub is as clear as bells. Hushpuppy and her father live in the "shacko in the backo." It has a "window made from a gas station sign." They fashion a motor boat from an oil drum and a refurbished motor. They put as much space as possible between themselves and the modern city, where Hushpuppy has heard of "fish stuck in plastic wrappers, babies stuck in carriages, and chickens on sticks." Other reasons for keeping away are the city's disapproval of the Bathtub's crawling-baby races, fireworks, and the crab and shrimp feasts (lots of meat and fish, like the Batture) as the storm approaches. New Orleans media's patronizing coverage of The Batture constantly depicted poverty, lack of ambition, irresponsibility, restlessness, and health risk of the miserable "river rats." Alibar and Zeitlin instruct their actors to

---

[26] "Rolling Along." Review of Macon Fry, *They Call Us River Rats: The Last Batture Settlement of New Orleans* (U. of Mississippi Press, 2021). By Nathaniel Rich. *The New York Review of Books.* Oct 7, 2021: 4, 6.

"Throw your fist in the air! These are the survivors, those who fight for their joy and their history to the last man." Hushpuppy had the next lines: "But me and my daddy, we stay right here. We are who the earth is for."[27] That is what the Batture River Rats believe. The moral of Fry's book might as well be, "Do not underestimate the old, weird America."

---

[27] *Beasts of the Southern Wild*. Final Draft. Written by Lucy Alibar and Benh Zeitlin. Typescript.

Figure 1-1: "Ain't going to be no more Bathtub": The Shacko in the Backo after a flood. *Beasts of the Southern Wild* (film). Google: BEASTS OF THE SOUTHERN WILD Clip: "Wasn't No Time For Cryin'"

Figure 1-2: The Auroch and Hushpuppy. Google: Best Picture breakdowns: 'Beasts of the Southern Wild' review.

Figure 1-3: Source "Breece D'J Pancake: A Short Life in the Hills." Thomas E Douglass, *A Room Forever : The Life, Work, And Letters Of Breece D'J Pancake* (Knoxville : University of Tennessee Press, [1998]), p.89.

Figure 1-4: "Somebody will come by sometime who will want to use the wood." E. L. Doctorow, *Welcome to Hard Times* (NY: Simon and Schuster, 1960). Collection of the author.

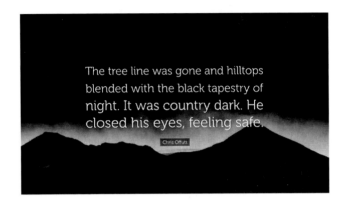

The tree line was gone and hilltops blended with the black tapestry of night. It was country dark. He closed his eyes, feeling safe.

Chris Offutt

Figure 1-5: Violence as Freedom and Fundamental Rightness, Beyond the Law—Chris Offutt, *Country Dark*. See https://quotefancy.com/quote/2018770/Chris-Offutt-The-tree-line-was-gone-and-hilltops-blended-with-the-black-tapestry-of-night.

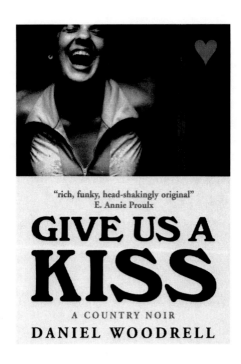

Figure 1-6: "Juicy and delicious." "Keep the jagged edges." Daniel Woodrell, *Give Us A Kiss* (NY: Back Bay Books, 1996). Collection of the author.

CHAPTER 2

From Mass Market Urban "Failure Stories" To Rural Adventures on the "Great Plains of the Republic"

However imprecise, the term "Country Noir" distinguishes this contemporary form of literature from 20th century "Newsstand Pulp" crime. Both kinds show a variety of perspectives regarding what crime is, and how that understanding motivates people trying to find a place for themselves. Both kinds of writing are about people in long-workable communities that have suffered economic enfeeblement, in an increasingly crime- and poverty-ridden 20th century inner city or in an equally distressed contemporary rural America with decaying infrastructure, shuttered hospitals, and unaffordable medicines.

The blurbs and reviews for country noir pulp crime stories are often interchangeable with those used to characterize newsstand paperbacks of the classic [1940-59] period: "official voice of working class literature"; "This is what noir is...blunt force drama stripped down to the bone"; "everything you want in crime fiction"; "The strange, fascinating, and dangerous fringes of American life"; "working class antiheroes as they indulge in theft, murder, and lawless shenanigans." All this is acknowledgement of the overlap between the 1950s readership of newsstand paperbacks and what sells country noir today. Both were replete with pulp characteristics, as the above quotations imply. Crime pulp of both periods could be a showcase of the hard-boiled: a communal degradation producing resignation, anger, and predatory action. It could also be noir, depicting psychosexual suffering either terminal or redemptive, depending on the capabilities of a protagonist.

The basis of pulp literature is formulaic entertainment. Salable product meant a template of straightforward plotting, colloquial language, and familiar point of view, whether the genre was Western, Crime, Mystery, Horror, Romance, Sports, War, Erotica, Science Fiction, or whatever combination got prospective readers under the sensational cover of the magazine, digest, or paperback.

James Cawelti[28] contrasts the formulaic aspect of a story read for escape with its "mimetic" elements—those that show painful consequences of shaping one's own future, or being condemned for trying. The differences and similarities between 20th and 21st century American crime stories—in distribution, points of sale, size of readership, narrative style, and authors' reputations— show stages in the shifting mimetic elements of crime pulp as it morphed from a twentieth-century mass market urban-focused genre to Country Noir.

"Not A Fragrant World"

Raymond Chandler, in "The Simple Art of Murder," discusses the essential contrast between the "mean streets" American and British "Great House," or "Locked Room" mysteries. In the latter kinds of stories, the detective solved the murder, however ingeniously the criminal had devised it. Poe described his own achievement in "The Murders in the Rue Morgue" as "unraveling a web which you yourself...have woven for the express purpose of unraveling it." Readers enjoyed themselves doing so, especially if they saw a divine purpose working itself out in the capture of

---

[28] James Cawelti, Adventure, Mystery, and Romance: Formula Stories as Art and Popular Culture (Chicago: U. of Chicago Press, 1976), 12-18.

the criminal. Often, the community is cleaned of the evil, regenerated, and, as Agatha Christie once said, innocence is protected.

In the American urban crime stories, which *Black Mask* brought to prominence when gangster violence proliferated after World War I, no innocent survived. Chandler states that "a world in which gangsters can rule nations and almost rule cities...is not a fragrant world, but it is the world you live in." Newsstand paperbacks appropriated many of these puzzle mysteries, but featured prurient blurbs and lurid cover illustrations. That in itself shattered the aura of innocence triumphant over evil. The vast majority of newsstand, cigar store, subway or railroad station spinner-rack browsers would not care to follow a puzzle mystery in which sporting detective vs. villain gamesmanship was distanced from the unfragrant world of inner-city desperation, illicit sex, and bloodletting. There were no village citizens or great House aristocrats. The PI, with his seamy reputation as transom peeper or small-con extortionist, was one of the people and shared their underdog vicissitudes.[29] His quirks—alcoholic, neurotic, bad-tempered, or war-traumatized—lent additional empathy. Sometimes he was a former policeman dismissed for insubordination. Newsstand pulp crime readers found the angry, hard eyed, indomitable man of the slums fascinating, Woody Haut pointed out, until upwardly mobile suburbanites, an increasing number of paperback crime purchasers and TV mysteries viewers, found it no longer a part of their own day-to-day confrontation with city life.[30]

When James M Cain described in *The Postman Always Rings Twice* the friendly contest between two lawyers totally unconcerned about the fate of Frank and Cora, the social and class distance between mere sportsmanship and helpless anxiety

---

[29] John Conquest, "The Making of *Trouble Is My Business*," in Maxim Jakubowski, ed. *New Crimes* (NY: Carroll and Graf, 1989), pp. 244-53.

[30] Haut, *Pulp Culture: Hardboiled Fiction and the Cold War* (London: Serpent's Tail, 1995), p.170.

of everyday life became clear.

Woody Haut's insight into moral authorities' "fear of a mass readership" when pulp writing caught the eye of the working class is invaluable.[31] He writes that middle class readers were wary that mass market paperback reprints of classics, with lurid covers, broke down distinctions between the educated and the hoi polloi A prime example is the "degradation ceremonies." They are well-orchestrated public events which denigrate public entertainments or self-expressive behaviors as "vulgar" or "degenerate". By doing so, they mark out as inferior certain beliefs, traditions, language, dress and food preferences, and means of entertainment—that is, aspects of the "habitus"—of segments of the population which create, distribute, or enjoy these entertainments.[32] The orchestrators of the ceremonies are in a position to insist on distancing them from the rest of the population.[33] Politicians, clergymen, school officials, and mainstream publishers conducted such ceremonies after World War I, to make sure the public, when it passed display racks on newsstands, five and tens, drug and cigar stores, bus and train stations, as well as bookstores, remembered judgments such as "pornographic," "perverse," "immoral,' and "commie-inspired." Booksellers had to stand still for confiscation of these items, before any court determination. The reason for this prior restraint was the "clear and present danger," These ceremonies worked

---

[31] Pulp Culture: *Hardboiled Fiction and the Cold War* (London: Serpent's Tail, 1995), p.5 and *passim*.

[32] "Bourdieu and 'Habitus'," https://www.powercube.net/other-forms-of-power/bourdieu-and-habitus/; "Habitus," Social Theory Re-Wired, http://routledgesoc.com/category/profile-tags/habitus#:~:text=Bourdieu's%20concept%20of%20cultural%20capital, of%20a%20particular%20social%20class. Both viewed April, 2022.

[33] Harold Garfinkel, "Conditions of Successful Degradation Ceremonies, "*American Journal of Sociology* 61 (March 1958), 420-24.

exactly as novelist Samuel Delaney said,[34] The goal was "social domination" of distrusted groups within a society.

Mass Market Crime Writers' Response to the Culture that Degrades Their Work

Kurt Brokaw, professor at the New School, film critic, and author of *The Paperback Guy: Words from the Sidewalk*, says of William Gresham's *Nightmare Alley* (1946) that the protagonist, Stan Carlyle's, fatal mistake is:

> 'reaching beyond his means.' This is probably the most frequent cautionary message in 1850's story papers, 1880's dime novels, and a fair amount of early pulp magazine stories from the 1900's through the 1930's. Stay cautious and know your place…'See what happens if you don't' is all the awful stuff that happens.[35]

Carlyle starts his circus sideshow life at the bottom, rises to become a renowned expert in the clairvoyance racket, but is unprepared for his own gullibility when the country's leading "mentalist," recognizing his threat to her supremacy, exposes, shames, and destroys him. Subsequently, the only job he can get is back in the degrading sideshow act where he started. "I was born for it," is his last sentence in the 2021 Guillermo del Toro film adaptation. Gresham starts each chapter with an image of a Tarot Card—mysterious validation of the power of Fate.

Isolation; stoic, resolute acceptance of one's fate; and terminal pessimism pervade the final pages of the typical newsstand pulp.

---

[34] Samuel R Delaney, *Times Square Red, Times Square Blue* (NY: NYU Press, 1999), p.121.

[35] Email to the author, Jan 8, 2021. Reproduced by permission.

Goodis's piano player says: "They've been coming here every night and waiting. But you just don't have it to give." Pulp crime's narratives of the prevalence of injustice implicitly inhibited an individual's ability to break free from anxieties that only salary, safety, and reputation could relieve. As several of Goodis' characters found out, "the street never lets you go." A mass market pulp writer focused on brutal mob bosses; infestation of racketeering, prostitution, alcoholism, and teenage gang violence on one's own street; and upper- and underworld collusion that sanctioned organized crime in declining or "blighted" neighborhoods. In a country where inner cities and their supporting institutions were losing stature, keeping what one had in the working- or under-class community pecking order was the first priority, however crippling that acceptance was for the citizen's American dreams.

One source of the common man's acquiescence was the war itself. In *From Here to Eternity*, James Jones describes (as only he could) the way the notes of the company musician's plaintively beautiful jazz embodied the "common soldiers'" resignation. They were:

> ...filled with an infinite sadness, an endless patience, a pointless pride, the requiem and epitaph of the common soldier, who smelled like a common soldier, as a woman had once told him. They hovered like halos over the heads of the sleeping men in the darkened barracks, turning all grossness to the beauty that is the beauty of sympathy and understanding. Here we are, they said, you made us, now see us, don't close your eyes and shudder at it; this beauty, this sorrow, of things as they are...The song of the mucky KPs, of the men without women who come to scour the Officers' Club—after the parties are over.

The deepest seductive power of the music is its salute to what Orson Welles called the "lost paradises" that so many people can only wish for, but are fated never to realize.

Despite the subversion of prefabricated class, ethnic, and political absolutes that lifted so many 1950s mass market crime stories above the level of ephemeral escapism, the courage and hard-won self-awareness of post-World War II pulp crime protagonists often results in stoic acceptance of impassive, callous fate. It is a basic truth in the time of The Big Fear. Cornell Woolrich's "First you dream. Then you die" sums up his work so effectively that Francis Nevins used it as the title of his exemplary biography. The following Woolrich assertion is shared by many twentieth century mystery writers: "Each man dies as he was meant to die, alone, all alone. Without any god, without any hope, without any record to show for his life…The burial-alive of the mind, covering it over with fresh earth every time it tries to struggle through to the light. In this kind of death you never finish dying." Jim Thompson's protagonist in *The Killer Inside Me*, cursed by child abuse and a misanthropic father, wanted readers to see his trauma as their own: "All of us that started the game with a crooked cue…That meant so good and did so bad." And then there is the last sentence in David Goodis's *Street of No Return*. The setting is the steps of a flophouse. Whitey, once a star crooner, has just seen his beloved for the last time. "They sat there passing the bottle around, and there was nothing that could bother them, nothing at all." The three stories from which I extracted these quotes are subversive of trust in authorities, faith in the future, fair play as a great leveler, and love overcoming despair. They may encourage readers, and many were working class, to fight for self-respect. Their protagonists, however, fail to find it.

Orson Welles once described American crime fiction as "failure stories" of personal fateful choices.[36] Striving to overcome the obstacles of their financial, familial, or amatory frustrations left protagonists stymied by "twisted sorrow" (Dylan, "Mr. Tambourine Man"): a fate beyond their control. "And so," Fitzgerald's Nick, Gatsby's only friend, concluded, "We beat on, boats against the current, borne back ceaselessly into the past." Protagonists in failure stories harbor insecurity and loneliness the anxiety of which they must resolve, or live with resignation, however noble in its acquiescence to the inevitable. This suggests that twentieth century pulp writers served a cultural consensus, despite their narratives' hard-boiled commitment to ruthless success and nuanced exploration of a protagonist's bitter rejection of the world that shaped them. "Every production of mass culture," stated Robert Warshow, acute observer of popular entertainment, "is a public act and must conform with accepted notions of the public good."[37] Even James Jones' poignant passage, in reinforcing the ordinary dogface's acceptance of "the sorrow of things as they are," is an instrument of the public good of a nation that needs common soldiers, and after the war, working stiffs.

Country Noir: "Sloughing [Off] the Old Skin"

This conviction of resignation to "things as they are," so constantly reoccurring in post war crime stories as to be part of the era's *Weltanschauung*, or sensibility, is what Country Noir gets

---

[36] Quoted in Kevin Tierney, "Orson Welles: Ten Years After His Death," *Kinema* (fall 1995). https://openjournals.uwaterloo.ca/index.php/kinema/article/view/768/62 6 "Almost all serious stories in the world are stories of failure with a death in it. But there is more lost paradise in them than defeat."

[37] Warshow, "The Gangster as Tragic Hero," in *The Immediate Experience: Movies, Comics, Theatre, and Other Aspects of Popular Culture* (1962; Enlarged Edition. Cambridge, MA: Harvard U. Press, 2001), p.98.

beyond. That does not mean that all such writing ends with new self-awareness, liberation from compulsions hardened into workaday habits, or with the knitting together of a sympathetic community. Many but not all, however, do limn "a sloughing of the old skin, toward a new youth." D H Lawrence stated that to be a keynote of American literature. Hushpuppy and her Bathtub friends exemplify it. If Country Noir is a revolutionary departure from the world of newsstand crime, it lies in this contrast (Figure 2-1).

Apart from the ambiguous closures of gothic-style mysteries by Annie Proulx, Harry Crews, David Joy, Denis Johnson, and Steph Post, the failure story is not the habitual closure of country noir. *Beasts of the Southern Wild* prefigures the direction they take: readiness for the impending disaster, knowing who the nemesis is, and staring it down (Hushpuppy); needing to get away from one's no longer livable home (the residents of The Bathtub and the women of the Elysian Fields floating jazz club); accepting compassion and responsibility as two equal parts of one whole (Wink); keeping stable despite vulnerability (Bathsheba); and the calmness under pressure to reevaluate oneself in the context of one's past instead of creating a body armor that isolates oneself inside it. Hushpuppy's preparation for stopping the monstrous Auroch is iconic of country noir, especially because it is as joyous as well as frightening, and a matter of family and communal love as well as gutsy belligerence. In *Beasts of the Southern Wild*, the *weltanschauung* of New Orleans entails an obedience to medical, educational, and legal authorities, a public good that Hushpuppy and her father want no part of. Surveying the city's storm surge barriers, He remarked, "Ain't that ugly?" He felt the same about the hospital where well-meaning physicians confirmed his leukemia.

On the last page in *The Great Gatsby*, Nick talks of "That vast obscurity beyond the city, where the dark fields of the republic rolled on under the night." Nick says this as he was "brooding on the old, unknown world...commensurate with man's capacity for wonder." Part of the wonder is the sense of wildness, the avoidance of any location tamed by law and order; and a sense of the exhilaration of self-discovery, not autocratically imposed restraint. Each of the following works are full of the subversive wildness that *Beasts of the Southern Wild* proclaim: Rudolph Wurlitzer's *Nog*, Harry Crews' *Scar Lover*, Denis Johnson's *Jesus' Son*, Allen Carr's *Opioid, Indiana*, Robert Coover's *Huck Out West*, Chris Offutt's *Kentucky Straight* and *Country Dark*, Martin McDonagh's *Three Billboards Outside Ebbing, Missouri*, J R Lansdale's Hap and Leonard thrillers, and John Williams's *Butcher's Crossing*.

Other country noirs do not have heroes as ebullient as six-year-old Hushpuppy, of course, but the central characters are emphatically not radically demoralized. In stories by Daniel Woodrell, Bonnie Campbell, Denis Johnson, Sheldon Lee Compton, and Chris Offutt, they prevail, despite the heavy load of financial stress, the inaccessibility to access health and child care, or the necessity to cooperate with criminal elements. Occasionally, they do so by leaving behind "guts on the ground," in defiance of the moral consensus and the legal and political authorities. They act with what they have decided is a fundamental rightness. Characters in newsstand pulp crime do this also. But there is a direct contrast between the open-ended possibilities of country noir's characters and the habitual grim conclusions of 20th century crime writing, visions of "lost paradises."

Failure Stories with Heartland Settings

Four examples are James M Cain's *Past All Dishonor* (1946, Signet paperback 1948) and his *The Butterfly* (1947), Charles Williams's *Hill Girl* (paperback original, Fawcett 1951), and James Ross's *They Don't Dance Much* (1940). They are set, as many recent noirs are, in the American West and Appalachia. The atmosphere is dynamically embodied by Stephen Crane's statement in his "A Man and Some Others": in it, he makes campfire a metaphor for "an ancient melody which surely bears a message of the inconsequence of individual tragedy—a message that is in the boom of the sea, the sliver of the wind through the grass blades, the silken clash of hemlock boughs." Each has an inevitable sinister trajectory from hope to despair: "twisted sorrow."

That is why they are unlike contemporary Country Noir. Inherent in the distinction are the nature of small- as opposed to mass-market publishing, and the very different experiences, and radically different endings, that the writers delineate.

In *Past All Dishonor*, the hero-narrator, abjectly involved with a prostitute, degenerates from a Confederate loyalist to a hired gun for owners of a Nevada silver mine. His own self-assessment: "A traitor, a killer, and a thief." His lover covers herself with stolen jewels just before being killed by the posse tracking them both. *The Butterfly* (1947) is set in Appalachia. The narrator has been trapped in a relationship he was certain was adulterous and is about to be killed by a relative of the woman's father, whom he had murdered. He has been wrong about who the woman's parents were, and about who was blocking his path to a marriage with her. The last sentence is "Here They Come." Williams's *Hill Girl* is set in Texas farm country. Bob and Lee are brothers locked in a love/hate relationship. When Bob marries Angelina, Lee's desire turns from erotic to monomaniacally possessive. The book ends with Bob dissolved in tears, as much for the loss of the brother as for the crushing of his wife's spirit. Finally, in Ross' *They Don't Dance Much* (1940), set in a small-town North Carolina roadhouse, the narrator is an observer of all kinds of racketeering, mayhem, racist brutality, and cold-blooded murder. He thumbs a ride out of time, grateful to still be alive (Figure 2-2).

The best-known western novel where all the protagonists meet with "twisted sorrow" is Oakley Hall's *Warlock* (1958). Cowboys employed by a cattle baron intimidate and humiliate the citizens, especially those who have struck silver ore. The cowboys have their own code, an illusion of honorable independence inherited from the agrarian South. They hate the law and order desired by those trying to suppress rustling, gambling, drunken shootouts, prostitution, and stealing of miners' goods. These "town yellow," as the cowboys refer to them, hire Blasdell, a brilliant shootist (based on Wyatt Earp), to stop explosions of violence with quick-draw effectiveness. The town stalwarts, knowing how to collect and distribute precious metals, are from the North; their law and order is thus pure hell to the Cowboys. The killing escalates as intransigence on both sides hardens, due not only to ethnic and regional ideological absolutes, but also to intergenerational familiar tensions. Blaisdell, in despair after an O K Coral-type shootout, throws down his guns and, his eyesight failing, leaves the town to its uncertain fate. The sheriff, a "one just man" who took the job out of compassion for the citizenry, is ambushed; the only way for a good man to find peace in Warlock is by quick, violent death. There is, Hall concludes, "no end but the corruption and the mock of courage and of hope."[38]

Would present-day writers hope for the mass market that characterized pulp of the mid-twentieth century? Something inherent in the latter's assumed meretricious effect on readers gave it power, even apart from its being a working-class genre. Its writers might have been exhilarated by freedom from the media critics' notions of character development, plot continuity, or satisfying closure. Contemporary writers may miss this freedom, but should be relieved not to have to conform to the prerequisites of editors demanding prurient sex and violence, predisposed length of text, sensational publicity, and a limited period of advertisement and distribution. They do not have to face the possibility, as twentieth century writers did, of one complaint by an individual or special interest group forcing a newsstand owner to remove all copies from a specific point of sale.

---

[38] Geoffrey O'Brien, "The Design of the West," *Bookforum,* 12.4 (Dec/Jan 2006), p.47.

"The Easiest Thing in the World"?

Crime story writers, for 20th century mass market or contemporary more limited readerships, face similar discouraging challenges placing literature sold for its entertainment value. Shamus award winning crime novelist Richard Helms, while publishing Back Alley books, had this to say:

> Getting published is the easiest thing in the world. All you have to do is convince one agent and one editor and one small group of marketing drones that what you have written will sell...The real problem is finding that one editor in the morass of agents and publishers in the business, and in catching the marketing department on a good day. And, finally, there is just no accounting for taste.[39]

Paperback crime novels are no longer considered throwaway distractions. However, middlebrow genre fiction is a denigrating enough category. Reviews are often segregated by a grouping such as "Crime and Mystery." A positive recent development is that that pulp hard-boiled novels of both the pre-and post-World War II period are now acknowledged to be of formative importance in defining the hostility, aggression, distrust, and despairing resignation of people striving to escape the anxiety, poverty, and decay of both Depression and Red Scare nightmares. Country noir is similarly respected as revealing the alarm, disorientation, and dread of communities whose institutions

---

[39] Posted on May 18, 2007 on the "Hard Boiled" (?) discussion group. Under the topic "Unpublished and better left that way." Reproduced with the kind permission of Richard Helms.

and traditions are no longer able to sustain their inhabitants. Harry Crews wrote, "The world that circumscribed the people I came from had so little margin for error, for bad luck, that when something went wrong, it almost always brought something else down with it."[40] That sounds like classic pulp crime: *Cassidy's Girl*, *The Postman Always Rings Twice*, *Kiss Tomorrow Good-bye*, *They Shoot Horses Don't They?*, or *The Nothing Man*. In both kinds of stories, protagonists lack the decorum and the self-restraint that inhibits public outbursts of emotions in middle class people. The results are sometimes disastrous, and sometimes beneficial, to the characters' fates.

Present-day editors have been known to warn against using subjects, although common in rural areas, which would cause bad reviews and sales: violence against spouses, child abuse, and killing of animals. Either acquisition editors or agents discouraged Eryk Pruitt (*Townies*, *Dirtbags*) from delineating cheating wives. His using a criminal anti-hero was also challenged. That does not mean that Pruitt or other writers—Charles Salzberg, for example, in *Second Story Man*—were successfully dissuaded from including such behaviors. They were not.

Do contemporary crime writers like the reality of having to reach a majority of their readers in eBook rather than print form? Like their predecessors, they sometimes have started in literary fiction and moved into crime, with its broad paperback, and presumably eBook, appeal. To have books displayed in stores and store windows is appealing. But not as much as a cover's display on a popular Internet home page. Most young writers yearn for established publishers of trade paperbacks, as pulp writers once wanted to appear in Fawcett's paperback originals.

---

[40] From his *A Childhood: The Biography of a Place* . Quoted in his obit in *New Georgia Encyclopedia* https://www.georgiaencyclopedia.org/articles/arts-culture/harry-crews-1935-2012/

Only the more established independent publishers can afford publicity campaigns, as was the case with pulp publishers. The word "noir" is becoming more saleable, but "thriller" has perennially been more so. Newsstand pulp crime publishers did not use the term "noir." "Noir" is a concept that critics need (not that readers and writers are not attracted to it). "Hard-boiled" implies adventure, sex, or suspense, which have always sold the crime genre, as have invoking the name of renown authors.

Steph Post, author of *A Tree Born Crooked*, *Lightwood*, and *Walk in the Fire*, puts it acutely: "Country Noir (or Grit Lit, or whatever) is an interesting genre, because it straddles a lot of other genre lines—working-class fiction, crime fiction, literary fiction, Southern, etc. It's hard to peg down and I think that's maybe why it's a genre title I feel comfortable wearing."[41] She's talking about the comforts of innovation and creativity. Therefore, the term "niche" cannot be applied to Country Noir, as it can be, for example, to Regency romance, apocalyptic science fiction, locked room mystery, or the police procedural.

Woodrell's concern about the term "country noir" being too limiting, or too niche, is another way of expressing what Post states. A writer's ability to put together elements of various kinds of naturalistic crime fiction attracts a mix of readers, women as well as men. But specifying a discreet group of possible purchasers is invaluable. Rusty Barnes (*Reckoning*, *Ridgerunner*) reports," I think my readership comprises cishet [non-trans heterosexual] white male small press [readers] ages 35-65." This being so, success in Country Noir publishing is especially dependent on sympathetic publishers and editors, whether on the staff of small presses or subsidiary imprints of established houses. Writers would be happy to enjoy the following marketing

[41] Steph Post, response to questionnaire, Nov. 6, 2020. I would like to thank the following for their thoughtful and helpful responses to my set of questions: Rusty Barnes, Eric Beetner, Rick Ollerman, Scott Phillips, Eryk Pruitt, Charles Salzberg, as well as Steph Post.

schemes, listed by Scribner's' "advance reader's edition" (2018) of Sarah Smarsh's *Heartland*: "Online advertising campaign"; Cross promotion with author's website"; Targeted email outreach"; "Discussion guide"; "Goodreads giveaways"; National print publicity campaign"; "National NPR campaign"; "Academic marketing outreach"; "Seven-city author tour."

Some Essential Components of Both Genres

The noir sensibility is just as engrained in rural noir writing as it is in newsstand pulp crime written a century ago. James Sallis makes this succinctly clear.

> Nowadays nothing tells us more about our society...than crime fiction. Hammett and Chandler recollect our attention not only for their precedence and brilliance, but as much because their tales occur at America's edge, with the frontier used up, at almost the very moment that our society was shifting from rural to urban. And perhaps nothing tells up more about the American psyche than the image of the West.[42]

Congruences of two kinds of adventure stories include confrontation with the mysterious, motivation for sinister actions, the exhilaration of survival, and even the capacity, or lack of it, for personal revelation.

Below are some categories which writers in both genres use extensively. The common denominator is violence. In 1950, critic Geoffrey Gorer wrote of the influence of American crime

---

[42] Introduction to On *Dangerous Ground: Stories of Western Noir*, ed. Ed Gorman, Dave Zeltserman, Martin H. Greenberg. (Forest Hill, MD: Cemetery Dance Publications, 2011).

novels in Europe, suggesting the appearance of a new myth of "a very strange society in which violence is normal, and normally unpunished."[43] Years later, critic Perry Miller observed that Europeans were enthused by the work of not only Hemingway, Cauldwell, Dos Passos, Faulkner, and Farrell but also Cain, Hammett, and other "tough" writers. Miller sees the American initiation into wild landscapes, decrepit mansions, and low-life dives as essential to finding a sense of identity, the price being "a foretaste of hell."[44] Contemporary rural gothic, especially Cormac McCarthy, David Joy, and Annie Proulx, gives more than a foretaste. See below.

Violence reaching the point of grotesqueness was a chief selling point for pulp paperbacks in America's 1950s mass entertainment areas. James M. Cain's most famous passage describes a wife and her lover making violent love with the body of the husband lying a few feet away (*The Postman Always Rings Twice*). It was alluded to or directly imitated by many pulp writers, most remarkably in Day Keene's potboiler *Home is the Sailor*. "His head plopped like an overripe melon…A peculiar look came into her face. Her upper lip came away from her teeth." Writers like Harry Crews, Donald Ray Pollock, David Joy, and Frank Bill integrate violence and brutality with the tapestry of the suddenly moribund American small town and farmer's field. They reveal the frustrated anger and morbid self-destructive urges of people with no way out due to lack of status and resources. Here are some hints at the shock twenty-first century noir crime can evoke:

—A young mother has to prove that her father, the owner of the house where she and her child live, is deceased, so that she can inherit the place. She is shown his corpse by his murderers, so that she can cut off a hand to make a case before the legal

---

[43] "The Erotic Myth of America," in *The Dangers of Equality and Other Essays* (NY: Weybright and Taley, 1966), p.236.

[44] "Europe's Faith in American Fiction," *Atlantic Monthly* (Dec., 1951), 52-56.

authorities. (Daniel Woodrell, *Winter's Bone*).

—A man sells his teenage granddaughter to nearby degenerates in order to pay for his wife's cancer treatments. She shoots him when she finds out. (Frank Bill, *Crimes in Southern Indiana*)

—A sheriff shoots a brave citizen fighting the power of the town's drug lords, out of sympathy for the town's addicts, who would be helpless without it. (Sheldon Compton, *Brown Bottle*)

—An obsessed game warden tracks down three poachers, killing two in the same way they waylaid their prey, and blinding a third. (Tom Franklin, "Poachers")

—The son of a drug kingpin who has been used as a hit man by his father chooses to walk into a stream of police bullets in an act of family unity. (David Joy, *Where All Light Tends to Go*)

—A novel's protagonist throws a bag of hornets at a gunman, who is half blinded and "webbed" with welts. Our hero can now use the gunman to find who sent him. (Chris Offutt, *Country Dark*).

Setting: Locale is as important as character in both rural as well as pulp noir and assumes the status of a protagonist or antagonist. In twentieth century pulp, it is underclass or working-class areas where mobsters, gamblers, hit men, and petty crooks do business. In rural noir, it is wherever people are hungry, needy, and have talents locked up inside them: the wild, wide-open spaces of the mountains, fields, and towns of Texas, Appalachia, the Ozarks, the deep South, and the desert Southwest. Prime examples include Brian Allen Carr's *Opioid, Indiana*, Rudolph Wurlitzer's *The Drop Edge of Yonder*, E L Doctorow's *Welcome to Hard Times*, Rusty Barnes' *Reckoning*, and Cormac McCarthy's Border Trilogy.

Protagonists: Both pulp and rural noir include characters marked by expressions of insecurity, bitterness, anxiety, and resentment. They suppress self-doubts with the aid of hard drinking and hard fighting. Schemes devised to improve financial or professional status collapse. Protagonists, living in urban or rural near-poverty with little ability to succeed in a workplace requiring cooperative division of labor, risk a well-meaning but desperate plan that lands them in jail or hospital. The hero with a "tough but tender" sensibility was conceived in the days of *Black Mask*—Philip Marlowe, Lew Archer, Peter Chambers, Daniel Port, and Peter Gunn are examples. In rural noir, there are Matt Phillips's Packard (*Accidental Outlaws*), Martin McDonagh's Mildred (*Three Billboards Outside Ebbing, Missouri*), Denis Johnson's Bill Houston (*Angels*), Rusty Barnes's Matt Rider (*Ridgerunner, Killer from the Hills*), and Steph post's Remy (*Lightwood, Walk in the Fire, Holding Smoke*).

Help from Unlikely Places. David Goodis's novels contain some of the best examples of the hero finding nurture not in an acquisitive bourgeois setting, but among rejects who have nothing left to lose and are open to empathy and charity. Peter Rabe, Steve Fisher, William McGivern, Gil Brewer, and Lionel White sometimes use this kind of story. The country noir stories of Denis Johnson, Chris Offutt, Bonnie Jo Campbell, Carolyn Chute, Ron Rash, and Larry Brown also do. In Crews's *Scar Lover*, Rastafarian outcasts are able to restore the protagonist's faith in himself and replace the brother he had irreparably injured many years ago. Many of Bonnie Campbell's stories are moving due to their writer's ability to look up from the bottom and get the reader to compare the characters favorably to those on top. In Campbell's "King Cole's American Salvage," the protagonist is a thief, but relief of his friends' needs is one of his desires, if not the primary motive. At his trial, they absolve themselves of complicity by lying in court. The thief goes to jail, where he consorts with people who know the difference, as he does, between purchasing security at the price of betrayal and taking responsibility for others as well as himself. In Denis Johnson's novels, people confront their visceral responses to horrific auto crashes, manslaughter, invasion of privacy, and aggressively asocial instincts until they discover a universality of human compassion. In Johnson's short story "Dun Dun" (in *Jesus' Son*), the narrator comments as follows on a drug addicted friend one of whose ambitions was to be a hit man: "If I opened up your head and ran a hot soldiering iron around in your brain, I might make you into someone like that." The men met in prison, and instead of threats and fights, they recognized how to support each other.

Fate, Cruel or Benevolent. Charles Willeford, in *The Woman Chaser*, writes: "I didn't have to be told that the siren was for me...I felt a welcome sense of relief combined with a feeling of dark depression and failure." An example of a twentieth century rural noir, published by the leading newsstand paperback publisher, Fawcett, is *Whom Gods Destroy* (Figure 2-3). Clifton Adams describes the searing prairie and the sweltering hard-scrabble settlements of the 1940s southwest. The narrator, Roy Foley, returns to his hometown to see "houses now unpainted, patched-up shacks stuck away here and there between junk yards and garages and used-car lots." Foley grasps for the gold ring in revenge upon the social structure that relegated him to menial jobs, bad housing, and contempt from patronizing citizens. These include a woman who scorned him in high school. He would take spiteful pleasure in becoming a member of the Big Prairie Country Club, which shows how fatefully bound he is to the institutions that have relegated him forever to the wrong side of the tracks, regardless of his upstart success. At the end, he is perfectly aware that his scramble for cash and status has betrayed him, and wonders when he will have enough guts to lift his pistol to his own head.

By contrast, a strain of spirituality and overriding benevolence is a bedrock motif in some rural noir. A character's fate can be resurrection of belief, not despair. In Crews' *Scar Lover* it appears as Rastafarian mysticism; in Brown's *Dirty Work* it is Walter's Christ-like sacrifice for Braiden, who sees angels and talks to God. Joy's *Where All Light Tends to Go* postulates a quiet time between life and a "resting time," implied in a mystic sense of light. Johnson's *Largesse of the Sea Maiden* and *Jesus' Son* are meditations on spiritual recovery. Chris Offutt's "Back Porch" depicts a terminally ill woman's strength and self-possession. Offutt makes her the only creative force in a community which has long accommodated itself to its meretricious stretch of fast-food and strip mall businesses.

Community

While many twentieth century crime novels delineate hostility and fear based on income level, race, ethnicity, and neighborhood, one of rural noir's defining contrasts is love of community and pity for long-settled families which can no longer offer their sons and daughters the house or livelihood of previous generations. Once-stable towns have become controlled by an underworld of drug dealers, loan sharks, and black-market operators, just as the inner-city urban neighborhoods did two generations earlier. Stories about the latter had noir endings, with even the toughest mob bosses agonizing for relief from their isolation. In rural noir, criminals who call the area home sometimes realize that they are essential to their hometown economy, and do owe something to their long-term neighbors. See Woodrell's *Winter's Bone* and "Joanna Stull."

I Wish I Were [Him or Her]; I'm Glad I'm Not"

The above conundrum describes a common vicarious response to a crime thriller. A character's aggression against law, religion, custom, or taste fascinates those who hear of it, perhaps stirring envy. Most people, as Pierre Mac Orlan, the French writer of adventure and erotica explained, are "passive adventurers." "Through the great suffering of men of action—incapable of common sense and caution—sedentary men obtain many delicate and varied little pleasures." Vicariously, they "savor the sweet anguish of thrills without consequences..."

This conundrum occurs in many kinds of communication. In media of mass communication, it surfaces when some viewers or listeners feel an identification with the subjects of news reports such as the following: an invader of the White House protesting an election; a member of a religious sect ripping off the facemask of a news reporter; a woman publicizing an episode of her boss' sexual misconduct which she suppressed while working for that person. In mass market pulp crime, evidence of the ubiquitous "I wish I were; I'm glad I'm not" or "passive adventurer" phenomenon results in stories with recurring figures: the gangster punished for success; the brave but morally compromised policeman (Francis Nevins' "noir cop"); the femme fatale navigating male attraction to her; the tough but tender, often hard-drinking and lonely detective.

Novelists hope their readers put themselves in the place of the protagonists. But there is a limit to that identity as the story unfolds and a main character either makes fateful mistakes or is victimized by malicious or weak-kneed characters, especially those the protagonist originally admired. Then the readers are glad they are not that hero, or anti-hero—but remain engrossed in his/her fate, vicariously. "I wish I were/ I'm glad I'm not" responses are more consistently present in Newsstand Pulp than in Country Noir. It is, like the stoic acceptance of fate endings discussed above, a form of social control that surfaces when a communication appeals to a mass audience. If a readership identifies with a hero of a crime story without sensing a safe distance from that character's social or cultural vulnerabilities, then the readers is more likely to become critical of the milieu that causes the hero's danger, as Woody Haut delineated in his *Pulp Culture*. Denis Johnson, Peter Heller, Barry Gifford, and Bonnie Campbell are markedly good at this kind of identification between reader and character.

Three Country Noirs, discussed in later chapters, work against the "passive adventurer" identification. The writers provide little chance for wishing themselves in the characters' shoes. In David

Joy's *Where All Light Tends to Go*, the protagonist is controlled by his drug-dealing father, participating in brutality against rival distributors. His eventual choice of family over manipulative law enforcement is heroic, and potentially sympathetic. But his entrapment is fatal, extending to choosing to die in a volley of police fire. At this point, few readers can vicariously identify. The same is true for Harry Crews' *A Feast of Snakes*. Former football star Joe Lon Mackey cannot find the exhilaration of decisive victory in his adult life, and refuses any compromise that would establish communication to even the most iconoclastic in his community. His only substitute for supreme vitality costs him the perquisite of living in any community. In Steph Post's *Lightwood*, the town's drug consumption is its major source of solvency. How this affects the major characters is epitomized by a misanthropic preacher's stranglehold over the lives of her congregation.

Since readers of these three novels are not likely to identify with the protagonists, they might consider more objectively what happens to the characters. They may even consider, as Mac Orlan does, that "a bad action never quite dies; quite the contrary, it bears fruit, with increasing abundance." What a character does, and how s/he deals with the heavy load of consequences, is puzzling, and in the end enlightening, to the reader, in a different way than the newsstand crime hero's fate was.

"Country Gothic"

Daniel Woodrell disavowed the term country noir, although he had originally subtitled his *Give Us a Kiss* as "a country noir."[45]

---

[45] See the "Reading Group Guide" appended to *Winter's Bone* (NY: Back Bay Books, 2006), p.6 (of the Guide).

It was partly because "noir" has maintained its twentieth century moorings as a film or novel where betrayal and failure were usually "the color of the air." Woodrell does not want the "form or structure" of noir to limit his writing to a genre-specific ending. He prefers the term "Gothic," as it describes Flannery O'Connor, William Faulkner, Harry Crews, or David Joy's work. These stories from rural America often feature suicide, rape, murder, sadism, impotence, betrayal, demonic gangsters, all in a carefully documented regional setting. Horror, the supernatural, and variating point of view and time sequences are other gothic elements. The shifting evaluations of amorality, madness, and crime test readers' tolerance for what begin as thrillers but defy classification, as Steph Post noted.

De Sade portrayed the gothic storytelling of his own iconoclastic time as "the inevitable product of the revolutionary shock with which the whole of Europe resounded." Country noir has not had the exposure to resonate like *Frankenstein*, "The Rime of the Ancient Mariner," *Candide*, or *Justine* did. The energy and imagination are present. Writers like Harry Crews, Annie Proulx, Daniel Woodrell, Chris Offutt, Joe Lansdale, Larry Brown, and Denis Johnson combine mystery, horror, the demonic, extreme violence, and dynamic responses to survival. They do have resourceful, publicity-savvy publishers. The first quarter of the twenty-first century has been as culturally revolutionary and counter-revolutionary as the period of the American and French revolutions.

I doubt a 1950s mass market crime novel editor would suggest a writer do a Gothic story. The plot would be too convoluted, a single naturalistic setting would have to be replaced by unfamiliar ones, the presence of the supernatural and the fantastic would be puzzling, and the array of characters would probably require that each be identified before the narrative began. There could be classic pulp blood and violence, prurience, suspense, and spicy, hard-nosed dialogue. The length of the book would, however, increase the cost. However, straightforward pulp crime thrillers also had points at which the action could accommodate the ominous setting, sinister motivation, psychic imbalance, gruesome killing, and ambiguous perspective on what makes for "justice." Notable mid-twentieth century pulp crime novelists merging pulp and gothic include Woolrich, Chandler, Thompson, Gerald Kersh, Jonathan Latimer, McCoy, Goodis, and Michael Perkins.

Country noir deals with such dire loneliness and confused loyalties that it tempts writers to suggest radical alternatives to current practices regarding family loyalty, community leadership, and spirituality. The resulting complex sensibility is typified by Larry Brown in *Dirty Work*, a powerful anti-war novel of sacrifice and inspiration in which horribly injured veterans of Vietnam reach out for the presence of Angels and God. It is also remarkable in Steph Post's three novels about recovery of self-respect by overcoming racketeers and fear-mongering preachers, and by Denis Johnson in his stories of criminals, including murderers, interminably alone in claustrophobic places. Protagonists in gothic country novels have complex, many-layered behavior patterns, signaling painful and sometimes weird but healing transformation. Sometimes a quest for money ends as a Kafkaesque glimpse of otherworldly light, as in Johnson's *Angels*, only seen by inmates on death row.

Gothic writing emerges when a culture's explanations for, and remedies for, divergent behavior no longer explain sensibly causes and results. People search out their own unique explanations for, and freedom from, loneliness, criminality, tabooed sexual compulsions, and unexplained and irresistible anxieties regarding supernatural presences. That is certainly what is going on in the novels of a wide variety of Southern, Ozark, Appalachian, Great Plains, and Big Sky novels. Whatever they owe to twentieth century noir or hard-boiled crime, the universe they create points in a different direction than failure, stoic resignation, shame and fear, or lack of love.

Figure 2-1: That a character's fate can be resurrection of belief, not despair, is a chief measure of the difference between 20th and 21st century noir. David Joy, *Where All Light...* (NY: Putnam, 2015). Collection of the author.

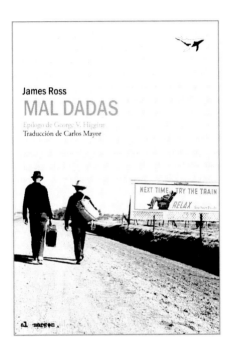

Figure 2-2: James Ross's *They Don't Dance Much* (1940; Southern Illinois U. Press, 1975) is set in a small town North Carolina roadhouse. The narrator, after watching a murder-suicide (the roadhouse owner and his wife), thumbs a ride out of town. "Have you tried the train," reads the billboard. The Spanish title means "bad luck."

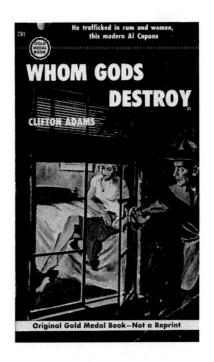

Figure 2-3: From patched up Oklahoma shack to country club, and back again, a bit like the geek protag in *Nightmare Alley.* The wind-up: a gun to his own head. Collection of the author.

CHAPTER 3

Contrasts: Sam Ross's *He Ran All the Way* (1947)
and Denis Johnson's *Angels* (1983)

This and the following two chapters contrast a highly regarded newsstand pulp and a country noir novel. The point is to reveal the contrasts in *Weltanschauung*, or sensibility, in response to overarching Fate as the narratives proceed toward their inevitable conclusions. In both kinds of crime stories, the sinister ambiance is a powerful presence. The responses to it differ, based on how the protagonists access freedom in their minds and hearts, or cannot do so. In Denis Johnson's work, and that of other country noir writers, the sinister atmosphere does not persist in the same way, with the same inevitable finality, as it does in many twentieth century crime novels, including Sam Ross's brilliant critique of his contemporaries' fear of the juvenile delinquent. His Nick is as sympathetic as Johnson's Bill. But fateful circumstance flattens Nick more totally and decisively than Johnson allows it to in Bill's case. As a result, Johnson implies a mysterious redemption for his protagonist.

Both *He Ran All the Way* (1947) and *Angels* (1983) reveal the American nuclear family's bedrock power in their respective time and place. Both concern a killer of a policeman, lifeguard of the people and a cornerstone of American justice. Both depict the consequences of botched holdups. *He Ran* takes place in industrial Chicago, where "roaring trains were sight and sound,

73

where the vibrations of factories throbbed." Nick, jobless and depressed, sleeps till noon. *Angels* is about an ex-con small-time drifter and a young woman escaping an abusive marriage. They pass archetypal small towns: "gas stations, barbeque joints, and vacant lots full of trash...the territory of mutilated billboards and stucco walls of black graffiti." The protagonist becomes part of a bank job poorly planned by his inexperienced, cash-poor brothers.

The two novels are recognizably American crime stories with pulp elements. Both describe community indifference to the main characters' troubles and the failure of their families to help them recover self-worth. In addition to violence and a hostile setting, there is unexpected inspiration from a person and a place, respectively. In *He Ran,* a young woman finds strength to help a fugitive, and then her family. In *Angels,* a condemned man recognizes in a bright light on a dark wall a sign of God's forgiveness. These responses occur as part of the climax of the works. It is left to the reader to decide in which direction they point.

"He felt exhausted, as though he had come off a battlefield" (*He Ran All the Way,* Figure 3-1).

Nick, a young tough, bungles a robbery, then takes a family hostage at gunpoint. On the run—he or his partner had shot a policeman during a robbery—he tries hiding in the crush of folks at the Lake Michigan beach. There, he meets Peggy Dobbs, a demure redhead. They hit it off. Both, Nick most desperately and Peggy subconsciously, are looking for something. She dutifully takes him home to meet the family, at which point, needing to stay out of sight, he holds them at gunpoint.

He desperately wants to enjoy the company of Peg. Several times, the couple contemplate making their escape together. Earlier, before he pulled the gun, she "saw his wrinkled forehead crush tears out of his eyes...Nobody had ever touched her so deeply." But family in danger comes first. "...the deep loneliness in him that reached for her, the sense of his touch and closeness and the way she yearned to get closer, closer...She had to hate him. He was dangerous. He was brutal...He was death." And, of course, sin.

Nick yearns after the mutuality of the Dobbs family. He tries to make a friend out of Peg's preteen brother, but the kid only wishes he were bigger so he could kill Nick. A poignant early chapter depicts Nick's disgust with his own mother, because, after her husband abandoned the family, she turned to street walking to feed Nick and herself. In the throes of a serious illness, Nick's father had left because he did not want to be a burden to a wife and son he could no longer support. This is a prevalent tragedy of both urban slum and rural village poverty, from coast to coast, in postwar and endless war America.

Sam Ross strikingly depicts the sadness of growing up in a poverty-stricken single-parent home. With no father to learn from, and a distraught, self-hating mother, Nick knew nothing of security or responsibility. He was a tough guy with no possibility of becoming tender. If his mother tried to show him love, he rejected it, and was proud of not (he imagines) needing it, until he met Peg at the point when he had become a frightened, hunted outcast. He may see Mrs. Dobbs as the kind of mother he wishes to have: self-effacing and loving. When Mrs. Dobbs runs a sewing needle through her finger, he tries to help her, although he's afraid her screams will attract attention. He does get the needle out. Mr. Dobbs's final plea to Nick is that he not take Peg with him when he makes his escape. It would be the end of their family and its cherished mutuality. He then begs his daughter not to go with Nick. That would be sacrificing herself: intolerable. It would be equally intolerable if Peg chose Nick over her father, mother, and brother. What would the neighbors say, or be incited to say, after the gossipy tabloid coverage of such a situation? And that would be the least of the turmoil encompassing them.

Peg's affection for Nick has been genuine, until the fateful climax. When she tells Nick she wants to go with him, and has arranged to buy an escape car, Nick is not sure this deeply religious young woman is about to abandon family responsibility.

On the edge of hysteria, he approaches her with a "crazy look of ecstasy." Although "frenzied with fear," she kisses him. As he throws himself upon her, wanting nothing but a release from tension, she gathers all her strength and plunges a knife she had hidden in the sofa deep into his back. Mr. Dobbs, who had reluctantly borrowed a gun from a policeman friend, was relieved from having to use it by Peg's act.

Ross, an experienced screenwriter, eschewed the more likely end of his hostage story. It was not the police, or the father, but the young, virginal woman on the edge of adulthood, who effected her family's escape. But at a heavy price. Attracted by Nick's vulnerability, Peg sacrificed those feelings under intolerable pressure. She is left to relive what she has done, and to weigh what she had lost. Ross implies the loss as well as the gain involved in inviolable family ties. Her father must now "pick up the scattered remains of his family and piece them together." Nick's home invasion precipitated responses that included a daughter's putting the invader off guard to kill him, a young boy's loss of security in his own home, a mother's mute passivity in her role as nurturer, and a father's puzzlement about how to defend his own family. They could not help but think about the fact that it was Peg and not her father who had to act. Would they recognize that the reason was his reluctance to kill? Or would they think that if he had borrowed that gun from his policeman friend, he would have won more respect as a protector of his loved ones?

The tabloids would ignore such questions, forcing the issue into a made to order melodramatic scenario. It would be sold as an example of all-American bravery when held at gunpoint by a "juvenile delinquent," or a "madman." With ratings in the balance, mass media will dismiss any mature approach in favor of bad faith melodrama that avoids confronting any serious dilemmas. If that is the kind of masscult propaganda Dwight Macdonald deplores, it is especially sad that he and his colleagues relegated crime novels and films such as *He Ran* to that category.

From his perspective circa 1960, he believed it essential to praise narratives that challenged accepted norms as if they were absolutes. That is in fact what *He Ran* does. But Mcdonald assumed popular "lowbrow" or "masscult" entertainments were like those concocted in *1894's* Ministry of Truth. They prevented citizens from thinking for themselves, and therefore were uncontrovertibly part of the problem.[46]

In the 1951 film, Mr. Dobbs does intend to shoot. Nick's gun falls to the ground as he prepares to return fire. Peg picks it up and, instead of giving it back to Nick, shoots him in the stomach (Figure 3-2). Ironically, the getaway car she and Nick ordered arrives, a few seconds before Nick dies. Crime doesn't pay, especially because Nick was not tough enough. He lacked callous contempt for other people.

Mr. Dobbs says, "Everybody gets to the point where they draw a line. When that line is drawn, you can't force them any farther. Not even with a gun. Not even if you beat 'em to death. People are like that." That is a bravely idealistic, American thing to say. It means that there is a point beyond which a people with faith in themselves will revolt against an oppressor and succeed in maintaining their honor. (In the classic Western *Terror in a Texas Town* [1958], the turning point occurs when the hired gun tells his oil-hungry boss that he just met a man who would

---

[46] I expected to find at least a few mass market crime novels, at least those first appearing in hardback (as *He Ran* had) discussed in Walter Rideout's *The Radical Novel in the United States, 1900-1954,* which documents working class urban suffering, but failed to find any. Writers such as Sam Ross, along with Benjamin Appel, Horace McCoy, Hall Ellson, Harlan Ellison, Whit Burnett, James M Cain, and Gerald Kerch were writing suspense thrillers with elements of pulp magazine style. It seemed that the genre precluded their consideration as radical social commentary. For the aspects of Modernist literature incorporated in pulp narratives, see David Earle, "The Modernist Genre Novel," in *A History of the Modernist Novel*, ed Gregory Castle (NY: Cambridge University Press, 2015), Chapter 16.

rather be shot than do as ordered). The problem Ross raises in his profound novel (and in the film, written by Dalton Trumbo, blacklisted for not following HUAC's orders), is how difficult it is to determine what that point is, and the fateful long-term consequences of the action. Mr. Dobbs did not take his policeman friend's advice at first, not through fear but because he did not want to make a horrible mistake with a deadly weapon. Blind fate relieved him of that choice, but it was his daughter who killed the family oppressor. What Peg did would be called "honorable" and "heroic" by the tabloid editorialists and local news broadcasters. But in fact, Peg will be haunted by her responsibility to family occasioning her killing of Nick. When she falls in love, she will be compelled to revisit the horror of Nick's alternating brutality toward her and his affection. The trust necessary for love may be paralyzed. Fate had let her in for more "twisted sorrow" than it had her father. Self-confidence may be hard for her to regain.

He Ran is one of the best juvenile delinquency novels in a storm of good ones that show the era's dysfunction. Ross's genius lies in his sympathy for Nick and his broken family as well as for the Dobbs family. Abe Polonsky, Academy Award (later blacklisted) writer and director, stated of Nick, "He defended his street boy's honor and they killed him for it." That would have made a great blurb. Lion Books republished the novel in 1950, with its own blurb equally pulpish and enticing: "We invite you to read the first half-dozen pages of *He Ran All the Way—* right now, at the book racks. Then we challenge you to put it down." Those pages concern Nick waking from a dream where he loses a bet, then having a fight with his mother, calling her a whore. "His fate was sealed; he couldn't struggle against it." His own family being broken, the boy forced entry into another one, frightened them into rejecting him, and was killed, not by the police, but by the one member of that family with whom he had established an emotional connection. Charles Williams, David Goodis, Jim Thompson, or Cornell Woolrich couldn't have written it better. To paraphrase Cornell Woolrich, everyone is afraid of everyone else. As many have said, including novelist Hans Fallada and Don Draper on *Mad Men*, everyone dies alone. In *He Ran*, it was Nick, not because he was a juvenile delinquent, which he wasn't, but because of slum-bred poverty and consequent desperation. The only solution seemed the gun, robbery, and hostage taking, all insuring loss of prerogatives as a human being.

Ineffable Blackness, but in God's Bosom

Nick's situation bears deep similarities to *Angels'* Bill Houston. They are both cop killers. These acts make them the kind of outcasts for whom execution is appropriate. Lawful citizens expect the state to relieve them of the burden of taking personal revenge. In both cases, compassion is assumed to be unthinkable. Both the newsstand crime writer and the country noir author provide that compassion to their readers. Sam Ross' Nick is fated to die alone, victim of the suffering a slum poverty upbringing, a misguided attempt to take control of his life, and an intolerable choice he has imposed on the Dobbs family. The characters are in the clutches of indifferent fate and the survivors will be in future. By contrast, Denis Johnson's Bill, also a doomed outcast, does die alone but not without hope or self-worth (Figure 3-3).

Angels is a hardboiled crime novel with many pulp elements. Bill Houston, an ex con with a tattoo of a female Satan to remind him never to remarry, displays occasional unrestrained rage, desire for assertion, resentment, and self-hate. His bothers share the same traits. "The vision of [Bill's brother] Burris' spirit was riveted on the single fact he could be certain of: he was a wasted and desperate human being who hated himself." Johnson's thriller has rape, theft, and the murder of a bank guard during a holdup. Bill does it on the orders of one of his brothers after the guard kills one of the gang. There are several classic Grand Guignol scenes describing physical but focusing on emotional suffering, ending with abused runaway Jaime's hysterics in a mental hospital and Bill's final minutes in the gas chamber. Bill asks how painful his execution will be, and his court-appointed lawyer tells him that his lungs will turn red before his soul drifts out of the death chamber with the gas fumes. It gets even more lugubrious when Bill is told to take off his pants so they won't get ruined by the fumes, but he can leave his underpants on. Bill's tears flow. In the chamber, he hears his heart booming and tries to hold his breath.

His last thought is to pray for another human being. This could be dismissed as pathos, but Johnson steers the reader in another direction, spotlighting an empathy lacking in the executioners and citizens, some of whom arrive in their campers at five AM to stare at the execution site. Johnson suggests that as death looms, the designated scapegoat can either pump up the fury within himself or conquer it. Bill does the latter. His lawyer, drinking coffee while waiting for the news of Bill's death, catches sight of a" portrait" of Elvis Presley behind the counter. "Rendered in iridescent paint on black velvet, hovering before a brilliant microphone, the face of the dead idol seemed on the brink of speech." Every evening, Johnson concludes, "this iridescent-on-velvet face of Elvis Presley [will] climb the twilight to address all the bankrupt cafes." The writer's language is extraordinary in the context of his narrative, becoming prophetic. The closing sentences of *Angels* are replete with spirituality. I think that portrait of Elvis, if it could talk, would commend the criminal lawyer, because he plans to stay in this arid desert town, which survives because a maximum-security prison supports it. "There is a part of [the lawyer] that wanted to help murderers go free." Perhaps Johnson was thinking of "Heartbreak Hotel," and Bill's final prayer to Jesus.

I looked over Jordan and what did I see
Coming for to carry me home
A band of angels coming after me

Coming for to carry me home...

Bill Houston, cop killer, is treated as a cipher by the guards. "Mr. Houston. Let's take you for a ride up the [exhaust] pipe" (in the gas chamber). But maybe he is free, in ethereal form, and with the angels. Johnson tells us that on his last night, "he had lain with the Unmade, with God, the incredible darkness, the huge blue mouth of love."

Denis Johnson's Challenges to Capital Punishment for the Murderer

Johnson creates characters who, although dangerous to themselves and others, develop a restraint and empathy. In the final story in *Jesus' Son*, one character finds a job working with the emotionally disturbed because their responses are not what are thought conventional, "sane," or "decent." Nor are his: his response to a woman crying when hearing of her husband's death is that her scream had the purity of an eagle's. In another story in that collection, "Dundun" (i.e., Fuckhead), a narrator describes a cell mate—an impassive thief, sadist, and murderer who "wouldn't mind working as a hit man"—and concludes by challenging the reader. "Would you believe me when I tell you there was kindness in his heart?...If I opened up your head and ran a hot soldering iron around in your brain, I might turn you into someone like that."

I know of no 1950s pulp crime writer who would go there. Horace McCoy's *Kiss Tomorrow Goodbye* (1948), Gil Brewer's *The Vengeful Virgin* (1958), and Eliot Chaze's *Black Wings Has My Angel* (1953) all have protagonists who, despite committing murder, could evoke sympathy. But these writers did not challenge the belief that murder was an irredeemable crime. Two of the three thrillers just mentioned are paperback originals. Their editors would redline any doubt about the death sentence for first degree murder. They had to have handy what could be explained to critics as a "crime does not pay" ending, in case they were caught in a degradation ceremony, as they were at least twice by congressional investigative committees in the 1950s. No one would accuse James M Cain of acceding to such redlining. Nevertheless, Frank, the protagonist of *The Postman Always Rings Twice*, narrating his story after being falsely convicted of murdering his beloved, Cora, acknowledges that his killing of Cora's husband had erased his prerogative of staying alive. Once again, as Robert Warshow observed, "The function of mass culture is to conform "with accepted notions of the public good." A narrative of a protagonist who cannot control events, and is therefore destroyed by impassive fate, does calm a reader's desires to revolt against the living conditions s/he chafes under. Thus, the pulp crime "failure story" reconciles the reader to his/her own place ("I'm glad I'm not the person in that story"; or, "I have family responsibilities, after all").

Johnson's perspective on the Houston brothers' ill-fated holdup is a challenge to societal moral judgement. Bill's brother Burris, watching a movie about Jesse James, sees the Northfield, Minnesota situation from the James-Younger gang's perspective. They were decimated by townspeople risking their lives to destroy the James family. Jesse had killed the cashier after he refused to open a safe and betray his fellow citizens and his employers. (The safe was open the whole fateful morning). The response of Northfield's citizens, a shootout with desperate outlaws, was self-sacrificingly loyal to their established institutions. Burris compared this dutiful, apparently redemptive violence to those who confronted the Houstons during their ill-fated robbery, specifically the bank guard. Instead of simply obeying the armed robbers, "he responded by ripp[ing] apart poor James Houston with a gunshot wound, throwing himself away forever in the effort." This may seem to be addled thinking: the guard was doing his sworn duty, just as the Northfield citizens were protecting their bank. The wealth of this growing community (two colleges, a railroad station) individually and collectively was in their bank.[47] Johnson suggests the chasm between civic duty and respect for private values, such as preserving one's life and therefore the welfare of one's family.

This is Burris, thinking of his own brothers: "The James Brothers did not know anything about sorrow, grief, or fear...as they risked everything, absolutely everything they could, to take their brothers home." That is also the case in the Houston brothers' bank robbery. After gut-shooting James Houston, the guard does not know what to do next. He is an easy target. His family, as well as Jameses', will never be the same. And, eventually, Bill Houston—who killed the guard because brother Burris told him to—is executed. Denis Johnson, like Sam Ross, is asking the readers to think about a conundrum: duty to law and order, or to family, can be a kind of straitjacket. Duty and familial responsibility prevent Bill from thinking about the bank guard's needs and obligations, as they prevent Jessie James from considering the life and family of the cashier at the Northfield bank. Certainly, the citizens of Northfield do not think of the James gang's fallen with any sympathy. The men who pulled the trigger, Jessie James, and the Northfield posse, are considered heroes to their communities. They have helped preserve the ideals of Confederate honor, or their community's

---

[47] A major reason for attacking Northfield's bank was that a Reconstructionist (i.e. Union) governor and a relative had a large amount invested there. Jesse James, as a Confederate soldier and sympathizer, wanted to end the post-war economic and political power of liberated slaves. The bank cashier's reluctance, with a gun to his head, helped buy the citizens time to shoot the James gang "all to hell." But Southern refusal to obey Reconstruction persisted, and increased regional pride. In fact, in the disputed aftermath of the 1876 election, Rutherford B. Hayes assumed office after agreeing to remove Union enablers of Reconstruction. African American integration in the South ended. Many former slaves had to work the land as sharecroppers.

law an order, respectively. The cashier's family and the bank guard's, and eventually the Houstons, all grieve for their irremediable losses. The body count, from the cashier to Bill Houston, is tragic.

As for the latter, his perspective, as the toils of the legal system close around him, becomes intensely personal. He asks his lawyer to tell Burris, "He's still my brother." Johnson directs his readers away from a belief system which prioritizes civil duty far above empathy for law-breakers, since they must not be thought of in halls of justice as fellow sinners, but as pariahs. His emphasis on Bill's weeping is one example. There's also Johnson's delineation of that mysterious, benevolent light appearing only to condemned prisoners at the hour of nine p.m. That is the time of an "angel light," symbolizing awareness of self and destiny, an angelic blessing at a moment when one approaches full maturity.[48] Finally, there is Bill's lawyer's staring at the "iridescent-on-velvet" image of Elvis, about to sing, maybe, "Heartbreak Hotel."

Angels' contrast to pulp noir is quite profound. Readers of pulp crime novels of the 1950s did empathize with protagonist-criminals. But in Johnson's work, and that of other country noir writers, the sinister atmosphere does not persist in the same way as it does in many twentieth century crime novels. He is able to raise questions for his audience about redemption, and about personal freedom from "sacred" obligations to law and justice.

To make the point, compare Bill's last tenuous moments with those of the protagonists of the aforementioned McCoy's *Kiss Tomorrow Goodbye*, Brewer's *The Vengeful Virgin*, and Chaze's *Black Wings Has My Angel*. McCoy's Ralph never conquered his incestuous fixation. Dying, he assumes a fetal position: "At last I was safe and secure in the blackness of the womb from which I had never emerged." Brewer's Jack feels no guilt at murdering desirable Shirley's husband because he is engulfed in this last

---

[48] "Angel Number 9 Meaning—Spiritual Significance and Symbolism," https://www.ipublishing.co.in/angel-number-9-meaning.

chance for a beautiful wife and therefore, to his manner of thinking, love and self-respect. After his conviction, he belittlingly puns, "There was time to burn. Then, after there was no more time, they would burn me." Chaze's narrator Tim is in the same position. With his wildly adventurous girlfriend Virginia, he plans an armored car robbery. The car and driver fall into a watery, hundred-foot-deep, black shaft. They must go back to the pit to see where the driver is, like sinners who have to come to terms with their fate. They think seeing the evil they did may free them from insufferable guilt. But Virginia falls into the shaft. When the cops come, they do not know about Virginia's fate but "They hit me a great many times before they took me off with them," probably for trial and execution. Tim, like Cain's Frank in *Postman*, is presumably telling his story from the death house. Neither he, Jack, nor Ralph would experience what Bill did in his final dream before being killed by the state of Arizona. "He slept along side of God, His darkness, His love."

The Nuclear Family in He Ran and Angels

Both the twentieth and twenty-first century crime writers reveal the nuclear family and community's bedrock power in their respective cultures. Maintaining it drives Mr. Dobbs to forsake his tolerant ideals and question his ability to protect and lead his family. It causes Peg to lie and then stab in the back a distraught, panicky young man who moved her to compassion. The act perfectly symbolizes what happens when fearsome intruders enter the space of an inviolable institution. That same attachment to family causes Bill Houston to kill the bank guard at his brother's command, even though Bill knew the robbery had already failed.

By accepting his role as outcast and adding to it the experience of a social isolate, Bill Houston becomes sensitive to his fellowship to all humanity and to mysterious supernatural presences. He joins other death row inmates in being able to see that cauterizing light from the jail's window every night at nine. The loneliness and fear are mystical in their intensity (like that in Kafka's parable "Before the Law" in *The Trial*). How to get through the barrier? On the other side is the light.

Sam Ross's novel takes account of the shadows as well as the sunlight of the American nuclear family in his time, in both Nick's tenement underclass and Peg's lower middle class. Ross makes Nick Robie not only sympathetic, but a tragic figure by showing how he ran all the way to the betrayal that awaits an outcast.

Denis Johnson's story also is about the institution of family and how it stifles connection with other people not in its orbit, as well as providing for those who are. He depicts a sensitivity to a supernatural world, only available to those outcasts who have suffered deeply enough to sense a spiritual transcendence. *Angels* is pulpish in its setting, its violence, and its tough but tender characters. And it is gothic in its final ambiguities regarding retribution, supernatural presences, and supernal finality.

I've indicated when I think a country noir novel has gothic tendencies. Country noir writing depicts the confusion and enervation of rural communities that results from corporate agricultural policies and the loss of jobs, homes, and health care opportunities. Partly due to the sometimes gothic shock its writers have the originality to employ, such as Johnson's angel light, Elvis' heartbreak, and Bill's soul forcing its way up the death house furnace, such a narrative is not only accurate social commentary but also healing, coming at a time when Americans need to know what—if anything—they feel in common.[49]

---

[49] Caroline Breashears,"'Riot Unrestrained'" and the Gothic Novel," Law and Liberty, https://lawliberty.org/riot-unrestrained-and-the-gothic-novel/

Figure 3-1: The underclass protagonist Nick, with no preparation for improving his prospects, is on the run from a mother who must support herself and Nick on prostitution. Nick runs: into a botched holdup, then into a working-class Catholic family which he holds at gunpoint. For the second time, he has isolated himself from a family which contains a loved one (first his mother, then his girlfriend). Dust jacket. Farrar, Straus, 1947; collection of the author.

Figure 3-2: Nick Robey's "Just Reward": Peg, choosing family over the desperate young fugitive, has just shot him. Not shown is Peg's (Shelly Winters') distress as she leans sorrowfully toward him, smoking gun in hand. Nick (John Garfield) displays in his dying moments the shock that the viewers must feel, along with sympathy for both protagonists. By permission of Metro Goldwyn Mayer Studios.

Figure 3-3: Noir setting, botched robbery, death row, last chance, a mysterious light that only condemned prisoners can see at the hour of 9 p.m., an "angel number." Collection of the author.

CHAPTER 4

Contrasts: Dorothy Hughes's *Ride the Pink Horse* (1946)
v. Larry Brown's *Dirty Work* (2007)

The previous chapter concerned family solidarity in crime novels published in 1947 and 1990. In the former, Nick Robey emerges from a broken home to make himself an enemy of a tight-knit one. In the latter, the family is a close one, but that firm knot results in Bill Houston's impulsive murder of a bank guard. The consequence for both protagonists is death, although Bill breaks through to a Christ-like consciousness just before he leaves this planet. Nick, in what was probably evaluated as justifiable self-defense, was stabbed in the back by a member of the family he was holding hostage.

The Hughes and Brown novels discussed below also concern personal isolation. In *Ride the Pink Horse*, Dorothy Hughes's Sailor is, like Sam Ross's Nick, from the mean streets of Chicago. A smart, mistrustful loner, he has allied himself with a politician who fought his way to the Senate by discarding his idealism. Now, Sailor has hunted him down and is determined to get the money due to him for his loyal service. He'll do so in the way he has done everything else—by fighting for it on his own. In Larry Brown's *Dirty Work*, dual protagonists are unable to fight on their own. Grievously wounded in Vietnam, they lie in adjoining beds in a military hospital ward set aside for those who will die there. One, Braiden, is black, and the other, Walter, is a rural white. Braiden's limbs have been blown off; his army companions, all of whom have visited him, hoped he would be spared from further suffering. But he has lain there for twenty years. Walter, who has just arrived on the ward, is literally a man without a face. And he has a bullet fragment in his head.

"A Stranger in an Alien Place"

Sailor has traveled to Santa Fe to confront "the Sen." It is Fiesta time, so the only lodging he can get is with Pancho, who owns a merry-go-round at the Fiesta site. Sailor sees a ragged prepubescent Mexican girl, whose aloneness reminds him of himself. He gives her a ride on one of the carousel's pink horses. It is his way of trying to make contact with an innocence torn from him on the mean streets of Chicago. Possibly it assuages his panic of "being a stranger in an alien place." Since he was a poverty-stricken street kid, he has trusted no one, been with no one, and buried his isolation under his tough, daring hostility to anyone with whom he deals. His alienation had become a mask that he could not take off. For him, the law, far from protecting and enabling, is a kind of sewer, disposing of uncouth upstarts from the racket-infested inner city if they cannot find ways to illegally succeed.

In one sentence, Hughes encapsulates Sailor's upbringing: sick mother having to care for eight kids; father quick with a beating; "vicious rats in the walls, shivering winters, stifling summers, bad teeth, pains in the belly, never enough to eat." But Mac, his boyhood friend, has had a different life trajectory. A police detective sent to Santa Fe to investigate the corruption of the Sen, he has a wife and kids, and, regardless of any malfeasance he has witnessed on the force, has forged a life of public service, giving him a stable sense of self. Sailor, on the other hand, is lost in a limbo of suspicion and alienation. The result is a kind of "panic of loneness," a "creeping loss of identity." Hughes carefully delineates this psychic isolation, which eventually sends Sailor running to the edge of the semi-arid region, part of what used to be called the Great American Desert, which lies just north of Santa Fe (Figure 4-1).

Mac tells Sailor the law will catch up with the Sen. He can get Sailor a short sentence if he reveals what he knows, including who is responsible for the murder of the Sen's wife. Then Sailor can start over, his efforts untainted by underworld associations. Sailor's paranoid distrust, and desperate need to force the Sen to give him what he owes him, results in his locking himself in an unmerry carousel of his own creation. There's an interesting contrast with Nick Robey in *He Ran All the Way*. Nick was desperate for love and forgiveness. He let his guard down when he thought Peg was sincere in arranging to escape together. If a lawman like Mac had given him the chance he gave Sailor, Nick could have trusted that he was sincere. Sailor responded with panic, forgetting himself. He ended Mac. Then Sailor ran, weeping, "plunging into the waste of endless land and sky." He seemed to hear Mac saying in a pitying voice, "You can't get away." It's actually himself, mourning his own self-inflicted loss of trust and fellowship, which not only Mac but Pancho had open-heartedly offered.

As he runs and weeps, Sailor think of Pancho, and that he might have been praying for Sailor at the moment he "damned himself": "Pancho who could have helped him." But Sailor disdained him due to his appearance (fat; grimy clothes; garlic- and whiskey-breath; yellow teeth). Sailor, like other Americans, feels such a fellow is "unclean." Pancho has proven himself to be a free, open-hearted, generous man who enjoys life and other people. "I am a proud man and a good man." He knows and disdains the passive escapism that characterizes vacationing Americans.

The Santa Fe Fiesta begins with the burning of Zozobra ("gloom"), a giant puppet tourists think of as entertainment at a parade, his burning symbolizing happier days ahead (Figure 4-2). Sailor thinks of it as evil. It is to him an uncanny representation of his subconscious—how he sees the world. In Zozobra, "He saw [his fatal vulnerability] and was suddenly frightened." This is the concept of Fate in twentieth cent pulp. It must be endured, for it is a soulless machine, just waiting to pounce. Hughes encapsulates this view of fate as "A fantastic awfulness of reality." It is totally alienated from natural rhythms implying eventual renewal. It defeats young people who have experienced bad housing, bad food, and impoverished parents before they are out of their teens. Sailor had internalized hopeless failure not just on the streets of the slums, but in school, where platitudes about gratitude to family, God, and nation rang hollow when Sailor went home to a drunken father, a sick and worn-out mother, and a rodent-infested home.

To Sailor, Zozobra's incineration represents the awful catastrophe that reduces the frowning, hostile loner to the ash from which he arose. The inevitable reality is self-imposed solitary confinement in sudden danger, and inalienable doom. It's the twentieth century pulp crime "failure story." I've quoted Orson Welles as using the phrase to describe how urban mystery narratives typically conclude. The implication that struggle against social and psychological conditions is doomed substitutes isolated self-awareness and fear-inspired hostility for any hope for a viable future. The hard-won awareness of the characters is admirable, whether they are awaiting execution, facing a future without the partner they needed, or simply inured to the point where "nothing can bother them." It's ironic that the pulp crime story, despite its hard-boiled and noir depictions of postwar anxieties, implied with its "failure stories" passivity and resignation. despite the characters' courage and defiance of the "keep what you have" admonitions.

"Fantastically awful," Zozobra is Sailor's nemesis. One's nemesis, like one's double, can control one's fate. Sailor has pre-programmed himself to allow it to, and it does. He has made himself "a stranger in an alien place. Immersed in the culture that produced and perpetrated his slum sensibility, he cannot see, as the poor Mexican who befriends him can, that the full range of Zozobra's story does not imply the subversion of hope and peace. It connotes a set of natural processes which bring, sometimes, tyranny supported by death-dealing technology, but, at another juncture, a return to order, sympathy, and community, all of which conquer loneness. To Sailor, lonely and bitter struggle is beginning and end.

Pancho and the Indian peoples see the fiesta as not just memorializing the Spanish conquest of Mexico, but as a round of nature, sun and shadow, full of both destruction and renewal. Pancho implicitly believes the Spanish juggernaut that conquered the Indian natives of Central America will pass away, as will the technological and military power of the wealthy gringos and their propensity for vacation dress-up in cowboy clothes. For Pancho, life does not go in one inevitable direction of degeneration, suffering, sin, and death. It offers people the chance for loyalty and commitment to those one is in a position to help. Thus, he takes a beating to keep Sailor's whereabouts from the Sen's thugs. But Sailor cannot rise above Pancho's spontaneous affection. His embarrassment at Pancho's openness suggests Sailor is a victim of the American tough-guy self-image. The complex interplay of its fearlessness, its cynicism, and its compulsion to repeat dangerous and self-defeating responses is as clear in Ross's hero as it is in Chandler's, Hammett's, Cain's, Cornell Woolrich's, and Peter Rabe's. Robert Warshow explains that the American gangster must act alone and with baleful aggression, leaving him "alone and guilty and defenseless against enemies."[50]

Pancho's kind of mutuality would have been impossible in the Chicago in which Sailor grew up. Even Mac could not absorb it. Pancho is the kind of outcast Harry Crews described as knowing that "It's better to be poor than be beholding." He has

---

[50] "The Gangster as Tragic Hero" (1948), rpt. *The Immediate Experience: Movies, Comics, Theatre, and Other Aspects of Popular Culture* (enlarged ed.; Boston: Harvard U Press, 2001), p.103.

transcended entrapment, while Sailor ends up running aimlessly, with no hope of putting aside the heavy load he constantly has carried since a slum boyhood. After his last irredeemable act, the phrase "you can't get away" ends the novel, echoing his destiny. Lost in the Great American Desert, he would encounter a landscape which epitomizes for him the one Mark Twain experienced a century earlier: "...the road was white with the bones of oxen and horses. It would hardly be an exaggeration to say that we could have walked the whole forty miles and set our feet on a bone at every step! The desert was one prodigious graveyard."[51]

"Ain't Many Ways to Leave." Courage Emerging from Unlikely Places

In Larry Brown's *Dirty Work*, both Braiden and Walter, despite terrible injuries, assert themselves against all odds. They have avoided the cages that cause paranoiac despair. "Jesus loves you," says Braiden, who had already had a vision of angels and of God. That vision, and the discipline of conceiving of a just, spiritual world, allows him to overcome helplessness. He is tougher than ever, and full of tenderness. Both Braiden and Walter make their own cosmic justice. Both are poor Mississippians, uneducated (make that: they had not been "schooled") and therefore had no defense against the draft. "Ain't no bars on the windows, but ain't many ways to leave."

Since he saw the Vietnam carnage, Braiden "has to cry for all them wasted lives, man, all them boys I loaded up like they loaded me up." Each one of Braiden's fellow soldiers has come to see him. There is a tight community. Further, he has created his own community inside his head, the "trips he takes in his mind." There, he is an African chief who instead of fighting intertribal

[51] *Roughing It*, ed. Harriet Smith and Edgar Branch (Los Angeles: U. of California Press, 1993), p.130 (Chapter 20). First published 1872.

wars, invites other chiefs to eat and dance with his people. Brown describes Walter's community too. He remembers a funeral his father took him to. The choral singing women made the hair stand up on his head. He could hear every one of them individually and if one of them was not there, the choral sound would be somehow lessened. Both men know how to bear heavy loads. The solution requires merging into a community the unity of which is age old, and as deep as it was in biblical times, or in the Native American dreamtime, when community was where one sensed the divine with faithfulness and trust, as expressed in sacred song and ritual movement.

At the end, Braiden, after twenty-two years in the hospital ward which patients never leave, gets what he has often prayed for from Walter, whom he had known only briefly, since he had been brought into Braiden's room only the night before. Walter gets his motivation from the company of Braiden's sister, and from a beautiful young girl who spontaneously falls in love with him, and who has, as it turns out, her own scars. One of their dates ends in the girl's death, after a fierce storm floods the roads.

Braiden and Walter are able to make radical, atypical decisions, acting—and the very fact that they can act is remarkable in itself—in direct contrast to law and military conduct. It's a perfect example of a twentieth century pulp theme: courage emerging from unlikely places, as explored in Dalton Trumbo's novel *Johnny Got His Gun* (1939) (Figure 4-3). Unlike the twentieth century noble loser narratives, however, these heroes change their universe. I'm not going to reveal Larry Brown's shocking ending, except to say that his title is double-barreled. In addition to being noir, ironic, and tragic, it solves the mystery of how to open a seemingly triple-locked cage. Brown's title refers to what put Braiden in bed for twenty-two years: the Vietnam disaster, and the function of the war hero: "Don't die for your country, let the other bastard die for his." A heavy load: "Jesus wept." That is Brown's final sentence. But as it refers to Walter's final, self-sacrificing gift to Braiden, the reader has to think carefully about whether the Jesus Braiden conversed with wept with grief or joy.

Pancho has no need to talk and pray. Instead, he accepts a Zozobran constant, the ineluctable rhythm of darkness and rebirth. He enjoys his life because he can accept what it gives and naturally takes. He manages a carousel, where those who wish, mostly children and their parents, can ride the pink horse. To Pancho, whose appearance Sailor feels is "unclean," mystery and personal loyalty are essential to accepting what life means— as it is for Braiden, who has lived a coherent, benevolent communal life inside his head.

Hughes used Zozobra to highlight Sailor's self-destructive aloneness. Braiden's God is not based on the "myth of eternal return," but rather on Christian redemption. He has a visit from a blissful angel child, who embraces Braiden for a long time as "things that wasn't said flowed from the child to me." The Lord himself is the epitome of impassive toughness, scolding Braiden's desperate pleas for death and reminding him of how sad his loved ones would be by his passing, which they would not know was the culmination of a loving pact between two men from neither of whom one would expect such defiance of a forbidden religious code. Braiden and Walter hold firm; the latter is a merciful angel of deliverance.

Brown is not alone (David Joy and Denis Johnson immediately come to mind) among rural noir writers in foregrounding the mystery of transcendence—and what it bestows, which is exactly the opposite of the panicked isolation seizing Sailor in the last pages of Hughes's novel. Jesus could truly weep at Sailor's lonely fate. There would be no mistaking the bleakness in those tears.

Figure 4-1: The Great American Desert, a wilderness into which Sailor flees as *Ride the Pink Horse* ends.
https://longreads.com/2018/07/02/taming-the-great-american-desert/

Figure 4-2: Zozobra ("old man gloom") burning. Source: "The Burning of Zozobra." Dorado Magazine. "The giant puppet is really mad now, flailing his arms about angrily. His eye sockets are glowing an eerie green, his pupils flickering a menacing red." But the event is festive. People write down what makes them gloomy and puts the paper in a box for burning with the giant puppet. Google: The Zozobra Goes Up in Flames.

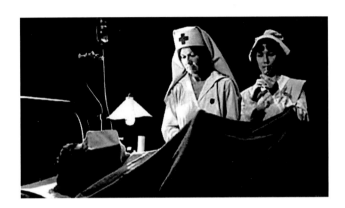

Figure 4-3: From the film *Johnny Got His Gun* (1971), alluded to in Larry Brown's *Dirty Work*. Johnny, horribly injured, had no arms or legs, like Braiden, and no face, like Walter. He requests permission to narrate what happened to him. The Masters of War deny him permission. Dist. Cinemation Industries, Inc. https://r7k2t3x9.rocketcdn.me/wp-content/uploads/2021/01/img-76070.jpg.

CHAPTER 5

Broken Down Dreams vs. Eyes Wide Open: Benjamin Appel's
Sweet Money Girl (1954), Robert Coover's "Sadfull"
Huck Finn (2017), and Barry Gifford's *Wild at Heart* (1990)

Appel's and Coover's books reveal betrayals of affection from
post-World War II New York and the Civil War-era Wild West
respectively. Barry Gifford's *Wild at Heart* points toward a way
of healing such a wound, beyond twisted sorrow.

Sweet Money Girl: Betrayal on Broadway

Benjamin Appel, who wrote over a dozen novels about New
York's union, police, and political corruption, created a narrative
that excels in both the hard-boiled and noir styles. The hard-
boiled aspect centers around "the spirit of Broadway," the giant
Bond (clothing) Sign, c. 1946 (Figure 5-1). On one side was a
scantily clad male, and on the other a woman in an undersized
toga, her pudenda blocked from view only by a wire. The sign
evokes the spirit of the prurient tease, in danger of being snatched
away. Bond was the leading retail outlet for men's clothing.

Seldom does a story make setting more of a perfect background
for human behavior. Appel, born in Hell's Kitchen, describes
Times Square's grinder movies and bookstores specializing in erotica. Other entertainments included "art" burlesques, peep shows,

taxi dance halls, outdoor auctions, flea markets peddling inflatable "honeys for your bedside," and "believe-it-or-not" museums. Freud called the interest in such attractions "scopophilia": the substitution of the eye for the penis. "For 69 cents," Appel reports, "you could make love to a beauty in Technicolor. At least the Technicolor women let you go when the movie was over." This saves money, precludes wooing women with dinner and shows, and opens up more time for gambling, numbers writing, and business deals. "Mr. 42nd Street; that's the nickname for all of us," including bank tellers, copy editors for ad agencies, writers for pulp magazines, talent scouts, peddlers of back date magazines, workers at grinder movie houses, and night club greeters and waiters. They all dreamed they could make a fortune moving up in their chosen businesses if only they kept their eyes and ears open. Broadway, an opportunity.

Appel's chief dreamer is Maxie Dehn. This "Joe Subway's" ambition, not far from that of the patrons of the 42nd Street mass entertainment centers, is to marry Hortense, a slim, beautiful dance instructor, a bargain basement femme fatale. He has convinced himself she will accept him if he can consummate a shady real estate deal worth scads. The co-protagonist, Maxie's best friend Hugh, tries to tell him to back off. Hugh should know. He is sleeping with Hortense, a fact he conceals from Maxie just as tightly as Maxie does his under-the-counter real estate scheme, and just as effectively as Hortense does the worthlessness of contracts she inveigles her dance students to sign. Sex and money; Broadway and bullshit. You have to be hard-boiled to ignore the guilt that nags at you for such self-deception and willed ignorance of what you are doing to people whom you string along until you have wrung out of them what you need. They may be relatives or close friends. As George Washington Plunkitt of Tammany Hall reminisced, "I seen my opportunities and I took 'em."

Maxie "loves" Hortense because he fools himself into believing marriage is all she needs to settle down. This from a man who survived World War II as a ball turret gunner. He is brave and smart, but back in New York, he lives with his mother. From the first time he was with a girl, he was impotent. His partner's ridicule was so hurtful, and so paralyzing to his self-image, that he could only experience orgasm with fat, older women. With Hortense, a very experienced call-girl, he succeeded in bed, although it does not relieve his shame. He is even more worried about being found out by the woman to whom he could never explain himself: his mother. Hortense is a possible substitute for her. Hortense knows Maxie is no different from her other marks, except that he really wants to settle down with her.

Hugh is ashamed of himself for his treatment of the army buddy who gave him a room in his mother's house when he was broke. He wants to wise Maxie up about Hortense, but will not confess why he knows so well she is a model of Broadway on the make. Instead, he betrays Maxie, chiefly out of jealousy. Hortense will kick Hugh out if Maxie really did swing that tricky real estate deal. So Hugh goes to Maxie's mother, asking her never to mention their conversation, then telling her all about her son and that femme fatale gold-digger. A few phone calls later, Maxie's relatives had decided against loaning him the money he needed. Hugh rationalized that what he did was no worse than Maxie's negotiations with the owners of the house he wanted to buy. Maxie wanted the deal so that he could remake himself as a secure businessman. There's no indication he wanted Hortense simply as a trophy wife, although he had little experience with how he might make her respect and trust him. Part of the pathos Apple creates is that, if given a chance by friends and relatives who really cared about him, Maxie might have been able to decide on his own how much he was willing to sacrifice to be with Hortense, and whether it was worth it. But the whole spirit of Broadway as opportunity works against that.

Hugh realizes that Maxie is incapable of seeing Hortense for what she has become. The fact is she never experienced a self-respecting family. But a Mr. 42nd Street like Maxie is too busy looking for the chimeric big score that will bring the Bond Girl down from her neon glamour to eye level, the perfect Pygmalion. Hortense has always equated security with material advantage, as does almost everyone. Broadway, an opportunity. Hortense, her cynicism protecting her from despair, has no faith in anyone, especially dreamers like Maxie.

Appel's hard-boiled story is as good a noir as ever was set in the Big Apple's Main Stem. In the novel's final paragraph, Appel echoes *The Great Gatsby*, and succeeds. Hugh, now a family man, reflects that always the open-eyed survivor, Hortense left Maxie when his shady real estate deal fell through. Maxie at least had the stubborn gumption to hope, "to go tilting against the facts."

> The gate in the sky, it would open again someday, in another time when we would dare follow our dreams and hopes into the universe...to ascend, always to ascend, instead of walking our lives away, with our hopes dragging behind us like unwanted shadows...

Gatsby was strong enough to dream he could resurrect the past with careless Daisy. He was "worth the whole lot put together." But he had been murdered for his gallantry, as Daisy and her husband chomped cold chicken. Nick concludes:

> Gatsby believed in the green light, the orgiastic future that year by year recedes before us. It eluded us then, but that's no matter—tomorrow we will run faster...So we beat on, boats against the current, borne back ceaselessly into the past.

These allusions to a classic American novel give a universality to Appel's story that in the hands of a lesser writer might have been a romance with a sentimental ending. The Broadway setting, the meretricious amorality, the guilt underlying the uses of sex and money, and the first-person perspectives Appel provides for the three main characters recreate a world, as did Algren in *Never Come Morning*, Weidman in *I Can Get It For You Wholesale*, Ellison in *Invisible Man*, or Green in *The Last Angry Man*. As for Maxie and Hugh, in their futures will be, instead of tenuous hopes and dreams, long walks through Times Square's ignoble fantasies, then back to suburbia, "borne back ceaselessly into the past."

Huck Out West: Betrayal by a Pard

Robert Coover seems to have channeled the spirit of Mark Twain as powerfully as Benjamin Appel did Fitzgerald as he concluded *The Great Gatsby*. The "damned human race" is on ghastly display. It's on an apocalyptic level, which is what it in fact was for the Native American tribes on the Great Plains. Mountain men meet to trade and exchange information, but also to gamble, fight, and drink themselves into oblivion, some emerging from the get-together, or "rendezvous," bereft of almost everything they worked for (in one case a scalp, in another a Native American spouse) (Figure 5-2). These annual events were organized by middlemen for the fur trading businesses to contract with the hunters and trappers for their very hard-earned goods. They brought high prices at urban markets in the US and Europe. The mountain men saw a scant amount of those profits, and their bitterness toward the entrepreneurs on both coasts fomented. Another reason was the prices exacted from them for equipment and tools.[52]

Early in his *The Drop Edge of Yonder*, Rudolph Wurlitzer delivers a breathtaking perspective on the rendezvous, by describ-

---

[52] Robert M Utley, A Life Wild and Perilous: Mountain Men and the Path to the Pacific (NY: Holt, 1997), pp.164-65, 168-70, 174-75.

ing his mountain man protagonist, Zebulon Shook's, love of these events. He gambles, has a quickie with a squaw, and smashes an opponent's "nose halfway into his skull." Then they go arm and arm to join others in drinking till dawn, eating buffalo liver and telling whoppers. Wurlitzer notes "these were the last days of the free-trapper, when a mountain man could ride wherever he wanted and perform any sort of mischief that suited him." The reader cannot discount the admiration in the author's tone even as s/he shudders at the drunken rowdiness. The Wild West's offer of radical freedom from a town's law and order was irresistible to men like Zebulon, for "mountain doings" were essential.

The Rendevous was a place for ferocious release a year's worth of danger. At one of these rendezvous, Huck's friend, Old Deadwood, is beaten half to death and his belongings are stolen. Violence and depredation are frequent in western expansion, and not only in boom towns before the lawmen arrived. Slaughtering buffalo, Huck learns, is a necessity because it means the Indians will starve. General Custer, whom his men call "Hardass," drives his men through snowstorms to surprise Native American villages, killing women and children and burning lodges. The troopers lynched any escaped slave they came across "for honor" (bounty). People were hung for a large variety of offenses. Huck did teamster-related work for Custer. At one point, Hardass orders him to shoot a large number of the Lakota's abandoned ponies ("enemy weapons"). Huck runs off. The sight of the raid on the teepees was the turning point: "eyes gouged out and ears tore off and bellies slit open with their innards spilling out..." He could not abide the "distressid" sight.

Nor could he look at a Sioux "Every-Hundred-Moons People Slaughter," with the Indians burning, eviscerating, and cannibalizing selected scapegoats. "Burnt and chopped up flesh everywhere." One of Huck's first experiences in the West was seeing a friend's ritually desecrated body, scalped, with arrows piercing it to the ground, and with his penis in his mouth ("eating what before was betwixt [his] legs, a most gashly [sic] and grievous sight"). The American troops may have been responding with viciousness to the Indians, but they at least equaled it, with no complaint from their officers.

Coover highlights the aftermath of the Sioux raid in Minnesota in 1862 that resulted in the rape and killing of settlers in response to American treaty violations. Troops captured 303 warriors and the military court sentenced them to hang. Lincoln commuted the sentence of all but thirty-eight. It was the largest mass execution in US history. Tom Sawyer explained to Huck that all Indians must be killed. They stand in the way of America's destiny. Later, Tom allowed, the country can build a museum or other monument in their honor (Figure 5-3).

On his way to a law degree ("Knowledge is power"), political fame, and personal wealth, Tom turns up periodically to enliven and bedevil Huck's life—he sells Jim to Indians as a slave and tells a Reverend it was Huck's idea. He sets up Becky, after marrying her, as a whorehouse madam. He thinks Lincoln was a coward for commuting so many of the Sioux's death sentences. It was the Civil War era, a war that, like all wars, continued to be fought after the soldiers from both sides went home. Tom has all the traits necessary for making the American dream into a nightmare. To him, life is a great big adventure into success. You achieve it by inveigling others into doing the groundwork.

So why is Tom Huck's pard? Loyalty and male bonding are deep in his value system. He understands Tom's resourcefulness in getting out of tight spots, while on his own he had gotten in deeper trouble with each change of job and location. Huck has been for a long time addicted to adventure, and Tom is a genius at this. Out West, he even saves Huck from hanging by shooting the rope. This and other adventures are right out of the 19th century pulp western dime magazines.

Coover's epigraph for his novel is "He had a dream, I says, and it shot him." It refers to the scene in *Huckleberry Finn* where Tom is shot by farmers trying to prevent Jim's escape, a childish scheme Tom dreamed up with no concern for the danger it put Jim in. To him it was a lark. It got him shot. As an adult, Tom is still playing the boy's games, but at the same time shrewdly enhancing his reputation. Maybe he has not lost the "plain level-headedness" Huck admired back in Missouri, but he is using it in a nasty way. He's an expert in manipulating friends. His own self-aggrandizement motivates all he does. Behind the bonhomie is meanness, casual violence, and cruel domination. Huck's growing sadness—a lifelong trait of an empathetic outsider—is a consequence of observing people like Tom and Colonel Custer, both dedicated to eradicating Indians and both equaling in sadistic domination the worst tortures and mutilations practiced by Plains Indians, especially the Lakota and Sioux. Huck endures the hardships of driving cattle ("dyspepsia, piles, and newmonia") because "The awful emptiness [of] the desert seemed as lonely and sadful as me."

Huck's other pard is the Lakota Indian, Eetah. Both are natural outsiders. According to Tom, Huck is "running away from the grandest idea what's ever been thought up...You're a coward and a traiter [sic]." And the same goes double for Eetah, "running off with a low-down white man just when [his tribe] needs him to fight and die for his people." Tom Sawyer, esquire, super-patriot and self-proclaimed "Sivilizer of the West," arrests Huck and Eetah, after the latter's "crinamal horse" went on a tear through the dusty street of the mining camp of Deadwood Gulch. They are saved by the arrival of Eetah's friends, causing quick-thinking Tom to cancel his plans. He is genuinely grieved by losing Huck's friendship, although too single-minded to guess why Huck has been keeping his distance. He invites "Hucky" and Eetah to live in his big house, where he can keep them close at hand. But experience had been too good a teacher for Huck to accept.

The novel ends with the two loners on a riverside with "no prospectors in sight." There are no Union or Confederate states with their banners and tortures, either. And no Tom with his business, legal, and rich-quick schemes ensnaring Becky, Jim, and Huck, each one far more a human being than he. Huck plans to fish up dinner, drink whisky, and talk about their mutual adventures as the light fades. "My pard yayed that." They can "ease through time, when the world 'lowed it." "All stories is sad stories, but not all the time."

There are inveterate outsiders in 1950s crime novels such as *They Shoot Horses Don't They*, *Ride the Pink Horse*, *He Ran All the Way*, *Kiss Tomorrow Goodbye*, and *Woman Chaser*. Lacking the option of a coherent, isolated community or a wild, untamed, chaotic world beyond submission to indifferent fate and adamantine criminal codes, people like Gloria and Robert (*They Shoot Horses*), Sailor (*Ride*), Nick Robey (*He Ran*), Ralph Cotter (*Kiss*), and Richard Hudson (*Woman Chaser*) can only suffer prison, suicide, or execution. It's fitting that Coover takes Huck out West where, as Whitman put it, "Pure luminous color fight[s] the silent shadows to the last." That is where many of the transfixing tales of social isolates like Huck and Eeta are set.

Wild at Heart, The Story of Sailor and Lula: A Life-Affirming Negation of the Failure Story

Barry Gifford said this novel was a "violent satire." If so, the severity would be directed at the pulp crime novels of the mid-century distributed to newsstands, train and bus stations, men's specialty stores, and erotica-themed urban bookstores. Prime consumer groups included returning veterans, needing help to deal objectively with their memories of blood and guts or avid to escape their nightmares. Gifford founded Black Lizard Books in the mid-'80s, which reprinted major noir writers of the post-war period. He applied the term noir to these novels, after the French term for crime films centering not on the crime itself but on the love and/or money that motivated it, and the sinister patterns of self-destruction that evolve from the crimes. A good Black Lizard writer fascinated readers with a protagonist's anxiety, revenge, possessive desire, betrayal, or entrapment in obsessive behavior patterns. If readers admired, and identified with, the hero's daring and resourcefulness, they had to admit that they would not want to be in such a character's shoes. Gifford avoids, and satirizes, this response.

Wild at Heart has suspense, pursuit, vengeance, murder, suicide, a femme fatale, a couple on the run, and descriptions of wild places, dangerous roads, "quickie" motels, and stunning sunsets. They reveal that "this whole world is wild at heart and weird on top." That could be said of the universe that any Black Lizard book (including Gifford's own *Port Tropique*, 1986) delineates. It fits just as well a characterization of any good pulp, noir, hard-boiled, or country noir (or gothic) crime yarn. Gifford is quintessentially aware of his genre. Sailor opines, "Anythin' interestin' in the world come out of somebody's weird thoughts." Pursuing these thoughts means identifying with the character throughout the story, noticing the reader's common humanity with them.

Satire, especially the most abrasive kind, makes people uncomfortable. So Gifford disarms readers by making Sailor and Lula perfectly endearing. They express themselves in southern dialect; what they say puts complex observations into short, telling phrases like the one just quoted; they go places everybody knows about even if they have never been to (a Motel 6, Variety Do-Nut, Nighty-Night Motel, Forget-Me-Not Café, and The Winn-Dixie); or never watched (Van Halen, the Braves, Kid Chocolate, The Holy Roller Rebel Raiders, Susan Hayward, The "Datin' Game," and The "Bleach" Boys.) That is why the wild-at-heart lovers tell what happened to people who have experienced these kinds of stage-and-screen stars and their presences. Joe Don Looney leaves pro football for study with a Zen mystic. Evil Knievel's motorcycle daring leaves him with eleven plates in his body. Marcell Proust's whole life story came back to him after he ate a cookie (it's true). Sailor and Lula pick up a hitchhiker on his way to Alaska with six Huskie pups he's feeding on calves' liver (whatta stink).

Sailor and Lula adore each other. What's more, they hate no one, not even Lula's mother, who hires Johnnie Farragut to bump off Sailor. ("He's pure slime and it's leaking all over my baby.") You gotta laugh, or at least relax, with Sailor and Lula. Nothing can bother them, nothing at all. Evil does creep in, however, near the novel's end, in the form of Bobby Peru, a stone-cold killer in Vietnam, and his partner Perdita Durango, a Lilith, whom they say killed her own baby. In the bible, Lilith became a demoness who tried to prevent childbirth. Bobby is fatally shot by Sailor. Perdita lives to star in her own eponymous novel, where she and her short-term boyfriend kidnap a pair of teenagers.

Gifford closes his story with Sailor and Lula meeting after he has finished his ten-year sentence for manslaughter and armed robbery. Sailor realizes his ten-year-old son never knew him, and he could not establish a father-son love with the boy. He walks away. No longer weird but prosaic duties are ahead for each. Separately. "You been doin' fine without me, Peanut. There ain't no need to make life tougher'n it has to be." It seems looking closely at life's choices, or lack of choices, as Gifford's Sailor does, is a kind of wildness in itself, simply because most people are not open to its matter-of-fact awareness of, and prioritization of, a loved one's need. It's a beautiful resignation one can live with, as Sailor and Lula do. It is the opposite of what possesses the heroes of Chandler, Horace McCoy, Charles Williams, Dorothy Hughes, Gil Brewer, Lionel White, Cornell Woolrich, or Benjamin Appel. The denouement of *Wild at Heart* has nothing to do with betrayal of a close friend when the latter is on the brink of success (*Sweet Money Girl*); or loneliness so deep in one's psyche that when help and affection is offered from an unexpected source, the result is violent resentment (*Ride the Pink Horse*). There is no abject self-hatred; emotional paralysis; or prolonged, self-willed physical suffering that would awe a medieval monk.

Barry Gifford, who expanded his Sailor and Lulu stories as time went by, rode the waves of change from urban to rural noir before most others did. He was as good at observation as he was at pop culture and as good at creating a setting as he was at showing how characters could enjoy their choices instead of letting them entrap them. It is all about, in contrast to the Black Lizard crime novels, an idiosyncratic, life-confirming perspective. The work reminds me of what Huck and Eetah do in *Huck Out West* "when the world 'lowed it." They practice the art of maintaining one's humanity, instead of being "borne back ceaselessly into the past."

Figure 5-1: "The spirit of Broadway." "What she's offering, she can deliver": Isaac Bashevis Singer.
https://www.walmart.com/ip/1950s-New-York-City-Times-Square-With-Massive-Bond-Clothing-Sign-Between-44Th-And-45Th-Streets-Print-By-Vintage-Item-VARPPI195894/779352884.

Figure 5-2: Fur Trappers at annual rendezvous. Source: *True West* magazine.
https://truewestmagazine.com/article/the-rendezvous
(Scroll down to "Free trappers).

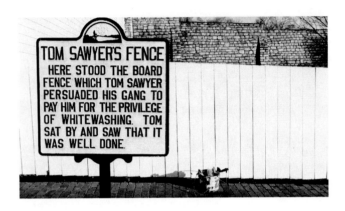

Figure 5-3: On his way to a law degree, as described in Robert Coover's *Huck Out West*. https://khmoradio.com/first-day-of-fence-painting-friday-at-national-tom-sawyer-days/

CHAPTER 6

The Heavy Load of Life in Rural Communities

In many country noirs, the protagonists carry a burden of anger and frustration. That is because, jobless and without access to wholesome food or health care, they depend on purveyors of drugs, medications, predatory loans, and dangerous, sometimes illegal, jobs (Figure 6-1). They are the ultimate victims of the wash of compromise resulting from the cooperation between legal authorities and criminal enterprise. Poverty level protagonists cannot afford to buy from legal suppliers. Because of an inability to work their town's arcane and often corrupt administrative system, they bear a heavy load. There is no possibility of leaders like Miss Bathsheba preparing Hushpuppy to stare drown Aurochs. Forget about cross-country frolicking like Sailor and Lula do, adoring each other and enjoying all the Nighty-Night Hotels and Forget Me Not cafes. Nor is there loyal and empathetic friendship like Pancho offers the tough guy from Chicago. Still less is there divine light penetrating Bill Huston's soul even as he approaches the gas chamber. When Appalachian, Ozark, west Texas, or Great Plains towns cannot maintain a viable economy, residents have little chance of being able to overcome hardship, cynicism, or paranoia by summoning the spiritual energy of Braiden and Walter in *Dirty Work*, Step Post's Ramie in *Lightwood*, or David Joy's Jacob in *Where All Light Tends to Go*.

117

Guts on the Ground

> ...before he could turn to see Brown standing
> above the three men he had just shot, there were
> only trees and ground, the scent of the fired gun
> and the odd hint of death excrement...He took
> careful steps toward Brown until he was standing
> over him, casting a shadow across the fetal-bent
> man...He didn't realize how loud Brown's dying
> was until the last breath was out and gone and
> the woods returned to the vacuum of quietness.
> (Sheldon Lee Compton, *Brown Bottle*)

Wade "Brown Bottle" Taylor is an alcoholic living in the
mountains of eastern Kentucky, the "prescription pain capital
of the United States." He had an abusive father and was not
able, despite all his efforts, to protect his mother and sister from
abuse. Sensitive to kindness when he sees it in others, Wade has
resolved to protect his nephew Nick, who's "into bad," immersed
in the drug and alcohol culture of the town of Sandy. It centers on
oxycontin or meth, which the town's young people turn to
because they have few prospects of leading independent, proud,
and useful lives. The behavioral patterns of the area had in the past
provided a code of loyalty. It was honed by lifelong friendships
and family traditions of bestowing farm land or stable businesses
to sons and daughters. Those days are over, due to agribusiness
forcing economic and cultural changes. Young people, some
suffering PTSD after reups to support their country's excursions
into Iraq, Kuwait, Afghanistan, Syria, Yemen, or Saudi Arabia,"
have been brawling, stealing, drinking, and growing pot to
anesthetize themselves from "the way things are."

Sandy's natives harbor a lot of self-limiting resignation and
suppressed anger. This has been the case with "Brown" (as people

derisively call him). Unable to help his relatives and parents find steady income, he has relied on alcohol to numb his sense of failure. His sudden decision to sober up in order to help Nick drives Compton's plot. He is at odds with Tuck Collins, the local drug supplier, who is protected by his savvy brother Stan, the town's car mechanic, and his wife Hen (her father expected a son, to be named Henry). When a state trooper shows up at Stan's while Nick is sleeping off a cocaine snort, Stan draws the law's attention away from Tuck by turning an addled Nick over to the oddly uninquisitive cop, who had to know Tuck's reputation. Brown recognized that this focus on Nick as the culpable party was typical of the practice of protecting the drug lords of the town from responsibility, while instead punishing their victims. Brown also understands that Tuck's drug business is a major source of Sandy's residents' resignation to hopeless cynicism. Threats, fights, and gunplay follow.

Why would Wade choose these tactics? For the same reason the urban poor in Jim Thompson's, Charles Williams's, James M Cain's, or Dorothy Hughes's books do: stubbornness rooted in lack of resources that might teach them effective ways of dealing with powerful people. There are other factors: the ineffective reliance on physical courage and the naive belief in elementary fair play. Thus, Brown tells Stan at an AA session about his problem with Tuck. The two grapple silently until they are both thrown out of the session. Later, Brown crawls on his belly through a corn field and marijuana plants to Stan's house, knowing it was silly but "the only way for someone like him." And he also thinks that it was better to be "feared and reviled and mocked than to be a laughing joke and mocked." A muddy crawl to knock on a screen door is risible, but self-assertion is as essential as food if one is starved for it.

Speaking of starving for essentials, in and around a town like Sandy, if a physician will not prescribe a pain remedy, or if a local health clinic gets shut down (as many rural hospitals have been), Tuck's oxys are all there is to keep a husband and wife working, and their children treated. "Nothing is anybody's fault. Everything just was, and you had to deal with it." That is an expression of fatalistic entrapment that a twentieth century pulp crime writer might delineate. The best example may be Jim Thompson's *Pop 1280*. In Daniel Woodrell's introduction to the Mulholland edition, he points out that the Oklahoma Thompson grew up in was a "frontier" environment. He explains that *Pop 1280* is a Southern noir, set in a remote Texas town where wrongdoing is excused in sheriffs, judges, and the wealthy, with guilt and brutal punishment reserved for Blacks, the poor, and others without status or hometown roots. Sheriff Nick Corey gets away with murder, extortion, thievery, and adultery. He then decides that God put him in Pottsville to fulfill His wishes. Thompson's nihilism is a faith-demolishing revelation. The God that allows murderers to escape but Who allows children to suffer abuse and near starvation, and condemns their parents to live with the emptiness of not being able to pay debts, feed the family, get medical treatment, or "being able to cover their poor bare asses,"—this God put Nick Corey on earth to bring them the relief of dying off. Corey sees himself as doing the will of this God. That is, his mission is that of the anti-Christ. In 20th-century "failure stories" there is a palpitating, uncanny devilishness lurking either in the human heart or in how fate sets up the protagonists for terminal despondency. There's a heavy load for you. Three country noir novels are very close to Thompson's vision: Woodrell's own *The Death of Sweet Mister*, Frank Bill's *Crimes in Southern Indiana*, and Jake Hinkson's *Dry County*.

The guts on the ground that *Brown Bottle* depicts culminates in Deputy Sheriff Dan Bell holding his gun on Brown Bottle, who had just killed one man and shot two deputies. The man killed was the sadistic killer Fay Mullins, who had slit Tuck's throat. Brown's disgust with that inhumanity toward another Sandy inhabitant leads him to kill Mullins. Dan thinks that there is only one way, however hateful, to prevent a "full out war"—

that is, there will be a struggle for control of the drug-dealing market in eastern Kentucky. Law enforcement in the "prescription pain capital," as Sheriff Bell sees it, requires being able to convince both users and peddlers that a symbiotic cooperation with the police is in their own and their families' best interests. In addition, such cooperation is good for more mundane business. Because of the many court cases to be adjudicated, lawyers and bail bondsmen move into town, buying or renting houses, purchasing high-end home appliances, and paying taxes. A multifaceted collaboration between newcomers and natives on the one hand, and underworld and elected officials on the other, has evolved. It injures any sense of community trust. A heavy load for the citizens is assured. To "return to the vacuum of quietness," one where, ironically, no one can breathe easy, Brown's guts must be on the ground. So, the lawman veers away from law, not toward vengeance but in search of what would maintain a quietly simmering resignation. And the man who only wanted peace for his nephew bleeds out.

But country noir has another, less judgmental and less assured, dimension, one where closure contains both deep shadows and an ameliorating benevolence. A few people experience a life beyond twisted sorrow. That benevolence suffuses the epilogue of *Brown Bottle*. A reformed Nick remembers his uncle's smile long ago, when he boarded his school bus. Compton's novel does not carry a weight of pervasive now-and-forever hate, fear, or betrayal in human affairs. That smile is what Wade died for. Very noir, but betrayal of self or others is not the ultimate reality in the novel. Facing the About the Author page in Brown Bottle is a photo of the author kneeling at Breece Pancake's grave (Figure 6-2). Pancake's great promise as a country noir writer ended with his suicide at twenty-seven. Brown Bottle shows the empathy Compton felt with Pancake's narratives. The heavy load which with Wade "Brown Bottle" Taylor coped through familial love, and a sense of who he was, is the same kind of response to ridgerunner living conditions that Pancake explored.

The Heavy Load of Western Small-Town Culture in a Time of Evolving Law Enforcement

This process of underworld/upperworld cooperation is similar to that in various Westerns about the coming of law and order to a boom town sprung up to serve the needs of homesteaders, cattle ranchers, or miners seeking a nearby gold or silver "strike." The ramshackle lawlessness of the place eventually gives way to a gutsy Marshall not afraid of gun-toting enforcers of the will of the powerful, be they either quick-draw cowboys working for cattle ranchers, or thieves as interested in putting more notches on their gun belts as they were in robbing banks and stores. The Marshall's world-class skill with physical force and quick draw makes him heroic; his connections to the dance hall gambling, money lending, and prostitution rackets are ignored. The unstable peace he brings only works until the town acquires churches, citizens' councils, fine houses, and a culture of respectability, all good for the trust that promotes business. Then the heroic gunman must find new adventures in still-wild places, or get hitched and settle down. Wyatt Earp's career before and after the O.K. Corral shootout is an example of the process. Earp had put down roots in his community, due to local investments.[53] Tombstone's business elite, at one time much relieved by Earp's repression of cowboy rowdiness and bullying, saw him as an outlaw instead of a hero after the O.K. shootout, which led to a vengeful feud as Earp took deadly revenge.[54] Similarly, Sheriff

---

[53] Jeff Guinn, The Last Gunfight: The Real Story of the Shootout at the OK Corral—And How It Changed the American West (NY: Simon and Schuster, 2012), Chapters 15 and 16.

[54] The events are similar to those which brought an end to Jesse James's career in 1882. He was idolized by Confederate supporters and pro-slavery sympathizers. As a loyal Confederate supporter, James after the war had joined Quantrill's Raiders, a gang that terrorized locations where Recon-

Bell of Sandy may give way to a more conventional, clean-handed lawman if the town ever wrests the area's financial viability from the drug kingpins. In Oakley Hall's *Warlock*, this process devastated Marshall Clay Blaisdell, Hall's version of Wyatt Earp. His quick-draw way of enforcing law and order, once praised, lost favor after his pursuit of thieving cowboys had led to a vendetta resulting in multiple deaths.

Stephen Crane's "The Bride Comes to Yellow Sky" depicts another facet of a frontier town's need for an unimpeachably correct lawman. "Correct" here means a seamless congeniality with the men in charge of the town's business, financial, and merchant affairs. The short story depicts the anxiety of Marshall Jack Potter as he and his bride take a train "from one end of Texas to the other." It is late in the frontier period, probably the 1890s. Potter told no one of what he had done, because the marriage would agitate the men of Yellow Sky, and especially the community leaders at the Weary Gentlemen Saloon. Potter had "jumped over the social hedges." They had trusted his decisions, his courage in making them, and his ability to not become involved with disruptive types, either outlaws, or the gambling and prostitution racketeers. But the wife was an unknown quality, and a stranger to the town's established social rituals. This aspect

---

struction was under way. During his train hold-ups, James pistol-whipped bank tellers and train passengers he spied out as Union men. Many western settlers were from the war-ravaged confederacy. Newspaper and dime novel coverage of his train- and bank robbing helped purvey the impression of heroism. But it also made Missouri a place "respectable" businesspeople avoided. The governor of Missouri worked out a way to offer a substantial reward to one of James's long-time gang members if he killed his boss. Hanging a picture in his home one morning, James was shot by Robert Ford in the back of his head. The state was now open for business. Ford became a saloon owner. Most of the reward he was offered went instead to lawmen who had planned James's demise. Ford himself was shot to death a decade later.

of the emerging West's male-centered belief system is described by Bret Harte in "The Luck of Roaring Camp," set c. 1850. The miners discuss whether or not to invite women to the Camp to care for an orphaned infant, named Luck. This plan to provide "female companionship" for Luck caused many to be "fiercely skeptical," perhaps because the good luck that the child brought had resulted in new challenges to deal with: flower-lined streets, improved sanitation, a proposal to invite "decent" families, and plans for a well-appointed hotel.

Yellow Sky is no rowdy boom camp, where most of the women were prostitutes. Female citizens' influence would help reconstruct a community with Gilded Age aspirations. Opera and lecture auditoriums would have been promoted by educated women. Their increasing influence made most of the men suspect the softening of their mutual power as wives observe and comment upon their husbands' affairs and behavior patterns. Crane tells us that Potter's newlywed had a "plain, under-class countenance," and "expected to cook, dutifully." But the Marshall's friends do not know this, and he feels he may have undermined "his duty" to them. Crane does not give the wife a name, perhaps to indicate her unknown quantity. Unknown to herself, as well. The future is still at hand. The bride, along with her husband, will bear a heavy load. Crane's extensive reportage on Western expansion as the frontier closed prepared him well for his fiction.

As depicted in the HBO series *Deadwood*, Seth Bullock, mayor of Deadwood, SD, is also similar to Compton's Sheriff Bell, who hates the compromises he must make with feuding drug distributors, especially one which requires that he kill Brown Bottle. Seth's heavy load is to fend off the persistent schemers who want to control the town. He must deal with two kinds of killers, first the strongman Al Swearengen, owner of the Gem, a watering hole/whorehouse. The Gem was an essential business when Tombstone was still a camp, yet by the 1890s it had gentrified into a cushy hotel. An even more repulsive enemy was the murderous "shitheel" George Hearst, who planned to capture and reinvent Deadwood for his expanding mining and communication industry interests. Seth stops—at the last moment—the enraged citizens from beating Hearst to death after he ordered the murder of a popular farmer. But Hearst's telegraph poles will go up. Tombstone will boast both a Gilded Age Nob Hill culture and would-be entrepreneurs avid for social status. Bullock had the flexibility and ambition to accommodate both kinds of citizens.

Some Country Noir Heavy Loads

A particularly hair-raising description of a deeply engrained and harmful equilibrium between underworld and respected citizens in a southern town is crafted by David Joy in his *Where All Light Tends to Go*. It's another case of "everything was, and you had to deal with it"—or pretend it isn't your problem. The citizens of Cashiers, North Carolina have inured themselves to the McNeeley crime family's narcotics transactions, which include murders of rivals. Joy's protagonist is Jacob McNeeley, outcast in his high school class due to his father's business, in which his son has little choice but to participate. He's the victim of a pernicious family loyalty, the opposite of Brown Bottle and his kin. *Where All Light* is a bildungsroman in reverse, in that it leads to the protagonist's death. The latter is a young man whose heavy load is his loyalty to a cruelly undeserving father, a man whose ruthlessness culminates in subjecting competitors to torturous brutality, which Joy describes in shuddering detail. Either intimidated or indifferent, the townspeople can only harbor silent contempt for the terrorist and his family. The result is trapping Jacob in his role as accessory to intimidation and murder. Loyalty to his father and brother has already cost him a prison sentence.

At the end is a brave and selfless suicide. It consists of the son choosing a hail of police bullets out of loyalty to his father.

Knowing the college-bound woman he loves cannot share his dilemma, he chooses the only alternative, that of loyalty to a loveless father. His antagonists are the exploitive police, his snobbish classmates, the fecklessly indifferent townsfolk, and his own father and brother. "Guts on the ground" here connotes not only self-inflicted mortal injury but a psychological prostration, being beaten down by isolation from love, camaraderie, community, and opportunity.

In S. A. Cosby's *My Darkest Prayer*, Nathan Waymaker is an outcast in Gloucester, Virginia. His family was biracial. His parents were killed when a sheriff's deputy ran them off the road, the event being ignored by the media and uninvestigated by local "law enforcement." Nathan was on the police force for several years, learning what Joy's protagonist learned about how it not only ignored, but actually served, a criminal power structure.

He was also a Marine in Iraq, where his assignment was preparing bodies for burial. The "thank you for your service" phrase makes him think about the scarred and burned pieces of young men in those coffins, their stories part of the reality that Capital Hill needed to ignore, just as the citizens of Joy's Cashiers, NC ignore the drug culture there. By making a pariah of Jacob McNeeley, they wash their hands of the hideous reality in their own jurisdiction. The community of Gloucester, VA does the same. Beneath the right-thinking, patriotic main street of a town busily preparing for its annual daffodil festival is a good imitation of Dante's hell. The town is a nest of poisonous drug distribution, racial bigotry, poverty, money laundering, and theft of charity funds. The Rev. Esau Watkins, much loved and a reformed thief, predatory money lender and drug distributor, has been killed. Nathan finds a thumb drive with images of the two clergymen, the wife of the wealthiest one, and a deputy involved in certain refinements of voyeuristic and group sex.

Nathan lives above the funeral parlor in which he works. That, as much else (including the orgies), is subtly reflective of the realities Cosby is very good at forcing upon his readers.

Nathan, despite being an outcast due to his skin color, violent past, and inclination for brawling, is part and parcel of the Gloucester ambience. He was, after all, a witness of deaths as veteran of battles in Iraq and on the streets of his home town. He is a violent man, built of anger and cynicism. He explodes on several occasions, and the results are literally guts on the ground: broken bones, fractured jaws, eyed smashed to jelly, and crushed groins. He is responsible for killing the man who ran his parents off the road. When he gets proof of the drug racketeering and sybaritic parties, he shows it to the sheriff who knew what happened to his parents, but denied them, and Nathan, justice. Nathan is all over him with the assurance that his legacy will be that of a shamed, incompetent crook. This results in the sheriff collapsing with a heart attack. Nathan gives him artificial respiration, so he can live to face trial and disgrace.

As Cosby and David Joy discussed in a well conducted interview, violence comes from "a multitude of variables."[55] A writer has to "earn the right" to feature it. Joy implies a spiritual realm beyond the bloody chaos in which a trapped Jacob can find rest. Cosby has Nathan recognize that living above a funeral home is not nearly the closest he gets to deaths for which he is responsible. With the recognition that paranoia, resentment, and grief frozen into hate and fear have enervated his spirit, he must face the desperate deputy and dominating preacher to find out who killed Watkins. He asks himself, "When did we become the arbiter of who lives and who dies?" It's suspenseful entertainment and also country noir that "allows for a balance of hope and fate," as David Joy stated in the interview.

Another moving, tragic novel is Steph Post's *Lightwood*, in which a fiery preacher terrorizes her aging, poverty-bound, tightly knit congregation. A gang distributing drugs and the extortionate preacher are equally accepted as inevitable. People

---

[55] "David Joy in Conversation with S A Cosby," August 20th, 2020. https://www.murderbooks.com/Joy-Cosby. Available on YouTube.

have no other source of escape from intolerable anxieties. The title symbolizes the fragility of those immersed in rural poverty. They are nothing more than kindling, useful only for exploitation.

In Rusty Barnes's *Reckoning*, young people want to leave the Appalachian northern tier of Pennsylvania because their choices and opportunities for personal growth are so limited. As the area gets less sure of a future, not only drug dealing, but gambling, porno, and prostitution move in. The criminal in this book, Lyle, terrorizes people with threats, beatings, and the money he has accumulated. The men and women, including the protagonist's uncle, are actively involved in the underworld. Car accidents, burned buildings, and assaults are seen almost as inevitable as forces of nature. Richard's father and uncle know everything about how to fix machines and cars that break down, and how to haul heavy materials around without getting hurt. The father "spent his life working a series of dead-end jobs…never being able to move away, getting older, sadder, and madder." "It didn't do any good to talk about the things you couldn't have and couldn't get, like food that other families ate, or chickens that did not have to be killed."

The kaleidoscope of rural noirs about the heavy load of dysfunctional communities requires brief mention of other notable examples. Donald Ray Pollock's *Knockemstiff*, Nick Kolakowski's *Slaughterhouse Blues*, Benjamin Whitmer's *Pike*, and Frank Bill's *Crimes in Southern Indiana* are all examples of "guts on the ground." Pollock's eponymous town is in Ohio, where insecurities and loneliness are hidden behind bullying and where escape is limited to muttering "Jesus, save me." Kolakowski's setting shifts from redneck small town to south of the border, as a larcenous couple flee from vengeful mob hit men. Whitmer's locale is Naticonti, somewhere in Appalachia but near enough to Cincinnati and one megalomaniacal cop; Bill's is in the hills and valleys of Indiana, remote enough to be centers for drug manufacture, dog-fighting arenas, clans who prostitute teen age girls, and bare-knuckle fighting tournaments. Bill's stories begin with a man who "loans" his granddaughter to a cabin full of pimps to get money for his wife's cancer treatments. With no money, no health care, no job or savings, he burns down his father's house for insurance money. He has destroyed his family. He experiences only panic and isolation; his terminally ill wife shoots him. The contrast with the "southern wild" of Hushpuppy, Wink, Bathsheba, and The Bathtub is complete. In Appalachia, the Ozarks, and the rural heartland, criminal desperation has settled in, and "where you are is no good unless you can get away from it" (Flannery O'Connor) (Figure 6-3).

After excursions into PTSD and suicide, *Crimes in Southern Indiana* concludes with a harrowing piece about a Salvadorian immigrant "schooled in selling meth at dog fights," colluding with MS-13 gangs and police to do so. (Immigrants from that country were escaping a vicious military dictatorship supported by the US.) His job includes burying dead dogs and other animals and gun-running for his boss, a scabrous Afghanistan vet who hates his country for not winning the war. At the end, the Salvadorian kills the scarred and bleeding dogs who "won" their battles and gets as far as he can, with money to start over far from his crimes, from Indiana.

A Weird, Primal Rightness as a Response to the Heavy Load

The narrator in Woodrell's "Joanna Stull" has a father, whom he calls Eugene, with "deep wrongness within him." Eugene is part of a gang of drug-dealing toughs who controls the town. He has raped five women, taking their driver's licenses so that he and his thuggish friends can terrorize them into keeping silent. The son observes Eugene's latest victim: the blood, the swollen face, the vomit, the terror in her eyes. His "bones sweeten[ing] to the root," he bashes Eugene's skull open. Wanting to help the woman, he takes her to the hospital to see and perhaps dispatch her comatose attacker. There, one of Eugene's motley crew implies there would be no retribution, that there was a fundamental rightness beyond the law, to what happened to Eugene. He goes on to say that most people's "goody-goodness" would lead them to condemn the vengeance. "If they haven't seen guts on the ground [the narrator is a decorated veteran], it's just too frustrating to talk to them." Those who can depend on legislation that provides them with material comfort and social status cannot conceive of how violence may be a way of getting justice. Vigilantism is seen differently by those for whom elected legislators have not provided livable wages, accessibility of bank loans, resultant protection from loss of mortgage, institutional health care, or a relief from addiction to OxyContin.

Eugene's son's vigilant attack on his father has a weird inevitability in a social context marked by indifference to crimes committed by people of influence. Sherriff Dan Bell (*Brown Bottle*) knew his deputy drew attention from drug dealer Tuck Collins by focusing on Brown Bottle's nephew Nick. Later, Bell realized he had to kill Wade Taylor to stop a further set of killings. This contrast between established law and a more primitive, ad hoc form of justice is further exemplified by Woodrell's *Winter's Bone*.

As I've notes above, many twentieth century crime novels, despite their compassion for their protagonists, conclude with their dignified resignation to inevitably destructive fate. Not so with the majority of country noirs. Examples include Frank Bill's Salvadorian immigrant; Eugene's son in Woodrell's "Joanna Stull," Frank Bill's addled father who pimps out his own daughter; David Joy's outcast hero who dies in a gunfight with local police rather than give them information about his callous father; and Nick Kolakowski's danger-loving couple willfully courting skilled mob killers. Such characters' lives may be just as unsalvageable as their twentieth century pulp counterparts. They may be just as unsympathetic. The difference is that the habitus or social structure of the rural crime universe is not shadowed by an overarching worldview that makes any fight against it futile. Thus, the Salvadorian escapes; Eugene's son is forgiven by his father's own gang; Joy's outcast hero dies sensing a quiet period of rest from his adversaries; Kolakowski's sexy couple survive the mob's worst plug uglies. Each of these might be justified in the conviction that fate, and/or social disadvantages, drove them down. But neither the father who pimps his granddaughter nor Brown Bottle, both of whom suffer mortal gunshot wounds, conclude that they "started the game with a crooked cue...[that they] meant so good and did so bad" (Thompson's *The Killer Inside Me*).

While the difficulties of forging satisfying human connections are clear in rural noir, the possibilities of securing mutuality can be realized, and enjoyed. Perseverance is fulfilling, not simply the mark of a noble loser. So it is in the work of Woodrell, Bonnie Campbell, Denis Johnson, Larry Brown, and Steph Post. The radical nature of the writing has everything to do with cleansing. Country noir writers do not want the readership to feel that they are better off for making safe, responsible choices. Nor do their narratives hint at predestined tragedy in the brave (however impulsive) choices of the story's protagonists. If crime does not pay, it is not because God or the State ultimately forbids and punishes it. It is because the spirit of resistance wins freedom from the bad faith and exploitation accepted by venal fellow citizens who resign themselves to slipping deeper into poverty and depression.

The Local Lawman as a potential Healer of His Community

Martin McDonagh's *Three Billboards Outside Ebbing, Missouri* is replete with angry, emotionally frozen, and cruel people. In contrast is Sheriff Willoughby, whose immediate task is calming a populace coping with a rape murder. The victim's mother has erected, on signboards, direct challenges to his handling of the case. He has no answers for her, and does not have the time to find them. He is dying. What he does do is write farewell letters, one to a deputy discharged for violent attacks on citizens who resent his bullying. The sheriff tells him, however, that he has what is needed to become a good detective. Willoughby arranges for one last loving picnic for his wife and child, then ends his suffering. Among those who weep for him are every member of his hard-bitten staff. Sheriff Willoughby's sacrifice brings a new awareness about what it takes to keep a town alive. Citizens begin to respect the hate-filled mother's actions; the fired deputy takes up his own investigation; and with that hard-won intelligence the mother and deputy join up not just to find the rapist but to consider what, beside punishing, they ought to do. That indecision may be due to the suspicion that PTSD from service in Iraq might have caused the rapist's violence.

Community peace, even if it only means time to discover the factors enfeebling it, is the goal, as we have seen, of Dan Bell. In the next chapter, I discuss Tom Franklin's novella *Poachers*, in which the sheriff in a backwoods community abides the constant insults of a shopkeeper because he knows the man keeps his provisions store open only to serve a few long-time local farmers with supplies. In Cormac McCarthy's *No Country for Old Men*, Sheriff Bell (was Compton's Dan Bell an allusion to him?) is up against a force as insuppressible as Fate was to 1950s crime writers. The latters' tales were set in motion by impulses to which the characters, both criminals and protagonists, had enslaved themselves. They were ants to the sugar of their compulsions. Sheriff Bell is up against Anton Chigurh, a renegade hit man that even the largest drug cartel in the country cannot stop. He's a "living prophet of destruction." And the sheriff has to protect "common people, common as dirt...that's a high compliment in my part of the world." The only advantage he has is his shaken belief that people's own moral and emotional failures produce evil, and therefore its representative can be defeated. However, this belief is just a hope, now that he is about to retire. He hopes he can remain a "spiritual person," like his wife. His country, which sent young men to Vietnam without sustaining belief in the country or its cause, "is in pieces." It started when the young stopped respecting their elders. He doesn't know why. Bell only wishes he could still make people listen to him, and then to let him "pull everybody back in the boat." Everything just was, [*but*] you had to deal with it. Perseverance is as much part of the American ethic as freedom itself.

No Heavy Load: Owen Wister's The Virginian and the Romantic Ideal of the Rural American Community

There was, contemporaneous with the closing of the frontier, a radically different vision of community than that dissected by twenty-first century rural noir writers. It was romantic and idealistic, projecting a mythical America where rowdy, strong-fisted, sharp-shooting westerners built a path to a peaceable, flourishing, church-going, and charitable democracy. It reinforced a connection between real and ideal, between expanding the frontier and heroic behavior. It thus built what Robert Warshow stated to be an "accepted notion of the public good." As for naysayers, the message was clear: "Smile when you say that, partner."

The western hero, as exemplified in Owen Wister's eponymous Virginian, was a commanding carrier of optimism and Americanism. He was so iconic that the author gives him no personal name. Today, the romantic Western hero can be seen as a prototype of the man or woman with skills as an astronaut, a video game last-person standing, a law enforcement undercover detective, or a life-saving surgeon. These protagonists make their audience proud to be Americans. This kind of hero was very much in vogue when *The Virginian*, and *Shane*, were written.

Teddy Roosevelt, friend of Wister and devotee of his hero, had *The Virginian* in mind when organizing his Rough Riders for the attack on San Juan Hill, key (he opined) to winning the

"splendid little [Spanish American] war." He had won the respect
of local mountain men when a cattle rancher and buffalo hunter
in the Dakota territory. Wister and Roosevelt both saw the
western hero as driven by an untainted love of country. "In
their flesh our natural passions ran tumultuous," reported the
narrator of *The Virginian*. "But often in their spirit sat hidden a
true nobility" that might redeem America from the venality of
cattle barons, railroad entrepreneurs, mine owners, proprietors
of circus and wild west show extravaganzas, and federal office-
holders. The patriotic Westerner believed in what Wister and
Roosevelt called the sober, respectable Anglo-Saxon virtues, and
the possibility of recovering them over not only robber barons but
foreigners, and people from ethnic and religious groups who did
not practice the "true nobility" of Americans like the Virginian.
Images of men like Vanderbilt, Rockefeller, and financial
speculator Jay Gould sitting in formal dress with wreaths on their
heads were emblematic for Wister and Roosevelt of high-hatted
moneybags who never had to plough a field, build a house, or
protect that house from Indians, thieves, Mexican rebels, sinister
Europeans, or assassins hired by land speculators to intimidate
homesteaders. Here, from Edgar Lee Masters' *Spoon River
Anthology*, is a passage praising the segment of that hard-bitten
true nobility still visible in the faces of aging pioneers:

With so much of the old strength gone,
And the old faith gone,
And the mastery of life gone,
And the old courage gone,
Which labors and loves and suffers and sings...[56]

---

[56] Masters, although a Midwesterner, had views similar to Wister regarding
racial and ethnic superiority of "the great race." He disliked Lincoln, believed
the Civil War as a Union strategy for invading the South, and felt slaves
could resolve their grievances without revolt. Christopher Benfey, "Exile on
Main Street," review of Jason Stacy, *Spoon River Anthology: Edgar Lee
Masters and the Myth of the American Small Town*, *The New York Review
of Books*, Dec 2, 2021, pp.41-44.

The Virginian, challenged to a duel, is magnanimous, allowing his enemy to shoot first. When his friend Steve is caught stealing cattle, the Virginian, as ranch foreman, carries out his "horrible duty" with stoic obedience to the law. Steve's composure on the scaffold touched the Virginian to the core. "You must die brave," the narrator concludes. "Failure is a sort of treason to the brotherhood." The Virginian had few words on this occasion: "Steve took dying as naturally as he took living. Like a man should. Like I hope to."

The Virginian's dry-eyed, unflinching resolve was also shown in his steady and gallant attention to his schoolmarm, whom he was confident he would eventually make his own. They lived happily in Wyoming, where he became part owner of the kind of ranch Teddy Roosevelt would have been honored to visit. This exemplary cowboy lifestyle won approval from critics of the sentimental romances, many by female writers. Admirers of male endurance and resolve, however, took fright at writing which softened the exclusively male virtues they assumed were needed to maintain manifest destiny. Depicting the female as a "tamer" of the hero's toughness bothered people who disliked reading about the lone riders who settled down, put their feet up by the fire, built a home with Gilded Age furnishings, and played cowboys and Indians with their children.

This American Dream was an artifact of American practical wisdom, optimism, chauvinism, colonialism, and exceptionalism. It is indeed a fantasy that rural noir writing about social conditions largely, but not entirely, negates. The humility, pride, and determination of protagonists in Whitmer's, Post's, Woodrell's, Proulx's, and Offutt's writing distantly echoes the Virginian's, in more realistic contexts. So does the belief that there is such a thing as a rural social unit dedicated to "the public good." That hope, however distant, also has a place in the narratives of the writers discussed in this chapter. It's a part of the deep attachment to one's territory. If those locations were allowed to flourish as self-sufficient small communities, they might even be like

Hushpuppy's hometown. (Wouldn't that scare the pants off Wister and TR, though?)

Figure 6-1: Still from film Ben Is Back (2018), about a young man addicted to opioids returning home on Christmas eve. His mother tries to keep him clean, precipitating feelings of hurt, isolation, and desperate need for trust, love, and self-respect. Lionsgate.
https://www.facebook.com/watch/?v=299816424191437

Figure 6-2: In Sheldon Lee Compton, *The Orchard Is Full of Sound: A Memoir* (n.p.: Cowboy Jamboree Press, 2022). Reproduced through the courtesy of the Press and Adam Van Winkle.

Figure 6-3: McDowell County, West Virginia. "Schools in poor, rural districts are the hardest hit by nation's growing teacher shortage."
https://www.wvnstv.com/community/health/coronavirus/state-of-emergency-declared-in-mcdowell-county/

CHAPTER 7

"An Insistence on Mystery as Inseparable from Any Honest Understanding of What Life Is About"

Brown's *Dirty Work*. Johnson's *Angels*. Coover's *Huck Out West*. Gifford's *Wild at Heart*. Joy's *Where All Light Tends to Go*. Each of these works embody an otherworldly or awe-inspiring mystery. Sailor and Lula's travels through the "weird on top" world and the interlacing of Eetah's kindness with Huck's escape from American "sivilization" are secular achievements. The other novels focus on a spiritual light that floods both Bill Houston and Jacob McNeely's beings just before their violent deaths by the Law's gas chamber and rifle blasts. Bill's last thought is for God to bless another human being. Jacob opts for loyalty to a careless father over a lying sheriff and seeks a resting place far from a world of betrayal and bad faith. All these protagonists have gotten free from "twisted sorrow."

The quote I used as title for this chapter is Griel Marcus's. It occurs in his liner notes for Dylan's *Basement Tapes* and is relevant to such songs such as "Tears of Rage" or "This Wheel's on Fire." In both, the recalcitrant, unsure singer recalls exploitations, cries out in anger, and threatens response, which may be aggression or may be resignation. Marcus says, "it is the quiet terror of a man seeking salvation who stares into a void that stares back. It is [an] awesome, impenetrable fatalism..." It is one step to confronting a mystery. Because of the problematical

141

efforts of the characters immersed in that endeavor, and the grotesque, otherworldly circumstances they must respond to, I will be pointing out the gothic style of the writers' presentation of these stories.

"Walking with the Woods"

In Chris Offutt's "The Leaving One," an entry in his *Kentucky Straight* (1992), Vaughn Boatwright, on the edge of manhood, finds in the brush a man in ancient buckskin, festooned in twigs and leaves. It's his grandfather Lige, exiled from the family for indecency. Returning home after experiencing hell in World War I, he derisively interrupted a preacher's baptism service. That set a tone for the rest of his existence. He sustained himself by living in the woods, letting nature show him how to survive. An example: foxes' urine erases any bad smell a human can make. Lige takes Vaughn deep into the woods for a mysterious walk, the grandfather's last journey. They climb a hill in the pale afternoon, Lige teaching Vaughn how to let animals and trees show them how to stay alive. The human must have a reverential passivity in order to learn. A deer shows itself. Lige sings: "The eyes in the woods you feel alone…The leaf be I."

Lige lies down. While Vaughn searches in vain for a heartbeat, the imprint of his body becomes outlined on his grandfather's. An old buck stands on one side. Cries of bear, bearcat, and hawk make it seem "all the hills were rushing to the oaks." Vaughn had forgotten the way back, but an uncanny force "moved to his back and stopped." He recognized it and proceeded unafraid down the hill and through the woods. The ending is an allusion to Thomas Berger's *Little Big Man* (1964). The eponymous protagonist, the former Jack Crabb, follows his Native American mentor and surrogate father, Old Lodge Skins, up a steep mountain where the Cheyenne sings his death song. D. H. Lawrence, in discussing Cooper's *Leatherstocking Tales*, specifies "The True Myth of

America":

> The old skin, the old form, hardens till it is tight
> and inorganic. Then it *must* burst, like a chrysalis
> shell…That is the true myth of America. She starts
> old, old, wrinkled and writhing in an old skin.
> And there is a gradual sloughing of the old skin,
> towards a new youth…

The stories of Lige and Little Big Man depict living and dying in a plane of existence alien to the practical, rational, community-oriented one now ubiquitous. The protagonists replicate that which Hushpuppy, her father, her teacher, and her fellow citizens have in a tiny island off the Louisiana coast. They have nothing to do with voting places; assemblies, churches, synagogues, or mosques; award ceremonies; saluting flags; or military service. Alone, the characters look into a void, and it looks back, as the Auroch, The Beast of the Southern Wild, does after rampaging through the world. But when it reaches Hushpuppy, it halts. She's prepared. So is Vaughn, who feels something at his back from which he intuits how to go back down the bear-infested mountain. So is Walter in *Dirty Work*, moving toward the throat of his roommate who already is talking to God from his hospital bed. So is Bill Hudson, praying for someone else while walking toward the gas chamber.

"Sloughing Off the Old Skin"

Finally, so is Pete in Harry Crews's Scar Lover. His guilt and impotence are replaced with love due to the efforts of two equally strange and magically restorative families, one Rastafarian outcast immigrants and the other his girlfriend Sarah and her parents. The girlfriend (with her "lovely, accepting, and caring" smile) and the Rastafarians get Pete to slough off his heartbreak, calcified in grief and guilt for his part in causing his brother's brain injury. Sarah prepares him to share her cooking and her lovemaking. Linga, adept in magic with a face "scarred into something arresting, compelling, and beautiful," and her husband George, immigrants from Haiti, believe in the possible divinity of a human soul. They find a boy in similar circumstances to the brother Pete disfigured. With his "new skin," Pete is prepared for reciprocal sharing.

It's similar to Pedro, always prepared to help Sailor in *Ride the Pink Horse*. But Sailor, stewing in the self-reliance that lifted him out of the mean streets, rejects Pedro as a peasant who has no money, class, or power. Newsstand pulp crime was full of such closures. In *He Ran All the Way*, Peg's inability to accept a stranger's affection is equally tragic. Out of allegiance to her family, she stabs Nick, whom she pities and may love. The way Shelley Winters shows Peg's confusion and grief with the gun still in her hand implies the full range of D. H. Lawrence's pronouncement that "sloughing off the old skin" may bring paralysis. Jane Russell, explaining her fortuneteller gig in the noir travelogue *Macao*: "Everyone is lonely, worried, and sorry. Everybody's looking for something." David Goodis, in *Street of No Return*, wrote: "yesterday could never really be discarded, it was always a part of now. There was just no way to get rid of it. No way to push it aside or throw it into an ash can, or dig a hole and bury it. For all buried memories were nothing more than slow-motion boomerangs." There's grim certitude in these observations—the speakers never gave themselves over to the mystery that implies a different tomorrow, albeit possibly not one in the mundane world. Pete, Vaughn, Little Big Man, Walter (*Dirty Work*), or Bill Hudson (*Angels*) are examples of readiness for tomorrow by psychic transformation.

A Rural Gothic About Communal Survival

Tom Franklin's Southern gothic novella *Poachers* (1999; Figure

7-1) brings together dirt, blood, murder, and retribution by a mysteriously implacable representative of the power of Law. The poachers are three brothers, for whom hunting is their life. They are illiterate, almost feral. Speaking in gestures and grunts, they are as much part of nature as the animals they kill. Kent, Neil, and Dan live deep in the woods, near a community of decaying shacks. Each year flood waters make them lean a bit farther toward the earth. The inhabitants grit their teeth and shovel the mud out of their homes. The community of Lower Peach Tree is representative of many remote, impoverished ones in the rural South where proud self-reliance is a virtue. The brothers share this trait, but do not bother to control their violent impulses. The representative nature of Lower Peach Tree may be why the author does not give the name of the state (one of the characters dies in the VA hospital in Mobile). One can see images of similar communities to Lower Peach Tree on covers of editions of books by Breece Pancake (*Stories*), Frank Bill (*Crimes of Southern Indiana*), Nick Reding (*Methland*), Jonathan Rabin (*Bad Land*), Ron Rash (*Something Rich and Strange*), as well as the anthology *Stray Dogs*. Two of Franklin's books, *Hell at the Breech* and *Mississippi Noir*, present dust jacket or cover photos of backwoods clapboard housing. They "seem to be slipping off into the gully," he writes.

A tyro game warden one day arrests the brothers for poaching. Uneasy, the warden shoots one of Kent's hunting dogs. Kent strangles the lawman. A store owner, Kirsy, who helped bring up the boys after their mother's death, provides an alibi for Kent. His store serves the few grateful residents of Lower Peach Tree who see it as the community resource it is.

A chief gothic element of the tale is the eye-for-an-eye "justice"—or is it inevitable fate?—that befalls the three young men. Parts of the narrative focus on the uncanny and the nightmarish: fear, murder, hideous injury, and carnage. Kent is strangled in what looks like a cottonmouth snake's doing. Neil is blown to bits by dynamite: the same kind that the brothers used to kill fish. Dan, in his turn, is hunted down. Either a venomous snake, or revenge exacted by a Black man whose daughter Dan molested, causes the youngest of the three poachers to go blind. Kirsy envisions a different scenario: all three events were the work of Frank David, retired game warden who had groomed the man Kent strangled.

Frank was the archetypal protector of state game land; as a lawman he might be compared in reputation to Wyatt Earp, sheriff of Tombstone, Arizona, and the last man standing at the O.K. Corral, or to *The Revenant's* Hugh Glass. They are forces of nature. a man and a force of nature: Frank "ris[es] from the black water beside a tree on a moonless night, a tracker so keen he could see in the dark, could follow a man through the deepest swamp by smelling the fear in his sweat, a bent-over shadow stealing between the beaver lodges..." Law, embodied in Glass' case by the Mountain Man's code, is relentless and stealthy in its rigor. It is built on what a culture has been conditioned to believe is timelessly just, even down to the biblical "an eye for an eye." That could be both Glass' and Frank's motto. In nature and law, action produces reaction, as sure as, for example, the destruction of rain forests results in greenhouse gasses, soil erosion, and species extinction.

That result is ultimately due to the nation-state's decision making and its enforcement powers. Nature does not know the concept of punishment, of course. Humans do, be they justices, police, or protectors of the state's forest and wilds. Kirsy recognizes that just as the poachers treated animals as trash, Frank, invested with the power of law, was "more than a match for the boys, [but] exactly the same as them." Relentlessly inflicting his will on others, he did his job cruelly, a vengeance for an otherwise unfulfilled existence.

The sheriff of Lower Peach Tree knows Frank will be back in town shortly and will want the deaths attributed to mere chance, to which the illiterate brothers were vulnerable. Frank has made himself an inexorable force, in addition to being calculating inside his vindictive brain and hard heart. Action (poaching, and killing a game warden) and reaction (Frank!) are basic not only to law, but to all life. The sheriff may be making it easy on himself by accepting Frank's explanation, but he may have his head screwed on right. He has a perseverant human-sized response to the inevitable. It may be similar to Sheriff Bell's in *Brown Bottle*, in that it allows for the community to go one with their necessary workaday tasks in relative peace. The townspeople respond to a spring flood and the decaying clapboard by bailing out and carrying on. That is what the sheriff is doing. That characterizes Kirsy also, who even though dying and grieving the death of his wife, helps all who need provisions by maintaining his store. It is therapeutic to him, as is helping the brothers. He is tough as nails and community minded on top. The sheriff's visits to Kirsy in his last days are probably due to admiration. There aren't many backcountry businessmen built like the storekeeper. All stories are sad stories, as Coover's Huck Finn says, but not all the time, if common sense and respect for community reign. Even in Lower Peach Tree, with its poachers, cottonmouth snakes, annual floods, and game wardens. If there is a mystery in communal endurance, Lower Peach Tree has intuited and acted upon it.

Franklin's story ends with an aging, bearded Dan meandering to the river's edge, listening to the birdsong, scattered leaves, and river run. He then feels the furtive and all-intrusive presence of Frank David, the Law itself, over his shoulder, "a strange and terrifying comfort for the rest of Dan's life." Frank, or his specter, is an uncanny, hidden presence, one who rises from the depths of the woods and reveals the consequence of brute domination of living creatures through shooting, skinning, evisceration, butchering, and devouring. In the case of the three brothers, it is a neck for a neck, an eye for an eye. Action breeds reaction, which, due to the actions of Kirsy and the sheriff, but certainly not Frank David, is benevolent.

It is the gothic elements of "Poachers" that make it an exemplary walk in the woods, and tell about the mystery of what life is about. The tools of the gothic writer include multiple points of view; archetypal hunters, poverty-beset towns, and hard-nosed lawmen; the passing of time; the merging of human with nature's actions and reactions; the weird indeterminacy of motives and events; the remote, grotesque yet communal setting; and nightmarish acts both instinctive and calculating. Especially haunting is consciousness of somehow needing the surveillance and the fear of the law, both of which invade the soul at a deeper level than does watching cockfights, molesting teenagers, or "treating animals like trash." As I said above, gothic closure (as in Johnson's *Angels* and *Jesus' Son* or Brown's *Dirty Work*) can signal a painful and sometimes eerie transformation. That might apply to blind, long-bearded Dan, silently walking in the same woodland he knew when his brothers were alive and poaching. If he cannot look over his shoulder at the presence of Frank the all-powerful warden, that only means he can experience him at a deeper level, as a cruel, murderous counter-force inevitably created by the poaching: the force of Natural Law that works in awesomely different ways than state ordinance. Sometimes it complements the latter, although the individual who does so can be vicious.

"Brokeback Mountain": Paralysis of the Will To Enforce a Sexual Taboo

Annie Proulx's story "Brokeback Mountain," which first appeared in *The New Yorker* in 1997, is equally dominated by an authority figure who lurks in the background. He acts, like Frank David, as a force of nature looming over the shoulder of the protagonists, in this case his own son, Ennis Del Mar, and Ennis' lover, Jack Twist. Like Frank David, Ennis' father is a kind of primordial Auroch, "a strange and terrifying presence for the rest of [Ennis'] life." For both Ennis and the poaching brothers, forbidden actions—poaching state property (a challenge to State control of access to nature) and homosexuality (the proof of un-manliness and thus a challenge to aggressive protection of nation and family)—must result in adamant destruction of the transgressors' lives and freedom. Keep in mind that while the brothers treated females and animals as trash, all Ennis and Jack did was passionately love each other. Proulx writes of the enduring homophobic panic in Wyoming, referencing the killing of Matthew Shepard, a gay young man tied to a fence and beaten to death near Laramie in 1998.[57] The impulsive hatred in the rural west of the same sex embrace, and impulsive scapegoating of offenders, is the creative motivation for "Brokeback Mountain," she wrote. Only in the remoteness of the "empowering and inimical" isolation of the Mountain could freedom from moral teachings about friendship be experienced. Ennis and Jack neve return there.

That is the fault of Ennis, who, unlike Jack, would never be ready for the psychic transformation needed to deal with his deepest desire. His father had made it too traumatic an experience for him. When, as a child, Ennis confides to his dad that he is being bullied, his father says he must attack, and hurt, his enemy until the latter is thoroughly cowed. The enemy was Ennis' older brother. After two days of unexpected attacks, Ennis' problem was over. Regeneration thru violence? When, after many days of ecstatic sex with Jack while the pair were sheep herding on Brokeback, Ennis unexpectedly slugs Jack, it is because he is uneasy with the consequences of being so much in love. Jack meant more to him than even his brother did. About to reenter the world of the cowboy, he needed to restrain, or bury deep within himself, his ecstasy—with an unexpected attack. When he was nine, his father, long dead when Ennis and Jack met, forced him to view the result of what happened when "two old guys ranch[ing] together" were torture-murdered. One of the

---

[57] Annie Proulx, "Getting Movied," in Proulx, Larry McMurtry, and Diana Ossana, *Brokeback Mountain, Story to Screenplay* (NY: Scribner, 2005), pp.130-31.

bodies showed the result of death by tire iron: "Like pieces a [of] burned tomatoes all over him." The corpse had been dragged behind the truck until the nose and penis were just bloody stumps. His father having taught him that lesson, all that Ennis could do is agree to furtive meetings with his lover at odd intervals.

"You just shot my airplane out of the sky," replied Jack: not because he was frightened by Ennis' story, but because "This ain't no little thing that's happenin here." He doesn't give a "flyin fuck" about the risk. He wants to live with Ennis on a remote "cow and calf operation." Ennis backs off. Twenty years later, there is a final confrontation. Amid all the "declarations, fears, shames, guilt, fears," Ennis simply collapses, "heart shot." "Twisted sorrow" claims him. And he knows he cannot contend with it. Jack, by contrast, is like Hushpuppy standing up to an Auroch, but unsuccessfully since completely without community or family help. Ennis' father has mysteriously embodied a version of his own horror of sexual transgression in his son. Its uncanny watchword was that tire iron. One remarkable example, and a chief reason "Brokeback Mountain" has such a gothic effect, occurs when Ennis hears of Jack's death in a freak accident, when Jack was trying to fix a flat. "'No,' he thought, 'they got him with the tire iron'."

His father's warning rises from the depths of Ennis' soul, like a sinister natural force, to repress his will to joy. As the years pass, the two men have acquired families and means of supporting wife and kids. In all that time, the only bliss Ennis had with Jack is in dreams, which include a long-handled spoon Jack used that long-ago summer. To Ennis, the spoon symbolizes not anything phallic, nor a vision of a camaraderie beyond sex. Freud, if he applied his theory of "The Uncanny," might say that the place of Jack's spoon/tire iron in the dream is a result of waking-life repression of what Ennis' father made certain it would always represent to his son: the hair-raising danger of same-sex intimacy.[58] Ennis is doomed to look over his shoulder at his long-dead father just as Dan must submit to the will of his oppressor, who blinded Dan and killed his two brothers. All for the cause of adamantine unwritten laws that to their enforcers were laws of nature. Ironically, Proulx observes that Jack's own father is similar to Ennis', "with an angry, knowing expression, a hard need to be the stud duck in the pond." But Jack never lost his ability to love. His impediment, ironically, was Ennis.

"Brokeback Mountain" is a Western gothic: The hellish irony is one aspect. Others include the inexorable and futile passing of years in which Ennis keeps Jack on a "short leash" while both men marry and eventually drift apart from their families; the varying and contrasting points of view, largely Ennis' but at key moments Jack's and their wives; the cinematic recreation of "the euphoric, bitter air" of Brokeback's high meadows, "the metal smell of snow coming on," and lightning reflected in a window "like a white sheet waving." Larry McMurtry praises another gothic element, Proulx's variety of settings, contrasting the expansive beauty of the land with the commonplace stores, bars, and eateries of the towns, all faithfully reproduced in Ang Lee's film.[59]

Proulx's kinetic skill and sexual frankness give mysterious depth to the explosion of passion on the partners' first night under the bedroll, and to their kiss-laden embrace after four years apart, so passionate Jack's buck teeth draw blood from Ennis' mouth. That suggests a gothic complexity of passion and blood. Both occasions reveal a feral desire that conquers for the moment any need to hide what is forbidden. The painful transformation of Ennis from lover to emotional cripple as his own will succumbs to that of his long-dead father's spirit is as grotesque a horror as

---

[58] Freud, *The Uncanny* (1919, NY: Penguin Classics, 2003), pp.135-51.

[59] McMurtry, "Adapting Brokeback Mountain," in *Brokeback Mountain, Story to Screenplay*, p.141.

The Misfit's gratuitous murders, which give him "no pleasure in life," in O'Connor's "A Good Man Is Hard to Find." The extreme violence exacted, possibly by Ennis' father, on the body of the gay man is as grim as the sudden beheadings in McCarthy's *Blood Meridian* and B Traven's *The Treasure of the Sierra Madre*. What Ennis' father may have helped do to the two gay ranchers is more sinister, being so engrained in the culture's world view as to seem instinctive. It epitomizes Wyoming's moral consensus regarding homosexuality, part of "the subterranean forces of the place."[60]

Finally, the uncanny: the way an everyday useful object for country people, a tire iron, becomes a fetish denoting the necessity of depriving oneself of the one person one loves. Ennis could not hold or kiss Jack unless from behind. He was always prying loose, even by refusing steady jobs for much needed cash to help his wife and daughters. Instead, he "yearned for low paid, long houred ranch work," a sterile way of reliving safely and secretly Brokeback Mountain. The "keep what you have" mantra explored in many 20th century crime paperbacks applies here.

After Jack's death, the final grotesquerie. Ennis substitutes a fetish for the never-to-return mutuality. On a visit to Jack's parents, he sees Jack has kept the shirt he had on when Ennis hit him, the dried blood still visible. Jack had placed one of Ennis' shirts inside it, "two in one." Ennis takes these shirts, hangs them in his trailer under a postcard of Brokeback, and weeps. Deep-rooted in gothic narrative is the contrast between self-assured characters and those drawn ever deeper into mysterious extremes of human behavior. The profundity of gothic suffering in "Brokeback" is delineated in Ennis' watchful carefulness. It tears him apart and throws what's left into a pathetic but safe corner. He inhabits that corner (in Ennis' case, the trailer in which the fetish hangs) alone, except for the looming ghost of an authority figure, his own father, who stands for an inimical

---

[60] Proulx, "Getting Movied," p.135.

feature of his culture. That is the story of Jack and Ennis. It's also the story of the game warden in "Poachers" and his sense of murderous justice. One critic has stated that American gothic is a "symptom" of forces of cultural degeneracy, located *inside* [italics his] the national mainstream." Annie Proulx and Diana Ossana (another essayist in *Brokeback Mountain Story to Screenplay*) would agree.[61]

There's an epitome here: "A man alive in shame is a man not truly alive."[62] Ennis never acknowledges to himself any guilt. That indicates how deeply "inside" his culture the force that inhibits his joy is.

Self-Regeneration after Humiliation: "And After That the Punishment Began" (Dostoyevsky)

The darkest Country Noir writing is full of compulsion, blocked paths to intimacy, and death. As such, it is comparable to, and shows the basic groundwork of, pulp crime and country noir. Offutt's "Old of the Moon" (in *Kentucky Straight*) is Grand Guignol, with an admixture of horror, the uncanny, and criminal transgression. As I've mentioned, that is true of Woolrich (*Waltz into Darkness*), Thompson (*Savage Night*) and Goodis (*Of Tender Sin*). Other examples include Appel's *The Raw Edge* and Cain's *Double Indemnity*. A significant difference between 20th century urban and 21st century rural noir lies in setting, but more in the nature of the struggles in the two kinds of noir mystery. In Offutt's "The Leaving One," and in Franklin's

---

[61]Eric Savoy, "The Rise of American Gothic," in Jerrold E Hogle, ed., *The Cambridge Companion to Gothic Fiction* (Cambridge, UK: Cambridge U. Press, 2002), p.168.

[62] Garry Lovisi, "Lead Poisoning," in Ed Gorman et al, ed., *Dangerous Ground: Stories of Western Noir* (Baltimore: Century Dance Pub., 2011), p.245.

Poachers, the ineffable strength of nature is the force the characters must adjust to. In urban mass market crime pulp, the struggle is with the acquisitive evil of the urban upper- and underworld. In Offutt's and Franklin's tales, closure is less bleak, and is imbued with a sense of mystery and even awe.

Peter Heller's *The Painter* has elements, as does Ron Rash's *The Risen*, of many pulp crime novels: first-person narrator, murder, and grief exploding into blood vengeance. It is radical in its treatment of justice and of a retribution both inevitable and welcomed by the protagonist. Jim Stegner is a celebrated "naïf" expressionist artist, hanging out in Santa Fe, New Mexico. The other setting is the deep woods of Colorado, where he fishes, paints, and confronts the dark rivers of cruelty and sudden violence flooding the hearts of people like him who have had something they love taken from them. Jim's teenage daughter was murdered while trying to buy drugs. He drinks, paints, fishes, remarries, but he does not recover. In the woods, he comes upon a big man beating a roan, fights him, and returns to the scene to smash the guy's head in. That man's brother is one of the strongest and most prototypical wilderness-bred Americans one could imagine. He has a little of the commitment to freedom of Daniel Boone, a little of Harry Crews' defiance of polite acquiescence, a little of Shane's need for isolation, and a little of the fearless assertiveness of Wyatt Earp. Most essentially, there is more than a little of Jim Stegner in him. The way these two men confront each other and discover what they have in common, stemming from the loss of a daughter and a brother, makes for a kind of retributive justice that will last two lifetimes. It is all about the process of moral and emotional restoration.

Heller has great descriptive power. His chapter headings are all titles of paintings. "An Ocean of Woman" depicts the narrator swimming for shore, not knowing if he will make it safely. "It looks like the man is doing many things at once and this may be his downfall. Or maybe it's the root of his joy...I am a fish myself, making small darting turns against the slower background rhythms and sway of the swell."

The Risen is a novel about the unsolved disappearance of a vivacious, life-affirming but reckless beauty. It carries the same mysterious openness as the Offutt and Franklin tales. The narrator is a depressed alcoholic with a neglected gift for writing; his brother is a respected physician. The setting is a small Carolina town, with a persistent sheriff, promiscuity, drug and alcohol problems, and malicious stereotyping. But it could be The Land of Nod or St Petersburg, for there are undertones of Cain and Abel, *Crime and Punishment*, and the work of James M. Cain and Nathaniel West. The novel's connection to rural noir is the heavy load its characters bear, and an enigmatic closure. A seventeen-year-old girl, with whom both brothers had made love, disappeared. For many years, the brothers agonize what each might have done to prevent her death, with good reason. Sibling rivalry, and the tyrannical hand of the town power broker, their grandfather, were both crucial to the girl's tragedy. The woman was a murder victim, and for many years the physician knew it. Both men realize they, especially due to the girl's impulsiveness and involvement with drugs, should have protected her from her fate. But redemption, rather than crime, is in the offing. Guilt brings the possibility of renewal through a self-lacerating, humbling self-assessment, which may be why the novel's epigraph is from *The Brothers Karamazov* (see subhead above), and its title is *The Risen*.

The name the narrator gives the woman is Ligeia, from Poe's story of a beloved rising from the dead. The first paragraph of *The Risen* describes the murdered girl's body emerging from where her killer hid it and flowing to freedom in the sea. The final paragraph imagines her life if she had been able to live it, in a house near the sea, as a "mermaid." She is—at least in the narrator's account of events—the risen one. Rash leaves it for the reader to decide whether to include among the risen the narrator and his brother. The writer's water imagery carries the same mystery of irresistible force of violence and redemptive healing as Heller's does. A similar growth in redemptive tolerance after anger and heartbreak pervades Martin McDonagh's film *Three Billboards Outside Ebbing, Missouri* (2017), discussed in the previous chapter. While searching for the rapist, Mildred's goal changes from revenge against her daughter's killer to musing about the mind of the killer and what might have incited the crime. In Mildred and the once-violent cop who accompanies her, a more complex and incisive view of violence and forgiveness has taken root, as it has with the brothers in *The Risen*.

In both Rash and McDonagh's endings, readiness is all, but it is a readiness to "slough off the old skin." It is not a readiness to accept with a martyr-like bravery an irremediable act, as is the case with newsstand pulp crime stories. Charles Williams's *The Hot Spot*, originally *Hell Hath No Fury* (1953), Gil Brewer's *A Devil for O'Shaughnessy* [written c. 1970] and *The Vengeful Virgin* (1958) are about sons locked in hateful competition with fathers and men who commit crimes to insure the love of women. They leave readers feeling pity and fear for the tragedies of the common man, resolved with a mysterious fervor to endure a death-in-life.

Readiness for Everything, Although "Straight Flat Bad"

Most of Offutt's "Old of the Moon" is narrated into a cassette tape by a lonely old man who died soon after. Cody, a former hell raiser turned preacher, finds the tape. It tells of a bear who had eaten a baby's head being hunted by three relatives of the baby's mother. The hunters kill and skin the bear and recover the head but are beset by panthers. One of them falls. To save him from attack, the others have to shoot him, for they do not have enough bullets to kill the panthers. They miraculously find their way out of the ridge, made sinister with the hunting and tracking of men and animals. A comparison can be made to Vaughn in "The Leaving One"; *Kentucky Straight* is a series of linked tales. The setting of the latter is indicated by a map of the hillside depicting the site of each tale in this microcosm "nobody visits" (Figure 7-2). "Old of the Moon" has some indebtedness to gothic elements as Flannery O'Connor uses them. The character who tells us his experience is a kind of Ancient Mariner, with a tape recorder instead of an evil eye. Offutt's time sequence, points of view, colloquial language, violence, and embodiment of uncanny superhuman forces are certainly gothic. A local legend grows about the ridge being haunted by the dead hunter looking for his gun and the bear looking for his hide. The consequences of feral blood lust suggest a preternatural reckoning. The tale ends with Cody's fate. Recognizing the evil that the tape recorder records, he destroys it. A fierce lightning storm blows in, ripping his bible from his hand and a tree out of the ground. It is about to crush the preacher. Reverting to when he was "straight flat bad," he "wished he had some whiskey and a gun."

The futility of this wish hides the fervency of an adventurous man who realized he had to become part of a community (Figure 7-3). Before that, the reverend Cody was a sadistic drunk capable of manslaughter. The tree is going to fall on him with the crushing irrevocability of that safe that just missed conking Flitcraft in *The Maltese Falcon*. Hammett used the event to show that the urban everyman is trapped in habitual patterns. Flitcraft flees his obligations only to find a similar job and wife in another city. In other words, he keeps his old, too-tight, and restricting skin. He flits, or flutters, lightheaded and unstable, from one place to another, still as pathetically unprepared for changing his life as he ever was, and no safer. (A good detective like Sam Spade needs to understand an unusual response to a shocking event by recognizing the compulsions of the person involved). Offutt's country preacher, with no future left, reverts to his old habits, the booze and the firearm. He once had a life-changing moment when lightning struck his horse; that is when he joined a church. His last thought is that he wants to fight back, at which he was a ruthless expert when "bad." He's hardly sloughed off his old skin, but he's not scared. Nor does he flit. Those are facts. As with much country noir, writers allow the reader absorb the perspective from which they tell a mystery-rich story.

Surviving Two Unearthly Communions

Denis Johnson's *Train Dreams* (2012) is probably the best reviewed novel categorizable as a rural noir. It's a thriller in all the ways that a Southern gothic can be so designated: a regional setting, shifting time sequences, sadistic violence, horror, the supernatural, tragedy and responsibility for bringing it about, and madness. Works by Flannery O'Connor, William Faulkner, Edgar Allan Poe, Cormac McCarthy, and Cornell Woolrich are representative. As a boy, Robert Grainier came across a dying man who asks for someone to talk to before his gangrenous leg ends his existence. The man who robbed him had cut the tendons at the back of his knees. He tells Robert, "I've got just one or two things that must be said." Robert brought him water but departed instead of listening to what seemed to be "a mouth hole moving in a stack of leaves and rags and matted hair." It took many years before he learned what these "one or two things" might have been.

As an adult, Grainier lives in the Idaho panhandle and does skilled labor for the now-intercontinental railroad, helping build miraculously intricate bridges over deep gorges. He marries and lives with his wife and child in a wooded area. While he is away, a forest fire claims his home, wife, and baby daughter. Seeking some evanescent remnant of family, he returns to the site of his cindered house and rebuilds, first a lean-to and then a cabin. He consoles himself with "The brilliant pastels of the last light...beneath the wonderful sky the black valley, utterly still." The passing trains and their "lonesome whistle" are a solitary presence as he sleeps.

At one point he sees his wife Gladys's bonnet flying in the

BEYOND TWISTED SORROW

wind. Her mourning spirit appears to him in a dream, "broad-casting" without words that she can find no peace because her daughter is not with her but still alive in some form somewhere on earth. Robert does finally see the girl, but she has become feral, and does not know language. Grainier believes this nightmare was set in motion years ago by forces borne of his leaving the dying man without letting him tell his tragically fateful story. He believed his "punishment was too great." Those forces are the work of a messianic God; thus, Johnson's protagonist must work toward redemption. That time comes. The effort he makes involves his daughter. It is unsuccessful, but it is all that is possible. After he does so, he continues to live in the place he once shared with his family. The nature of his world contains ineffable tenderness as well as wolfishness. *Train Dreams* takes place just about the time that the frontier was declared closed, due mainly to the promise of—and to the native Americans, the death knell of—the Iron Horse.

This is how Johnson tells us Robert's wife dies, surrounded by fire but not claimed by it: "The water stroked at Gladys until by the very power of its gentleness, it seemed, it lifted her down and claimed her." A very similar event occurs in *The Risen*. *Train Dreams* has an omniscient narrator, who might have God-like qualities. S/he describes, as does Offutt in "The Leaving One," the beauty as well as finality in the feral yells, and the sub- and superhuman behavior, of animals (who weirdly share human traits). The mixture of depredation and steady perseverance in country folk, working toward preparedness, make Denis Johnson an archetypal country noir writer. Elvis is in the novel too, as he is in *Angels*. The elderly Grainier glimpses him on a train: "the mystery and grandeur of a boy so high and solitary."

Figure 7-1: "Trees grew bigger, the undergrowth thicker, the shadows very black." "Back Porch" by Chris Offutt, in *Appalachian Noir*, Larry Smith and Charles Dodd White, eds., Huron, OH: Bottom Dog Press, 2015, p.162. *Poachers* in collection of the author.

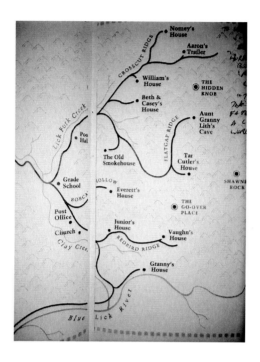

Figure 7-2: Chris Offutt, *Kentucky Straight* (NY: Vintage 1992), n.p. Map on two-page spread (detail). Collection of the author.

Figure 7-3: Photo for Italian essay on Offutt's *Kentucky
Straight*. Original photo: Arthur Rothstein, "Post Office Porch,
Nethers, Virginia", 1935. https://ilmanifesto.it/chris-offutt-
verso-ovest-passaggio-alla-redenzione/

CHAPTER 8

The Untamable Social Isolates: Amoral Vitality, Endurance, Solipsistic Willfulness

A social isolate is a person who, like Shane, Huck Finn, Sailor in *Ride the Pink Horse*, or Jacob McNeeley in *Where All Light Tends to Go*, cannot embrace the personae, behavior patterns, prejudices, and taboos which make him/her part of a community. S/he is not furtive or introverted, nor does the isolate suffer in silence. Social isolates, like Melville's Bartleby, "prefer not to" join in the aspirations, institutions, or rituals that identify a citizen as "one of us." They have no interest in the public good or in shaping themselves after any available exemplary role model. Many are dare-devils, who live distant from institutional protection. Some must fight for life against wild animals, fierce weather, alien wilderness, and hostiles who will not accord them human status. If an identity requires adopting a criterion for behavior that earns one trust from a social unit, then someone isolated, for whatever reason or with whatever motive, is at least as close to death as someone cursed and banished from civilization. The border between freedom and isolation is a unique test of human resourcefulness.

In Pete Dexter's *Deadwood*, Bill Hickock and Charlie Utter come across the body of a young Indian. He was a tribal outcast.

'There's a part of you,' Bill thinks, 'that anchors

to what common people think. There's a body of opinion you can't get away from, even if you lived by yourself twelve months a year...When the Chinese took away their opinions of this boy, they took away the biggest part, and he might not have been strong enough to keep his spirit by himself.'[63]

Many social isolates have chosen to live without the world view, habitus, and comforts of a social unit, although they may have tried and failed. Their "opinions" have strengthened, toughening them for a path ending in behavior either more malicious or more sympathetic than that of the average citizen, who is taught to keep what he/she has in the community.

James Sallis's *Drive* and *Driven* both tell the story of a stunt driver with magical skill in handling the most ubiquitous vehicle with which people equate practical needs, cultural status, and sex drive. "That's all he does." Driver has the effortless mastery of many rural noir characters, such as Amos Edwards (*The Searchers*), who has spent the greater part of his life on horseback. His willpower over his automobile is similar to that of John Grady Cole with horses in McCarthy's *All the Pretty Horses*. He has the brute strength of Boone Caudill (*The Big Sky*), the daring of Ree Dolly in *Winter's Bone*, the resolution of Edward Abbey's *Brave Cowboy* (who broke into jail to tell a friend to break out before the sheriff offered him a deal), and above all the mental agility and survival instincts of both Natty Bumppo (*The Last of the Mohicans*) and Little Big Man, the hero of Thomas Berger novel by that name. Both Natty and Little Big Man (born Jack Crabb) preferred life in American Indian nations to that of frontiersmen. Driver much prefers Latinx, Mexican, or newly arrived immigrants to comfortably settled Americans. I will discuss these social isolate protagonists later in this chapter.

---

[63] NY: Vintage Contemporaries, pp.108-09.

A Fisherman Isolate in a Trailer Park Who Only Does One Thing

Merle Ring (Russell Banks's "The Fisherman," *Trailer Park* [1983]) is an ice fisherman; he lives at the far edge of a trailer park in the "north country" (New Hampshire). Merle lives for winter. With the skill of a master carpenter, he builds a shack (a "bob house") on the lake when the ice becomes ten inches thick. Those who live near him recognize him as an eccentric loner who bothers no one and needs no one, even as an old man. He has a stunning ingenuity for keeping himself fed and warm in a structure every inch of which serves to a perfect tee the lone purpose of survival. He's had several wives and sets of children, but no fond memories of family.

Then he wins two lotteries, one for forty-five hundred dollars and another for fifty thousand dollars. He is only too happy to "loan" money no matter how disingenuous and merely self-seeking the plea. He keeps a number of hundred-dollar bills in a cigar box for his practical needs as a fisherman and for his favorite whiskey. He is a one-trick pony. What he is not is a misanthrope testing the extent to which his neighbors demean themselves to get ahold of his second windfall; nor was he when he let people bullshit him into giving them part of his forty-five hundred dollars. Struggling to keep their heads above water and their trailers warm and stocked with enough food to keep their families healthy, his neighbors feel they must take advantage of every windfall available. The narrator of the story observes that the fisherman's neighbors include people who are, like him, basically alone in the world: single mothers, closeted homosexuals, black people in a white culture, divorcees, alcoholics, or drug dealers.

They discuss what to do with the fifty thousand dollars. It's a consensus that everyone deserves Merle's luck. One resident puts down Merle as a fool. "Money demands to be taken care of in a responsible manner." Another suggestion is that the trailer folk should take the cash before Merle dies and the government dips its beak into it. His neighbors wind up chasing hundred-dollar bills over the ice, endangering themselves in a feeding frenzy to make their lives easier and relieve their sense of lonely victimhood. Later, they are ashamed to talk about their cold scramble. Merle is indifferent. He does not see himself as better than anyone; he is not proud; he always is polite and soft-spoken. Nor does he see himself as a victim. He does not evaluate himself by such criteria, or any other that his neighbors use to convince themselves that they have had bad luck. For them, money brings community status, self-respect, and possible inclusion in elite-level events. For Merle, fishing is all he does. When the ice melts, he prepares his rowboat for summer.

Merle, like James Sallis's archetypal isolate, Driver, has one overriding, obsessive trait. He only does one thing.

The Social Isolate and Other Rural Noir Protagonists

Rural noir rejects a fundamental starting point that is part of the twentieth century mass-market crime thriller's cultural zeitgeist: a stoic resignation to social and emotional restraints, to "keeping what you have," is not the final resolution of protagonists. Novels such as *Sweet Money Girl*, *He Ran All the Way*, and *Ride the Pink Horse* have such closures. Many rural noirs do make betrayal and motiveless cruelty part of the story, and often attribute it to the conditions of financial and emotional survival in small towns facing job loss, poverty, drug use, and failing schools, churches, and health care. But they usually do not end with the resolution that trust, and open congeniality with, one's fellow citizens and even one's family members, is impossible in a town challenged by poverty and isolation. There is instead a determination to find *either* a path to recovery of community trust, *or* an anarchistic

166

freedom a person can only reach alone, apart from any cultural duties or prerequisites, in that "vast obscurity beyond the city."

In novels by Rusty Barnes, Steph Post, Daniel Woodrell, Sheldon Lee Compton, Peter Heller, Larry McMurtry, or Willa Cather, protagonists struggle to survive with people they care for in their communities. In Woodrell's *Winter's Bone*, Ree Dolly must accept as a gift her dead father's severed hand so the fact of his death will allow her legally to keep the house where she can raise her daughter. In Barnes's *The Last Danger*, Matt Rider defies an extortionate drug mob. They kill his brother. He kills two of them. He can't help getting an adrenaline rush, but that doesn't help him protect his family, the goal he continues to strive for. In Post's *Lightwood*, a preacher's power is so hypnotic as to criminally subjugate members of her congregation. The protagonists, a loving couple, survive the tyrant and decimate the drug gang with which she is confederate. Heller's *The Painter* is about two men responding to a murder committed by one of them. Eventually, the characters learn to depend on each other to revive their empathy for their world and each other.

Rural noirs with social isolates, by contrast, present a rare perspective on aloneness, and the consequent self-empowerment it encourages, even if self-destructive. Occasionally, there is indifference to or instinctive contempt for other humans. At other times, the lone individual has achieved unique survival skills which he uses to rescue a town from the bad faith, and predatory power, of its authorities. Then they are on their way to a new, unsettled territory. Such narratives are as tightly wound into the mosaic of American literature as the Western itself. The craving—sometimes brooding and sometimes exhilarating—for freedom from ritualistic duties to community and family is as many-sided as the heavy load of survival with dignity among the folks in the mountains, hollers, plains, and fly-over heartland.

There is one overriding commonality in these two kinds of rural noir. Social isolates have the same resolution, courage, physical strength, and endurance as western cowboys, ranchers, prospectors, and homesteaders. Both twenty-first century kinds of American crime fiction—the struggle for recovery of community wholeness and the isolation of the lone rider—can offer brilliantly crafted eruptions of deep-seated need for freedom from suppressed guilt, sexual frustration, bursts of violence, and violated intimacy. There are two contrasts. Not only are the isolates uninterested in participating in community or family, but they relish for its own sake the battle with recalcitrant wilderness, and with people as keen as they are on keeping their own will pure and dominant. The judgments of legal, religious, social, or professional authorities have no potency. They do not pursue ownership of property, nor any of the responsibilities it entails. Their stories provoke admiration, but of an essentially different nature than that given to those whose accomplishments are recognized as making their society a more workable, "decent" place in which to live. James Cawleti has delineated these two contrasting ideals of the American character. See Chapter 9.

"You want to trap beaver and fight injuns, and live like a natural man. Can't miss it and still shine as a man" (The Big Sky)

In the splendid series of novels known collectively as "The Big Sky" Series, for one of which A. B. Guthrie won a Pulitzer, the recurring character Boone Caudill is an extreme social isolate. He is a runaway from a father who beat his sons and put them to hard labor. His surname honored Daniel Boone, quite ironically. That Kentucky icon, although a remarkable hunter and trailblazer, was a founder of places where people could collectively, and peacefully, pursue hunting, tending to crops, animals, and the needs of neighbor farmers. Nothing prepared Boone Caudill to be with fellow humans. His oppressive father's attitude replicated the institution of slavery, a destroyer of innocence. It was an extreme example of the division of labor in families whose crops were the chief sustenance. Unlike his siblings, Boone will not have it. One day, he knocks the old man unconscious. Believing he has killed him, he escapes. His father, like a slave owner whose minions are his fortune, is in desperate pursuit. Reaching St. Louis, Boone is on his way to becoming a mountain man of great skill in living off the land, repairing equipment, hauling provisions, fighting with Indians, and coping with the harshness of unsurveyed wilderness. He has found one friend, Jim, another road kid on the way west, circa 1830.

Boone Caudill fits D. H. Lawrence's description of an archetype of the American experience. He has "sloughed off the old skin," in his case the role of obedient son in the hierarchy of family responsibility. His new identity, naked of contact with other people, is raw, without any attempt at a civil persona. Any trace of refinement in cultural manners or mores is absent. That may be necessary for his self-respect. But Caudill's defining trait is his severe unkindness. Lawrence called this state of existence "The essential American soul…hard, isolate, stoic, and a killer." Caudill kills an Indian for his horse, steals a man's dog after beating him up, rapes a woman whom he knew when they were children, and picks fights so he can make his opponent beg for mercy. Finally, he kills Jim on false suspicion he has had sex with his Caudill's Indian wife, Teal Eye. Then he abandons the wife and her son, who was born blind, not, as he thinks, because of any degeneracy in Jim, who in fact was too loyal to Boone to sleep with Teal Eye. The blindness was more likely due to Boone's VD. He gave his own son "no fucking chance."

Caudill is archetypically "tough," or "too tough," but that word connotes a comparison to other people in a particular culture. He lives in another dimension. He survives beatings, the arduous piloting of a flatboat in swirling river currents, a bad case of the clap, an Indian massacre, attacks of nature in the form of ice, snow, clouds of gnats, and an exploration of an abandoned native village with its smallpox corpses. Most amazing is his escape from the massacre by swimming with only his nose above water while the victors were busy slaking blood lust by eviscerating the bodies of some of his companions. Proximity to death is his enduring experience.

The intractable freedom from the restraints needed to be part of a family or community was never clearer than in Boone Caudill. Most tough as nails mountain men hoped for a sociable future, as stated by one member of his friend Dick Summers's party:

> It was the little things that made one feel at home in the world, that made him happy and forgetful: neighbors to hail and supper on the table and a good woman to love and the tavern and fire and small talk and walls and roofs to shut out the terror of God, except for glimpse enough to keep the sinner Christian.

Caudill is comfortable only when confronting wilderness, "the raw, vast, lonesome land" with all its terrors. He was a guide and expert hunter, as was Dick Summers and Natty Bumppo in Cooper's *Leatherstocking Tales*, with which, states James Cawelti, he "invented the Western."[64]

John Williams's *Butcher's Crossing* describes an 1870s buffalo hunt during which two mountain men and Will Andrews, a novice from Harvard, must endure near death from hunger, thirst, stampede, uncharted wilderness, a diet of raw buffalo liver and rot-gut coffee, and a snow-bound winter in a makeshift dugout. After returning to the Crossing, the former novice sets out alone, not knowing where he is going, but addicted to the danger, beauty, and vastness of the Rockies. He has learned to survive as a social isolate. Perhaps he is going back, without the equipment needed

---

[64] John G Cawelti, *Adventure, Mystery, and Romance: Formula Stories as Art and Popular Culture* (Chicago: U of Chicago Press, 1976),193-209. (Direct quotes on p. 193, 209.)

to kill buffalo, to a wilderness that tests human endurance to its apex. That was what he experienced on the hunt. He had left Harvard to learn who he was. The answer has nothing to do with how Caudill lives, for Will's temperament, shaped at Harvard Yard, is politely curious. His similarity is to Natty Bumppo. He has proven his manhood by surviving the trip and spending many nights with a tavern prostitute who intimidated him when he first arrived in town, a town on which he now turns his back, taking none of its creature comforts. He has internalized an irresistible attraction to natural vitality, as is the case with with Offutt's "The Leaving One" and with Little Big Man in Thomas Berger's novel by that name. Will has had a revelation of what Scott Fitzgerald called the "capacity for wonder" inspired by "the dark fields of the republic." The novel ends with him riding out of Butcher's Crossing, not knowing "where he was going, but he knew it would come to him later in the day. He rode forward without hurry, and felt behind him the sun slowly rise and harden the air."

Similar to Andrews's story is that of Jim Bridger in Michael Punke's *The Revenant: A Novel of Revenge* (one of several Westerns employing the names and character traits of historical personages). The revenant is Hugh Glass, an almost superhumanly resourceful mountain man abandoned by two partners after suffering grievous wounds while killing a Grizzly (Figure 8-1). He does make it back, at first by crawling, then by knowing the country, nourishing himself on animal carcasses, and using every trick in his "possibilities bag." He had vowed to kill the men who left him, as such an abandonment made survival of the group impossible. He beats one of the offenders, young Jim Bridger, almost to death, but stops himself because of Jim's silent acceptance of punishment. The novel ends with Jim, ignoring the wish of his Captain, volunteering to scout a canyon in the Big Horn Mountains.

He raised his eyes to a horizon carved from

snowy mountain peaks, virgin white against the frigid blue sky. He could climb up there if he wanted. Climb up there and touch the horizon, jump across and find the next.

Greil Marcus, in *The Old Weird America*, conjures up the cowboy's anthem: "The shape of the land, its vast expanse, its indifference to who you are or what you want, looms up as this solitary figure says his piece. I am the first cowboy and the last. Here no one sees me, myself least of all, I am happy, I am free."

Solitary Boone Caudill of course is never happy, or free from unbounded hostility. When Caudill returns home after years of hunting and scouting for westward travelers, his brother tells him that his father asked often about him, and, until suffering a lingering death, was a faithful provider. Despite the tears of his mother and brother, Boone inwardly sneers at their being weak enough to justify such a mean-spirited tyrant. Perhaps he cannot face the similarity in temperament between himself and the father who treated him as an unmanageable workhorse. That is not how his mother and brother remember the man, but one of the traits of the social isolate is his/her obduracy, which appears to all the world as mulishness but really has a dimension of fervent conviction. In the case of Caudill, it is the fervor of a killer, unlike the humane purpose in Natty Bumppo, Shane, or Harmonica, the hero in Sergio Leone's epic *Once a Upon a Time in the West*. These free spirits live by a code essential to their survival, and to that of those they ride with. Ironically, it isolates them even more completely from others, in that they see them as potential betrayers. Hugh Glass felt fully justified in killing the fellow hunters who abandoned him. They had betrayed their manhood, their group bond. Such a personal unwritten accord is bone-deep, closer to the heart and soul of an initiate than any contract formulated and enforced by a political or financial entity.

Some writers explain Caudill as enmeshed in a drama of hubris. His sin is the killing of Jim, who has established a friendship with

Teal Eye. Jim thinks his death is deserved, since God frowns on excessive sensual desire for a married woman. The hubris explanation does not fit Jim or Caudill. Jim did nothing sinful. Caudill's murdering Jim and abandoning his wife and son is horrible; he must have a psychic awareness of that. But he does not admit it. To say he is the clutches of hubris diminishes the chasm between the asocial isolate and people with an advanced sense of being part of a moral community where disregard of religious commandments is a sin. He has learned nothing but aggression from his father and submission to her husband's will by his mother. He sees as betrayal any challenge to his integrity as complete in himself alone. To him, his physical strength and icy emotional control comprise his individuality, his ability to "shine as a man." When Summers confronts him with his treatment of his wife and best friend, he responds as he did to Jim when he suspected him of making love to Teal Eye.

This kind of truculence is a trait the western pioneer often learned by fighting Indians, rustlers, maddening wind, blizzards, dust storms, and sweltering heat, possibly while living in a sod dugout on the plains, or passing a brutal winter in a wickiup, awaiting for nature to allow competition with other miners digging for a gold strike . When enemies appear, they must be dominated and thoroughly neutralized. One example is Hugh Glass, who would not have been a revenant without his determination to kill those who left him to die. Another example is Breece Pancake's farmer in "The Honored Dead," who disdains those who quit putting their strong backs to the soil. "Well, when everybody's going this way, it's time to be going that way, you know. Somebody's got to dig in the damn ground." Annie Proulx's Wyoming stories often delineate this belligerence conviction. In her "What Kind of Furniture Would Jesus Pick,"[65] Gilbert Wolfscale inherits a farm his sons are forced to work on, until they are old enough to choose to turn their

---

[65] In *Bad Dirt, Wyoming Stories 2* (NY: Scribner's, 2004), pp.61-86.

backs. Gilbert tries all the tricks in his arsenal to make them feel as he does. He is a relic of a period when there were fewer choices, with a profound love of the land and the livestock. He displays an "affronted hostility, as if he had just been insulted," especially when "ecology-minded freaks" or ambitious contractors come around to buy his land, and must be put in their place. At the end, he's thinking of furnishing the ranch house with simple pine chairs, "pegged, no nails or screws"—Jesus' own furniture. That's Gilbert's way of "shining like a man."

Guthrie contrasts the pugnacious Caudill to the generous, savvy leader of his hard-bitten troop of hunters, traders, and Indian fighters, Dick Summers. They were friends until Boone killed Jim and abandoned his wife. In *Fair Land, Fair Land* (1982), Summers is obsessed with Boone's aloofness from any iota of sympathy or moral awareness. When they meet, he wants to bring Caudill to an understanding of his perfidy. It is intolerable to Summers, a devout Christian, that such a man as Boone can act as he has. Caudill's lack of any accommodation to neighborliness, trust, and restraint negates the principles Summers has lived by. When the two men meet, Summers confronts Caudill with the murder of Jim. The response is "a look of torment changed to black rage" and an attack.

Summers does not want to respond violently, even though in mortal danger. To him it was not a "killing matter," but a moment when he might lead Caudill to repentance not through violence but through the birth of a humble self-awareness. That "look of torment" and Caudill's earlier confession while visiting Summers might indicate either guilt or, at the least, repressed self-hatred. Summers's primal duty is to forbearance. Caudill is on the point of strangling him when Dick's traveling partner shoots Caudill in the head. His statement "He didn't mean nothin' to me" is doubly powerful. First, it spotlights by contrast how committed to trust and fellow feeling Summers himself was. It makes the reader weigh carefully the character of Boone and Dick, two representative westerners, and consider which one is indeed more representative of their young, restlessly expanding, and deeply divided nation. Secondly, Dick's partner's exclamation echoes an overwhelmingly common response to social isolates, whether by people who have personally been in their company, or have read about them or seen them on stage or screen. Such a man or woman has lost his/her entitlement for being part of a social unit. He cannot be reined in by any code. He/she refuses to be judged by its benchmarks for trust. The fate of such outsiders will not be met with commiseration. Caudill dies quickly, with an involuntary shudder. The description is much like that of Amos Edwards's sudden death in Alan Lemay's *The Searchers* (1954). Caudill dies so that a man capable of guiding others to their goal might live. Edwards' death allows for Mart and his sister to live. Neither he nor Caudill is permitted any future. Nor did Caudill create one for his blind son, Nocansee, abandoned after his father killed Jim and disowned Teal Eye. Dick Summers, by contrast, can leave a civilizing legacy.

But Caudill remains a fascinating human being, all the more so because human status is denied him by less daring, less resourceful, and less courageous people. In Guthrie's complex narrative, Summers also does not have the time to fulfill his potential. A victim of the Indian holocaust, he and Nocansee are shot by federal troops raiding an Indian village with the implicit mission of killing all its inhabitants.

"He Didn't Mean Nothin' To Me"

This pronouncement by Caudill's killer epitomizes the life of Phil Burbank in Thomas Savage's *The Power of the Dog* (1967). Phil's abilities as a cowherder, horse breaker, outrider, trail boss, rope braider, brander and castrator of bulls, and banjo player make him as exceptional a 20th century cowboy as Boone Caudill was a 19th century Mountain Man. Phil proudly displays his racial, gender, and ethnic prejudices, his brutal efficiency with animals, his dirt-smeared clothes ("I stink and I like it"), and his refusal to wear gloves for even the harshest ranch tasks. The novel is set in 1920s Montana, at a lucrative ranch ran by mercurial Phil and his phlegmatic brother George, who handles the financial affairs. Phil has a lean elasticity as an outdoorsman. He bathes once a month at a secluded pool; his hair and body reek of contact with horses and cattle. He enjoys telling tales of the old days when men were still men; the exemplar is his own long-dead mentor, Bronco Henry. No one wants to be in his company, except George, whom he addresses as "Fatso." He is a supremely intelligent put-down artist. Annie Proulx sums him up: "a vicious bitch."[66]

When George marries, Phil tries to use his wife Rose's 16-year old son Peter to increase her despair at his virulent contempt. He has made her feel unwanted, incompetent, and dishonest, telling her she has no right to be part of his family. "Don't call be brother." Already having lost her physician husband to alcoholism and suicide, to see her son manipulated by Phil could lead, Phil hopes, to Rose's final breakdown; she is already drinking heavily. But Peter proves to be Phil's doppelgänger, walking with him, flaunting with each effeminate step what Phil most disdains. Both are brilliant. Both can see the shape of a running dog in a mountain's sloping rock. Peter meets the ranch hands' sneers with aloof disdain; Phil does the same with his own parents. Phil studies many subjects deeply; Peter knows all about diseases, infections, and medicines. Peter is overtly gay; Phil is a closeted homosexual.

Peter, as doppelgänger, is a copy of Phil, superseding him, somewhat like the 19th century college educated lawyers, judges, and peace officers replaced the charismatic quick draw sheriffs and Marshalls like Wyatt Earp and Seth Bullock, who enforced

---

[66] "Afterword," (c.2001) in *The Power of the Dog*, by Thomas Savage (NY: Little, Brown, 1967), pp.277-93. Proulx analyses Savage's body of work, his background in "bronc-stomping Montana," and his publishing career.

the mining or cattle town peace with fists and guns. Phil can observe people carefully, and control them as a result. But Peter can also manipulate, despite his outlandishly mincing body language, which is really a self-assured assertion of identity, in contrast to Phil's militant repression of desire. Peter is therefore free and proactive, while Phil is reactively suppressing what he had with Bronco Henry. When he considers replacing the long-lost Henry with Peter, he actually feels, with pride, that "the boy wanted to *become* him" (Italics Savage's). As his doppelgänger, that is what Peter does. One's doppelgänger embodies a secret self, with its buoyant freedom to satisfy yearning. In Savage's novel, it replaces and negates what turns out to be its original, weaker copy.

As Annie Proulx points out, Phil shuts down his sexuality in an unreachable space deep inside himself. Being an unerringly hostile social isolate allows him the space to do so. But it also prevents him from escaping his self-imposed prison. His imperious nastiness is a shield preventing people—and himself—from knowing that he is what the he-man cowboy most despises, a homosexual.

"What had love to do with Phil?" Nothing, no more than it tempered Caudill's rough edges. The latter's father made him hate people; he distrusted his wife and best friend so much he killed the latter and abandoned Teal Eye and his own blind son. A social isolate whose death is very similar to Phil's is Amos Edwards, in Alan Le May's *The Searchers*. He is killed by a cousin kidnapped by Comanches years ago, whom he has been stalking as a race traitor. She tells her brother that in shooting Amos she acted out of sibling love. Amos had kept secret his love for his brother's wife, so, not having experienced family togetherness, he would not have recognized the depth of his cousin's resolve to save what was left of her family. Ironically, protecting the family (from the blight of Indian blood) was Amos' ambition also. Peter had the same fervid desperation to protect, at all costs, his mother. Phil, not having had any filial love, did not consider that his new friend would turn on him if he destroyed his mother's sanity. An affectless social isolate can have this reticence to hurt someone who respects and has befriended hm. Natty Bumppo has it for the Temple family. It's a single-mindedness that sometimes can be fatal, as it almost is for Will Andrews on the buffalo hunt outside Butcher's Crossing, and for Little Big Man when, after living in an American city, he had returned weaponless to the Cheyenne tribe where he spent his childhood.

Having recognized Phil's unspoken attraction to him, Peter asks Phil to teach him how to braid rope. He had rubbed the rawhide strings with a dead cow's tissue. Phil, quintessentially and overtly tough, has not bothered to dress a deep cut in his hand. He dies within days of anthrax, of which Peter must have read in his father's books. In Jane Campion's film of the novel (2021), Phil's negation is brilliantly depicted by his coffined body. It is impeccably dressed, clean shaven, with hair slicked back and hands folded. The coffin closes on a young man devoid in death of his cowboy persona, the very identity he had clung to until Peter exploited it. In removing Phil, Peter, with poisoned pieces of rawhide, has relegated to the dusty past a late representative of the hardnosed solitary tamer of the American wilderness, with all the qualities, let it not be forgotten, needed to do so.

The film has other preternatural, eerie, and gothic features: one is the brooding, monochromatic landscape, composed of sand, rock, and vast mountainside, dwarfing the machines, buildings, and put-putting automobiles of 1920s Nevada. Another is the running dog image only the antagonists Phil and Peter can see. A third is Peter himself, his bat-like, freakishly awkward figure in its stiff new Levis, with veiled eyes and frozen expression, proving him to be an inscrutable force hiding in a 16-year old's body. He is stronger than Phil, especially because he has none of Phil's misanthropy, the latter's strategy for hiding the homosexuality that would brand him in his own milieu as a weakling pariah. Peter's stunning lack of any insecurity, so unlike his mother and father's self-destructive sensitivity, is his more potent for being unexpected.

Another way of putting it is that Peter is Phil's nemesis. As such, he can never be defeated. A nemesis implies that one has committed hubris, and will suffer something as dreadful as a death in convulsions. Under Campion's direction, Benedict Cumberbatch and Kodi Smit-McPhee act out a drama of a man encountering and succumbing to his fate after encountering his double.[67]

The Power of the Dog is among the darkest of rural noirs. A pernicious individual's doppelganger goes about his business of negating and replacing his double. Peter wants to be a doctor, possibly one specializing in infections passed from animals to humans—and how to prevent that death-dealing sickness. Who would know better, and have more power over life and death? One aspect of a doppelganger is its function as "an evil twin." Peter is, and always will be, Phil's murderer. He has also shown, at 16, the power of the dog.

"Hard, Isolate, Stoic, and a Killer"

Readers may deplore the failure of Boone Caudill to repent, or dismiss Phil Burbank as a sheer monomaniac, but that is imposing a moral stance on a sensibility addicted to the untamed struggle for survival. Caudill defines himself as on a mission to fight to the death with those he rashly judges to be alien, be they the Indian peoples; his own father; his best friend, after he thinks he slept with his wife; his Indian wife, whom he assumes encouraged the friend; and his caring mentor. A similar character is Amos Edwards, in another classic Western, *The Searchers*. He has

---

[67] See Otto Rank, *Double: A Psychoanalytic Study* (Chapel Hill: U. of North Carolina Press, 1971), pp.6-33.

spent his adult life almost entirely on horseback in the Texas badlands. His brother's family has been slaughtered by Comanche raiders, who kidnapped the two daughters. With his nephew, Amos spends years searching for the surviving woman, planning all the time to kill her because she has been living with savages.[68] "We be Texans," says Amos. "Someday this country will be a fine good place to live in. Maybe it needs our bones in the ground before that time can come." This social isolate is addicted to danger and confrontation to the point of death. The careers of Amos Edwards and Boone Caudill have at least something to do with death, as do those of Driver, McCarthy's Lester Ballard and Culla Holme, McMurtry's Hud, and Terrence Malick's Kit Carruthers (see below).

Lawrence's "hard, isolate, stoic, and a killer" resonates when one thinks characters discussed earlier, such as the predatory preacher in *Lightwood*, the fanatical game warden in *Poachers*, Jacob McNeely's heroin-dealing father in *Where All Light Tends to Go*, or several characters in *Crimes in Southern Indiana*, especially the meth-peddling owner of the dog-fighting ring in the final story, who hates America because it did not close out the war in Afghanistan, where he had served, and witnessed the death of companions. Two archetypes are The Misfit in O'Connor's "A Good Man is Hard to Find" ("no pleasure but meanness," since he has never been in Jesus' company), and The Judge in McCarthy's *Blood Meridian*, for whom violence is a

---

[68] The film *The Unforgiven* (1960), from the Alan Le May novel and directed by John Ford, is about a young Texas woman who was rumored to have been born and raised by Kiowas. A strange man with a saber he says represents God's vengeance spreads the word. The result is ostracism, contention between families, attempts by the Kiowas to capture the woman, and a revelation of the ugliness ("dirty Injun") of racist fear and contempt. The woman's courtship and possible marriage to a Texan exacerbates the violence.

quasi-religious creed: "If war is not holy, then man is nothing but antic clay." (That, by the way, is an echo of militant evangelist Billy Sunday: "I have no interest in a God who does not smite.") The historian Richard Hofstadter sees a "a Rooseveltian note here."[69] The only people who count, who are worthy of respect, are those "who know the sanctity of war." That knowledge isolates one in a sensibility that knows no fear. S/He sees himself as one of the elect.

There is also a Calvinist note, especially the espousal of "total depravity" as a result of original sin. Only God's grace can save a soul. It comes without any deeds that humans can attribute to their own good works. God's election is beyond human understanding. The strong, defined as the righteous, must dominate the weak. The careers of Caudill, O'Connor's Misfit, Savage's Phil, and Lemay's Amos Edwards exemplify this kind of manliness. With Promethean hubris, they act as if the will of a God whose acts are beyond human comprehension has implanted itself in their own souls. The result is powerfully stated in McCarthy's *Child of God* and *Outer Dark*. McCarthy captures the weird integrity of those who can embrace the solitary impulse to destroy without sentiment of any kind. Lester, "Child of God much like yourself perhaps"—note the Calvinist view of depravity—is progressively isolated from his Tennessee community, lives in a cave, has necrophiliac tendencies, and keeps body parts of murder victims in his dwelling place. In *Outer Dark*, Culla Holme exposes a baby, the result of raping his sister. He travels throughout his region of Appalachia, suspected of being a thief or carrier of disease. His sister, meanwhile, is greeted kindly as she looks for her baby. Culla is followed by three evil degenerates who exemplify his sin by killing people with whom he has been in contact. Finding that the child is alive, he locates it, but the three avenging devils have killed the man who took it. They inflict burns on the child and one of the three cannibalizes it. Years later,

---

[69] Anti-Intellectualism in American Life (NY: Vintage, 1962), p.119.

Culla, passing a "landscape of the damned," encounters a blind man who says he will pray for him. The man walks toward the blasted country—Hell—while Culla thinks "someone should tell a blind man before setting him out that way." Culla's dispassionate observation reveals that he has been incapable of being that someone. His isolation from humane response is as complete as that of the three degenerate child murderers who have been following him. Everyone he meets senses that. His total depravity has prevented him from empathizing with a person sufficiently to reach out a helping hand.

Another stunning example of a nihilistic isolate, set in the American west, informs Terrence Malick's classic film *Badlands*, preserved in the National Film Registry. It follows Kit Carruthers and girlfriend Holly, as they go on a killing spree through 1950s South Dakota and Montana. He Kit kills a half dozen people, including her father. Holly shows little remorse; her father's capacity for love ended with the death of his wife. Kit's killing of a friend who has sheltered him and two of his visitors is gratuitous. His finishing off three bounty hunters is also. Kit's and Holly's only emotions are for each other, especially when they dance to Nat King Cole's portentous romantic ballad, "Autumn Leaves." After his capture, the police and national guard officers, disarmed by Kit's wit and aplomb, accept gifts and wish him well. There is something distinctly American about Kit. It is coherent in his resourceful survival tactics in the empty, silent dust of the Great Plains; his service in Korea; his respectful acquiescence when appearing before police; his openness in admitting what he had done; and his physical resemblance to James Dean, the rebel without a cause. But his silence regarding any responsibility serves as a shield against empathy or responsibility. "Do you like people?" a deputy asks him. He replies that they are mostly okay. Holly's diffidence regarding responsibility is similar. She marries the son of the prosecuting attorney and apparently lives happily ever after. She describes Kit's execution on a sunny day six months after his capture as if she were reciting the ending of a fairy tale.

Yet another isolate who knows no fear is Larry McMurtry's Hud, "more reckless than the best of the thousand wild-ass cowboys in the Texas cattle country." The title of McMurtry's novel *Horseman, Pass By* is elegiac. Set in the mid-twentieth century, the prideful endurance of the aging, neighborly ranchers atrophies as their land comes under the control of oil companies, to whose impassive acquisitiveness Hud adds a human-scale dominance. Neither sympathy nor respect are part of Hud's nature. He has contempt for everyone, including his grandfather, nephew Lonnie, ranch hands, and any Mexicans or Blacks, especially his opposite, the impulsively sympathetic, healing housekeeper. The marvelous film *Hud* used a father-son confrontation to explain Hud's hardness of soul. "You just don't give a damn," said his father. McMurtry makes Hud an isolated force of brute nature, one facet of the ugly replacement of a coherent, once vital small town by one accommodating the changes which oil rigs and massive slaughtering plants signify.

I've mentioned Dick Summer's death and that of Caudill's son Nocansee at the end of Guthrie's *Fair Land*, and that both were victims of a U.S. cavalry raid on an Indian village. Summer's last word is a puzzled "well." He may be thinking about whether or not the murderous troopers are replicas of Caudill's hard isolation and proclivity for fierce assault. The difference is that the brutal troopers are have been trained to be part of a body of men serving a nation-state. Caudill, with a profound and limitless contempt for organized, admired causes, is a law unto himself, a social isolate, as is Hud.

A Wandering Isolate of The Fields and Camps, Canceled Out.

In his 1975 Spur Award novel *The Shootist*, Glendon Swarthout presents a social isolate named John Bernard Books, afraid of nothing, skilled gun handler, scourge of hypocrisy, fighter against illness and pain, impassive killer (as many as 30; five on his last day) and personification of "bone lonesomeness." He most closely resembles three western heroes. One is Lassiter, in *Riders of the Purple Sage*. "He packs two black-butted guns...hard to see...He takes no chances with men" and exudes "the set changelessness that came from years of silence and solitude." He was someone "forever looking for that which he never found." A second is Hugh Glass, the Revenant. When companions leave him to die after a maiming by a bear, he crawls back to camp, fired by the need to kill those who broke the Mountain Man's code. He acts not for personal revenge but to keep workable a code without which duty would be overpowered by chaos. Finally, there is Sergio Leonia's Harmonica, who knows his kind of eye-for-an-eye justice is about to give way to impersonal law and prison. He will not be a part of a social unit that outlaws personal tests of courage and integrity, replacing hunting for food with game wardens. Lassiter, Glass, Harmonica: all hard men, who know their kind of man about to die off. We might add Shane, Rudolph Wurlitzer's man of "mountain doings" Zebulon Shook, and even Natty Bumppo.

Swarthout has given J B Books a fallible humanity that sets *The Shootist* apart from other heroic narratives of the plains, mountains, and camps. The writer makes Books unique by having him face extremely painful death through prostate cancer. Books acts with resolve and dignity, like the silent resolve of Harmonica or Shane, but existentially greater even than that of those men. Lawrence's "hard, isolate, stoic, and a killer" connotes behavior both amoral and, equally, at the limits of human endeavor. At one point, when Books' laudanum cannot alleviate his suffering, he challenges God. "Maybe I don't believe in you, but you damned well better believe in me...I kill bad men, you kill good. I have reason, you don't...God, face me now. Be a man and face me now if you have the guts."

This gargantuan contempt for God and man is the result of

betrayal by El Paso's solid citizens: a minister, a former lover (who wants him to sign a contract for a ghost-written tell-all), a photographer, a pulp writer, and an undertaker: all trying to exploit Books' shootist fame. Books alone has generosity, expressed toward those who face suffering alone. And the reverse of the medal is there also. When he is waylaid by an old, desperate thief at gunpoint, Books shoots him and offers him only an easy death with a shot in the robber's head.

On the cover of the Bison Books edition is a cartoon of a man dancing, swirling, holding a gun in each hand. It is not Books; it is Gillom Rodgers, the landlady's son, Books' successor. Books has decided to choose his final gunfight. After, Gillom is in possession of Books' Remingtons, which he will display, for a price, to anyone in the upscale bars of Gilded Age El Paso (The Continental, reminiscent of Yellow Sky's Weary Gentleman). His ambitions and feckless pursuit of them is much like the Tom Sawyer in Coover's novel. Swarthout concludes:

> [Gillom] strode head up, shoulders back, taller to himself, having sensations he had never had before. One gun was still warm in his hand, the bite of smoke was in his nose and the taste of death on his tongue. His heart was high in his gullet, the danger past,...and the sweet clean feel of being born.

These are the very terms the author uses to describe how Books feels after a shooting. But Books and Gillom are doppelgangers. The latter, man of business, cancelled out the wandering isolate of the fields and camps. Books and Gillom's mother had hoped the young man would go to school and learn about himself. But that misjudgment is a sign of the times, as well as a many-leveled irony. Gillom steals the money Books had given Mrs. Rogers. With Books' guns, and Gillom's own sense of how to successfully "jump into the scene" of turn-of-the-century El Paso, Gillom begins a career as a successful entertainer, starting with that stolen money and lying about Books having given him his guns. He's on his way. In the film, starring John Wayne, an ending which would have damaged Wayne's image as depicting heroes was replaced by one in which Gillom shoots the bartender who killed Books and then, under the influence of the latter, throws away the gun.[70]

The Value of the Social Isolate on the Frontier

Despite his/her equation of detachment from others with personal freedom, the social isolate is valuable as an agent of Manifest Destiny. In this context, it cannot be said, as the man who shot Caudill said of the latter, that people like Caudill "don't mean nothing." Andrew Jackson's quasi-religious colonialism was grounded in and supported by single-mindedly aggressive men like Caudill, Hud, and even Kit Carruthers, as well as by people dedicated to establishing societal institutions. Historian Richard Slotkin explained that territorial expansion (the Nazis called it *lebensraum*) required regeneration through violence.[71] The social isolate's behavioral traits—toughness, obdurate willfulness, indomitable progress toward a goal, single mindedness, pragmatic resourcefulness, and proclivity for scapegoating—contributed to the success of institutions of national expansion in politics, the military, industry, and education. It was these habits of mind that finished the Indians, uncovered precious minerals, broke the sod, closed the frontier, and made the Westerner a figure of patriotic song and story.

The archetypal loner's need to test human capacities for

---

[70] See the Introduction to *The Shootist* in the 2011 Bison Books (U. of Nebraska Press) edition, by Miles Swarthout, who wrote the screenplay.

[71] Richard Slotkin, Regeneration Through Violence: The Mythology of the American Frontier, 1600-1860 (1973; Middletown CT: Harper Perennials, 1996), pp.556-62.

merging with nature is an essential contribution to the myth of the American West. Nothing is more indispensable to the westerner's' self-development than the ability to keep what Harry Crews called "the rough edges." That meant many protagonists championed individual strength over the influence of the railroads, the steamships, the mechanical reaper, the Pinkertons, the banks, the opera houses, and the Wild West circuses. Natty Bumppo was the first protagonist of this type. It was Mark Twain's genius to make Huck Finn a similar disdainer of progress, someone whose deepest personal attachment was to an African slave. In Robert Coover's novel *Huck Out West*, Huck's closest friend, like Natty's, was an Indian. Huck was also the increasingly disenchanted pard of that exemplar of American initiative, the congenial, ruthless, amoral Tom Sawyer, who had his own rough edges. They were the kind that led to control of mining, cattle-herding, and railroad businesses; the near-extinction of the Indian food source, the buffalo; and political power.

The western social isolate could herd stampeding cattle, crawl through hostile territory after a mauling by animals or Indians, pursue killers for hundreds of miles to exact justice, strangle enemies, persevere in a dugout while snowbound for months, or calmly seek food while half dead with fever and starvation. But Amos Edwards, The Judge (McCarthy's *Blood Meridian*), Joe Lon Mackey (Crews's *A Feast of Snakes*), Hugh Glass (Punke's *The Revenant*) and Boone Caudill, as social isolates, could not join the stalwarts of the western frontier in celebrating the triumph of law and order. The isolates are what John Cawelti describes as men of "lawless openness," as opposed to the settler, be s/he a homesteader, shopkeeper, lawman, or cattle rancher. Cawelti's encyclopedic knowledge of American history and popular culture lead him to define the Western as the struggle between, on the one hand, the impulsive lawlessness and solipsistic motives of the isolate of the high country and plains and on the other, the creators of order, piety, law, and a Gilded Age town culture of assembly halls, churches, schools, clothing emporiums, opera houses, women's clubs, and other showcases of gentility and polish: the kind of civilization that made Huck Finn want to set out for "the territory ahead of the rest."

Popular films made from *The Big Sky* and *The Searchers*, needing to insinuate the "public good," recast Boone Caudill and Amos Edwards as tough, high spirited, and supremely courageous. Viewers could walk out of the theater admiring them. Dewey Martin's Caudill, after a contest with Jim Deakins for Teal Eye's hand, finally wins her love. In the novel, he was about to kill Dick Summers when the latter's partner killed him. John Wayne's Edwards is a contemptuous and vengeful loner, once shooting the eyes of an Indian corpse so the man's spirit will never find his way to the afterlife. He refuses to enter the family house to which the "rescued" Debbie is returned. In the book, as stated above, Debbie killed him as he was pursuing her with deadly intent. John Ford shows Edwards to be "hard, isolate, stoic, and a killer," but at the end he rides off proudly into the Texas sunset. Interestingly, Martin's and Wayne's acting made their characters attractive because their courage and resilience were foregrounded by the actor's posture, voice, gait, gun handling, physical strength, and self-assertiveness: all traits (of course not exclusively) of the social isolate.

In Western films, the heroes with such traits often end up accepting and helping other men, and marrying women attracted to a vulnerability integral with male bitterness. Great actors can make this softening of rough edges convincing. Examples are Robert Mitcham in *Blood on the Moon* and *The Man with the Gun* or James Stewart in *The Far Country*. The lure of rescuing a sympathetic community struggling for freedom from exploiters wins out over their desire to meet the test of survival in the wide-open spaces. In the script for *The Shootist*, written by the son of the novelist, El Paso was the community and Gillom the man who came of age by bringing law and order to the town, thus negating the possibility for another man of Books' fearlessness or his primitive clarity of self-awareness.

Figure 8-1: Hugh Glass, right, and as played by Leonardo
DiCaprio (upper left). The Daily Mail.com: "Exclusive: Savagely
Mauled by a Female Grizzy, Hugh Glass Trekked 200 miles..."
Google: Hugh Glass Daily Mail UK.

CHAPTER 9

Binary Ideals Of The American Character: Personal Confrontation in and with Wilderness vs. the Comforts of Community

Boone Caudll, James Sallis' Driver, Amos Edwards, The Revenant Hugh Glass, Harmonica, Shane, Dexter's Calamity Jane, *3:10 to Yuma's* Ben Wade, Hud, Cormac McCarthy 's vicious Culla Holme and his John Grady Cole the horse whisperer, and *Badlands'* impassive killer Kit Carruthers—all are by choice isolated from the habitus, taboos, institutions and aspirations of an organized community. They do not want its legal protection, social acceptance, or religious comfort. They lead lives of high drama, saturated with resolve, iron clad resolution in pursuit of goals, and unique physical skills.

John G. Cawelti writes of the two contrasting origins of the American character: "advancing civilization and the free and natural life of the wilderness." The people just listed are in the latter camp. Neither the adjectives "free" nor "natural" have any moral or other judgmental implications, while the phrase "advancing civilization" certainly does. Cawelti writes that James Fennimore Cooper, in his saga of Natty Bumppo (modeled after Daniel Boone), "invented the Western." The characters may have ties to the eastern cities and have to visit a fast-developing acquisitive, law-saturated social unit. But the western hero is a "man of the wilderness who comes out of the old 'lawless' way of life." "The most significant aspect of the Western," he concludes, is the relationship between the hero and the contending forces of civilization and wilderness."[72] Lawless openness" is the mark of that confrontation with untamed nature and irrepressible human will that is contrasted to the other, and with closing of the frontier, predominant, American way of life in settled urban culture where property, decent manners, and moral consensus are valued legal and informal directives about decent behavior.

In Cooper's *The Pioneers*, Natty and The Last Mohican, Chingagook, encounter aristocrats, including the compassionate Marmaduke Temple, who restrict hunting on their lands and threaten Natty with fine and humiliation. They also offer him the comfort of their grounds and mansion in his declining years. He cannot accept. "The meanest of God's creatures be made for some use, and I'm formed for the wilderness, If ye love me, let me go where my soul craves to be agin!" Temple represents, as Cawelti shows, "progress": "the firm governance of order and decorum." Natty embodies "the marginal, lonely man of the wilderness" whose spirit of radical freedom, and embrace of social isolation, is doomed to end with the disappearance of the "territory" which Huck Finn wishes for himself, beyond the reach and ken of Aunt Sally.

Of course, the people of the Appalachian and Ozark mountains, the West Texas and Arizona badlands, the rural South and Midwest, and the states of Nevada, the Dakotas, and Wyoming still contend with wildness, sometimes flourishing as a result. Cormac McCarthy, Annie Proulx, Richard Hood, Daniel Woodrell, Steph Post, Rusty Barnes, Steph Post, Eryk Pruitt are some of the writers concerned with radical individualism and social isolation. The more the realities of urban injustice,

---

[72] *Adventure, Mystery, and Romance: Formula Stories in Art and Popular Culture* (Chicago: U. of Chicago Press, 1976), pp.192-201. The quotation about "the most significant aspect of the Western" is on p.194. The one about the "invention of the Western" is on p.195.

indifference to it, and resultant "failure stories" are inevitable, the more fascination exists with the lawless hero confronting wilderness and isolation "beyond twisted sorrow."

Single-Minded Purity of Purpose: The Grieving Loner in Once Upon a Time in the West

Sergio Leoni's film may be praised as a tall story, mythic in scope. It earns its effectiveness by manifesting the contradictions in the American character that led Fennimore Cooper to "invent" the western. *Once Upon a Time* features an indominable woman leading fellow settlers to cash in on the promise of a railroad depot. It depicts hired killers, criminals turned businessmen, a terminally ill railroad magnate determined to reach the Pacific, sadistic cowboys, and a lone quick-triggered searcher seeking righteous justice for being forced into involvement in his brother's hanging. This searcher is called Harmonica. The man for whom he is searching, Frank, forced a harmonica into Harmonica's mouth while he was required to hold his own brother on his shoulders. Frank's gang had thrown a noose around the brother's neck. When, inevitably, Harmonica collapsed, his brother was strangled. He played a gasping note as his brother died. The cruelest aspect of this torture is the guilt forced upon the helpless Harmonica.

Leone may have been recalling the way border state gangs of private citizens during the Civil War responded when they confronted enemies. Heads of families who answered political questions the wrong way were summarily hanged. (See Woodrell's *Woe To Live On*). One extreme example is the work of the Bushwhackers and Jayhawkers, Confederate and Union raiders respectively. Each side engaged in massacres, ambushes, and raids. Bushwhackers, in response to free-state (Union) anti-slavery actions, killed over 200 citizens of Lawrence, KS in 1863. From the Bushwackers came the nucleus of the James-Younger gang.

It's a particularly dark example of regeneration through violence: "something to do with death." What happened to Harmonica, and his revenge on Frank, are also.

It was the outlaw Cheyenne who spoke about men like Harmonica having something to do with death. He was talking to Jill, the woman who, despite losing her husband and suffering rape, organized the disparate settlers into the railroad town of Sweetwater. Jill had fallen in love with Harmonica, who told her she was creating "a beautiful town." But he was going to ride off, into whatever was left of the frontier. He and his brother had been victims of the viciousness of the Civil War and its aftermath, as embodied and refined by Frank and his loyal crew. Two cultures had mutually excluded each other from human status, forming mutually exclusive covenants. Social isolates cannot accommodate themselves to a community's institutions and social obligations. Maybe that, but also the following might have killed any affection in Harmonica: the cruelty done to him and his brother; Frank's killing of Jill's husband and family, which was his way of jump-starting a career in the railroad business; and a dying railroad entrepreneur's mad dream of seeing the Pacific from his window, a dream that entailed hiring killers to dispatch a whole family.

All of the above had a lot to do with death, as well as with contradictions in the American ideal. But none of it cancels out Jill's vindication of her husband's dream of a functioning community, or Harmonica's successful crusade to rid the region of Frank, shooting him and shoving the harmonica into Frank's mouth as he took his last breath. He wasn't being ironic when he told Jill she would lead the development of a "beautiful town." The scene where Leone depicts Jill leading the sweaty, sooty labor of building Sweetwater's train depot has a heroic, and democratic, cast. We last see Harmonica riding out of town and into the sunset of the Day of the Outlaw, while the Iron Horse chugs into Sweetwater station.

Harmonica leaving Sweetwater with Cheyenne's body may

be an allusion to Jack Schaefer's *Shane*, whose quick draw saved the homesteaders from the terrorism of the cattle baron. Shane cared for the family he interrupted his mysterious journey to help, as Harmonica did for the town Jill founded. In a famous episode, Joe, the farmer and community organizer, and Shane, the isolate from the wilderness, work together to pull up a gigantic tree stump by its roots without machinery, getting hungry for Mother's pie. Thus the vitality of the homesteader and the mysterious wanderer work together. Later in the novel they defeat the corporate power of the cattle rancher and his hired gun. At the climax, however, Shane prevents Joe from coming with him to the showdown because Shane has had experience with killing that a homesteader could never have.

Possibly, Shane had been a hired gun himself in the past, after having failed as a farmer. He rides off with no desire or capacity to live in a community, even one he has saved from a criminal extortionist and a murderer. Ironically, he may have a wisdom unusable in such a setting. Its regulations, its covenants, would be in his way. In that, he is like Guthrie's Caudill, Banks's fisherman, Denis Johnson's Jesus' son, Zane Grey's Lassiter (in *Riders of the Purple Sage*), or Harte's M'liss (see below). *Shane's* narrator is an adult recalling this key event in his youth. Shane has become a mythic figure, both to the narrator and, thanks in part to the movie, to many Americans. Recent editions indicate that young readers are a projected audience. Shane, like Harmonica, has qualities every boy admires but very few encounter in the "adult" or "civilized" world.

From Roughshod Camp to Gilded Age City

Leone was aware that Harmonica, Frank, and Cheyenne were the last of their breed in the West. The likes of the two-gun sheriff, the cattle baron, the rustler, the whorehouse/saloon entrepreneur, the stage and train robber, the miner competing with other desperate men for precious metals, the shootist cowboy, and the wilderness hunter-trapper would need to survive increased censure and legal scrutiny, or adopt a respectable enterprise and civil personae in the West's Gilded Age communities. In the final episode of the TV series *Deadwood*, the town's murderous strongman, his henchmen, the dance hall owner, and the hard-boiled provider of cheap immigrant manpower all become respectable. They had started as thieves of property and killers, then continued as pariah middlemen, providing tabooed services. As time passed, and the mining camp experienced progress, they ended up proud and relieved to shed their rough edges, and, as they aged, to exist within a compliant cultural unit.

Here is an enthusiastic request from one kinsman to another to be a part of the progress of camp to city, and from a Territory to the State of Montana:

> 'It takes a little time to civilize a new place, but we're almost there...We'll have better courts, better law enforcement, more churches and schools, a more general respect and support for the finer things.' He stood gazing as if these things had come to pass and he could see them—the sunny [Sunday?] schools, the Methodist churches, the happy law and order, the good life under God...Evans had to remind himself that here was a kind man...overgood, too blind by nice choice to what went on in sporting houses and who went in, or had gone. He put down the wild impulse to wise the man up.[73]

To account for the growing division between the West's violent, hastily constructed, and boom-or-bust towns and its

---

[73] A B Guthrie, Jr., *These Thousand Hills* (Boston: Houghton Mifflin, 1956), pp.332-33.

nascent cities, the centralized power of the federal government after the Civil War must be taken into account. It focused on land acquisition, and served best those who prospered most by acquiring it. Property brings power. Denis Johnson's *Angels* suggests his readers think about how duty to law and order, for the protection of property, can be a kind of straitjacket. A panicked bank robber, escaping the scene, wonders why a dutiful guard foiled the theft at the expense of his own life. He hides in a theater where a movie about the James Gang's rout after their Northfield, MN holdup is playing. A cashier refuses to open a safe, and is killed by James, who loses several men in flight from a well-armed, vengeful band of citizens, self-sacrificingly loyal to their established institutions. Some of them get shot. Johnson makes clear, and questions, the priority duty assumes over respect for personal and family welfare when property is threatened. It is a civic expectation difficult to challenge without loss of respect, even self-respect. Of course, the citizen expects his/her own land and home to be just as worthy of protection. But a bank's decisions, especially involving foreclosure deliberations, could work against that expectation. The conundrum of doing a citizen's duty as contrasted to the lone fight for victory over the untamed land involves the all the intangibles of human identity. Jill knew this in *Once upon a Time in the West* when she founded the town of Sweetwater, and Harmonica did when he said goodbye to her and to the town parameters, economic and social, over which she will preside.

Eric Foner, scholar of Reconstruction, describes the way the Washington bureaucracy became exponentially more important as a result of financial reforms during the Civil War. They were crucial to settling the West. After the war, the government instituted a common currency, greenbacks or bank bonds, unlike the various forms of exchange in the confederate South (one form of which depicted laboring slaves). Wealthy southerners hated federal currency reform; it meant increased taxes. But it helped post-war pioneers and made easier the enforcement of the

Homestead Act, allowing settlers to acquire free land, and helping farmers pay taxes.[74] Property brings power, and security, both yearned for by American pioneers.

Nevertheless, the relationship between the US government and the settlers of the plains was often contentious. Part of that was energized by a growing urban—rural hostility. Pioneers protested Washington's failure to clear the Indians from the locations in which they settled, instead allowing them to remain in reserved areas as a result of treaties (while they lasted). Farmers, ranchers, and miners all felt Indian peoples were "holding captive" land they were not using, by the White Man's definition of use. Later, and with much more validity, settlers blamed the federal land offices for bureaucratic ineptitude and dishonesty in specifying where on public domain areas they could live and work. Even the Homestead Act had its inequities, condemning some would-be settlers to the Sisyphean task of making success out of semi-arid and weed-infected earth.[75]

As the intercontinental railway was built, new opportunities generated grudging respect for federal and state institutions governing the administration of the frontier. Street lighting, telegraph lines, mechanical sod-breaking equipment, and barbed wire made the West's farm and town workers more productive and their futures more secure. Banks became essential for both homesteaders and ranchers, as well as transportation and mineral

[74] Eric Foner, "Ways and Means," review of Roger Lowenstein, *Lincoln and His Cabinet and the Financing of the Civil War, New York Times Book Review,* March 10, 2022, p.10.

[75] Patricia N Limerick, *The Legacy of Conquest: The Unbroken Past of the American West* (NY: Norton, 1987), pp.44-47, 58-62. She quotes (p.61). Malcolm Rohrbough, author of *The Land Office Business*: "The land was there to be taken, and...the rules and regulations of the government did not change their natural rights as citizens." David Danbom, *Born in the Country* (Balt.: Johns Hopkins, 1995), p.114 points out, however, that startup costs hindered poor people from considering the Homestead Act.

companies. A town's main street federal agencies, media outlets, and office buildings became crucial to it getting on the map. Men of stature at work in elite locations, with the help of politicians, could control the production and distribution of gold, oil, and silver. Although some hard-working miners struck it rich, the real winners in the discovery of precious metals turned out to be mining corporations. Manufacturers of needed clothing, goods and packaging flourished as well. The middle-class establishment grew to include storekeepers, hardware merchants, hotel owners, craftsmen, physicians, contractors, restaurateurs, theater impresarios, livestock entrepreneurs, clergy, and educators.

Citizens blasted the stinginess, corruption, and insensitivity of state capitols and of Washington. But the larger the city, the more its inhabitants required law enforcement, as well as financial support, especially in the form of bank auditors, District Attorneys, and judges. As C Robert Haywood explains, a western town, if not abandoned after a failed search for precious minerals or grazable cattle land, separated itself into a rowdy proletariat and a sedate, respectable neighborhood. Social class and the Gilded Age values and tolerances inherent in it became all-important to an increasing majority. "The ability of individuals to pass on social and material advantages to their children" was key to this ideal in urban centers from New York to Dodge City and Deadwood. Haywood cites the career of Dodge's dapper, cocky, increasingly wealthy gunman and Front Street saloon entrepreneur Luke Short. In his Long Branch Saloon, innovations such as singing prostitutes set off a contest with other dance halls which, despite Short's strongarm men, neither side would win. Instead, the civic-minded do-gooders, with support from Christian reformers, educators, politicians, and business interests among the "decent" community in the county-seat market town, shrank the Front Street district into insignificance."[76]

---

[76] Haywood, *The Victorian West: Class and Culture in Kansas Cattle Towns* (Lawrence, KS: U. Press of Kansas, 1991), pp.13-21.

In boom town after boom town, sophisticated peacekeeping tactics replaced vigilante violence, administered at state and federal courthouses by district attorneys and judges. District marshals now stood alongside local sheriffs, or competed with them, for the protection of law and order, US Marshals and their deputies were privileged to carry guns wherever they went. Business leaders and bankers, and clergymen with sanctioned credentials, built showplace houses, and assigned their wives renewed responsibilities for bringing Gilded Age culture to prominence. They donated money toward lecture halls, schools, and prestigious public entertainments.

Rarely, a gambler like Doc Holliday, a train robber like Jessie James, a rustler like Billy the Kid, a volatile, quick-draw killer like James Wesley Harden, a tall-tale entertainer like Calamity Jane, or Belle Starr the Bandit Queen would provide fascination, entertainment, and outrage, depending on the prestige level of the individual. The "uncivilized rowdies" were representatives of Greil Marcus' "old, weird Americans," those with Harry Crews' "rough edges" and possibly self-destructive but stubbornly self-assertive traits. Few solid citizens of the newly flourishing cities would want to run into them in a saloon or a dark street. The older settlers, the stage coach drivers, the rowdy hard-bitten cowboys who raised hell on Main Street and in saloons offering gambling tables downstairs and "soiled doves" upstairs, the men who rode in posse after rustlers and thieves, and the early sheriffs who actually did confront outlaws on the Main Streets of gerry-built camps when court houses were days away, all had to share prominence in the community with less heroic folks, who soon outnumbered them.

The Frontier Marshall: Both Fearless Gunman and Agent of Law and Order

Bat Masterson's reminiscences of his fellow lawmen specify two

Machiavellian traits: fearlessness, and circumspection. Wichita's "Rowdy Joe" Lowe ran a brothel and saloon. Ben Thompson killed many men, "always in an open and manly way," wrote Bat. Bill Tilghman fought and defeated the Doolin gang in Oklahoma after serving, and cannily buying much-desired property, in Dodge City. (He starred in a 1915 film about these exploits). Wyatt Earp knew how to elevate his reputation in any confrontation. Thus, he refused to return money a gambler had been cheated out of, because of the gambler's bad reputation in the town. That left the latter with two choices, a gunfight he was sure would get him killed, or leaving town before other, lesser men took advantage of his loss of face. Earp first won respect by the "courage and coolness" he displayed in the then-lawless Dodge City, both with a sneering alderman whom he unceremoniously dragged off the jail and with a cowboy shooting up a theater whom Earp shot dead before he hit the ground. In Tombstone, the Earp brothers, and especially Doc Holliday, saw their opportunities and took them: James had a saloon, Virgil rode shotgun on a stagecoach, and Wyatt headed a gambling establishment.[77] Holiday way mixed up in stagecoach robbery. Masterson, possibly by contrast, gives an example of his magnanimity before closing: he declined Pres. Roosevelt's appointment as Marshal in an Indian reservation, on the grounds that he would have to meet inevitable challenges by killing young men.

Frontier Marshalls such as Masterson, Bill Hickock, and Wyatt Earp sometimes persuaded dangerous men to leave town or cooperate, instead of standing trial. It might not have served the ideal of justice, but it prevented a lot of bloodshed, which would have made it hard for a camp to gain the status, and the variety of citizens with administrative and technological skills, that a growing and prosperous town needed. Wyatt Earp often made deals and shared information with Ike Clanton, later an

---

[77] W B (Bat) Masterson, *Famous Gunfighters of the Western Frontier* (Mineola, NY: Dover, 2009), pp.30-59. For Joe Lowe: Haywood, p.21.

opponent at the OK Corral shootout.[78] Bill Hickock's confrontation with impulsive young killer John Wesley Hardin while Marshall in Abilene is exemplary of the frontier Marshal's conciliatory tactics. Hickok enforced the no-guns-in-town ordinance. According to Hardin, Bill tricked Hardin into getting the drop on him; he cursed Bill for intending to shoot him. Hickok denied it and then told the teenager, "You are the gamest and quickest boy I ever saw. Let us compromise this matter and I will be your friend."

There were also strongarm tactics. A frontier "peace officer" like Wyatt Earp was invaluable for a *modus operandi* that worked for his time and place: when confronted in the street by a cowboy opponent, he once confessed, he "slapped him in the face with my left hand and drew my pistol with my right...I hit him on the head with my six shooter and walked away."[79] Historian Tom Clavin observes: "The way to tame a notorious town was not to outkill the bad guys but to intimidate them, sometimes with the help of a gun barrel to the skull."[80]

Bill Hickok held no office in Deadwood, was having trouble with his eyes, and seemed to have been in a different dimension of existence than that of a gunman Marshal. It may well have been that Wild Bill realized that his time and usefulness as a frontier marshal were receding. In Deadwood, Bill knew and could still display the required skills: athleticism with firearms and fists, a need to establish superiority, or the ambition to calm and control a group of westerners. But he spent so much time in saloons that he was once arrested for loitering, probably a message to make a better example of his renowned heroism

[78] Tom Clavin, Tombstone: The Earp Brothers, Doc Holliday, and the Vendetta Ride from Hell (NY: St Martins, 2020), p. 217.

[79] Lubet, p.142.

[80] Clavin, Tombstone: The Earp Brothers, Doc Holliday, and the Vendetta Ride from Hell (NY: St Martin's, 2020), p.13.

and initiative. The day he was shot, he was not in his habitual seat with his back to the wall, simply because another card player was occupying it and Bill did not ask him to move. All frontier marshals had to take such precautions; they all had long lists of suspected would-be assassins.[81] And Hickok had an imminent threat to deal with. There were rumors that he was to be appointed Marshal, in order to stop the dance hall racketeering (including pimping), extortionate loans, rustling of horses and cattle, the wild shoot-ups and shoot-outs by drunken cowboys, the bawdy plays and skits in the bars (especially Al Swearengin's Gem); the thievery and intimidation of prospectors, and the defiant carrying of firearms in the streets and eating places. Hickock's response was "Those fellows across the creek have laid it out to kill me, and they are either going to do it or they ain't. Anyway, I don't stir out of here unless I'm carried out."[82] He stopped those rumors with a warning that he was still a champion sharpshooter.

One of the most intractable of the frontier Marshal's tasks was the political tangles that inevitably ensnared them. Earp and Hickok could have had a long sit-down about it. If Hickok had to squelch rumors of his being designated to clean out the rowdy and quick-fingered elements in Deadwood, Earp, as U.S. Deputy Marshal in Tombstone, contended literally to the death at the OK Corral and its aftermath with the squatting, rustling (in Mexico as well as Arizona), bullying, card-sharping, stagecoach robbing, shootout-provoking cowboys (often from Texas) and their Democratic supporters. The animosity was deeply related to the Union-Confederate post-Civil War situation. I've referred to this while discussing Oakley Hall's *Warlock* in Chapter 2. The cowboys had deep Southern allegiances. Their support of the

---

[81] Deputy Marshal Sam Sixkiller presided very successfully over the Indian Police in Muskogee, Indian Territory. The town was notoriously dangerous. He was ambushed and killed in 1886, joining many other lawmen and government agents killed in the vicinity.

[82] Tom Clavin, *Wild Bill*, p.273-75.

Democratic sheriff meant that he did little to punish their stagecoach robberies. Wyatt Earp was a Republican, and a Kansan, which to Confederate supporters from Texas and Arizona translated to "Easterner."[83] Looming beyond the immediate grievances that caused the shootout at the corral was the pre-existing hatred simmering between southerners and easterners, Democrats and Republicans, riders of the range and men connected to and protecting town businesses. "The ways of those saddle tramps/tin horns are not our ways, and never will be."

The immediate cause of the OK shootout was an explosion of frustrations on the part of both cowboys and lawmen based on the specific crimes stated above and the Earps' hard-handed enforcement of the peace.[84] Three of the five cowboys, included two brothers, died. Wyatt was the only one uninjured. The night of the shootout, The Earps expected a visit from the Tombstone Citizens Safety Committee, and/or the vengeful cowboys. They sat up all night with their rifles, willing to use them to resist arrest or kill enemies. The rumors had it that the mercurial cowboy leader Curly Bill Brocius and his men were on their way. It's true that in the West, protecting members of one's family took precedence over everything else: personal reputation, law, job, and any financial considerations included. But brotherhood, personal bravery, and even legal exoneration weighed little when balanced against the political tensions, with Tombstone's reputation in the offing as well. "How long are our people going to stand for this kind of thing?" editorialized the *Tombstone Epitaph*.

At trial, the town newspapers took opposite sides. The cowboys' lawyer stated the Earps' real motive was to finish once and for all their political enemies. The judge had to weigh that

---

[83] Steven Lubet, *Murder in Tombstone: The Forgotten Trial of Wyatt Earp* (New Haven: Yale U Press, 2004), pp.21-26.

[84] Clavin, *Tombstone*, Ch.22.

supposition against the importance of a federal marshal's power to control acknowledged criminals. The Democratic sheriff and the Republican marshal gave conflicting testimony. The Earps and Doc Holliday were exonerated, for they were basically upholding the law.[85] What followed was the cowboys' revenge: the maiming for life of Virgil Earp and the murder of Morgan. The Earp response, their "vendetta ride" of 1882, resulted in the killing of several men, some at a shootout led by Bill Brosius, himself possibly killed there. The hatred of the two factions survived, as fear and contempt for groups with contrasting moral, economic, and social values do. Such duels, feuds, or wars are never over, at least while the world views that give them life are vital to the ideal of lawless confrontation. Twenty years later, a cowboy shot Warren, the youngest Earp, to death during a confrontation in an Arizona saloon. He pled self-defense. Warren had become obsessed with the righteousness of his brothers' part in the OK shootout, and often bragged of it. Wyatt, Virgil, Morgan, and James had long since left for California. A federal or state team of officials had emerged, with access to resources that could take advantage of a more precise body of criminal law, and, if necessary, might call on troops for support.

What a contrast Wild Bill made to the Earp brothers at the O K Coral. For the surviving Earps, there would be no loving monument erected, as Charlie Utter had done for his best friend, helping him become a figure of mythical stature (Figure 9-1). Hickok was not alone in being soft spoken and well dressed, but the kindness in his voice, and a sincerity in his gaze, were uniquely endearing. He proved the western lawman need not be simply without fear, tougher and more impulsive than others, and unerring with draw and trigger-finger. Bill Hickock could talk to citizens, from both sides of the tracks, as equals,

---

[85] Clavin, *Tombstone*, chs. 23-24.

and they could see in his eyes that he meant it.[86]

Stephen Crane's proto-Country Noir Tales: Virginia City's Masonic Vigilantes; A Newlywed Frontier Marshal's Dilemma; An Outcast's Fate in a Brand New "Met-tro-pol-is."

Stephen Crane's "Twelve O'Clock," set in 1875, starts with some hopeful merchants discussing drunken rowdiness on the town's main street:

> Upside-down-F ranch [hands]shot 'em up—shot 'em all up—an' Rickets lyin' on his belly in th' store a-callin' fer 'em to quit it. An' what did they do! Why, they laughed at 'im!—just laughed at 'im! That don't do a town no good. Now, how would an eastern capiterlist"—(it was the town's humour to be always gassing of phantom investors who were likely to come any moment and pay a thousand prices for everything)—"how would an eastern capiterlist like that? Why, you couldn't see 'im fer th' dust on his trail.

In at least one example of a mining camp morphing quickly into an organized town, attitudes exactly like the one just quoted led to vigilantism by organized citizenry. The place was Virginia City, Nevada. After a gold strike in the area in 1863, thousands showed up, building shacks, primitive log cabins, and tents. That first year was a chaos of drunken brawling, thievery, and murders. There was no sanctioned enforcer of law and order. A Vigilance Committee of men who had established roots in the area was formed, headed by a Chief Executive Officer, a President,

---

[86] Tom Clavin, Wild Bill: The True Story of the American Frontier's First Gunfighter (NY: St Martin's Griffin, 2020), pp.171-72.

and an Official Prosecutor. On January 14, 1864, Committee Members, implored to "do their duty," hanged five "road agents" (highwaymen), displaying the graves prominently on Boot Hill. Altogether, about thirty undesirables met the same fate. "Truly the rush to prosperity was on." By 1866, there were butcher shops, hardware and tool businesses, a brewery, a "shaving salon" (tonsorial parlor?), a book store, hotels, restaurants, a newspaper office, an Episcopal church, a Chinese Temple, a fraternal lodge, a library, schools, and a comfortable residential area.[87]

A very similar progression from camp to city took place in Tombstone, a silver-mining boom town, and known as well land for cattle raising and homesteading. The first hotel was a tent. Within a year, there was a post office, two stage lines, a rail line, various restaurants, a bowling alley, a theater, and a variety of fine theme restaurants that were compared to those of San Francisco.[88] This was at the same time as Wyatt Earp and his brothers had their hands full with rustlers, gamblers, thieves preying on miners, drunken and violent cowboys, and illegal uses of land.

The Virginia City vigilantes had been sworn in at a midnight ritual modelled after a Masonic ceremony. There had been no need for a fearless shootist sheriff who could face down belligerent miners, cowboys, and dance hall rowdies. The vigilantes sufficed, particularly because their rituals legitimized them as protectors of property, in the same way banks and assay offices did, with their deeds, stock certificates, mortgages, and federal and state sanctioned investment opportunities. The same westerners requiring the challenge of brute nature, like Shane, Lassiter, Huck Finn, or Harmonica, who turned their backs on the sanctity of

[87] Evalyn Batten Johnson, *Virginia City*, Images of America Series (Charleston, SC: Arcadia Pub., 2011), pp.9-60.

[88] Clavin, *Tombstone*, pp.105-09.

property, would disdain this ritualized legitimizing of vigilantism to create and protect a sedate community. Whatever was left of the frontier offered them trials of self-sufficiency that civic obligations would not allow. They needed the "vast obscurity beyond the city," even if it had "something to do with death."

In Stephen Crane's aforementioned classic "The Bride Comes to Yellow Sky," the respectable man's watering hole of choice was The Weary Gentleman. That town was burgeoning with new-found respectability, at the same pace as Virginia City had. Its patrons were mightily displeased when old, drunk Scratchy, longtime resident from the wrong side of the tracks, started shooting up the place and looking for a gunfight with Marshall Potter. When young, as an Indian fighter (he knew "Apache scalp-music"), he was necessary; now he's a nuisance. On that night, the Marshall is returning to Yellow Sky, Texas, with his bride. Both were concerned with how the town would respond, aside from platitudinal congrats. The new Mrs. Potter is horrified, but when her husband explains he does not have a gun because he was just married, Scratchy congratulates him and apologizes. Yellow Sky's gentry would be harder to deal with. Would a married Marshall Potter be as daring as formerly in fighting off gangs wanting to free convicted pards from the train to prison? Would he be as effective as formerly in protecting homesteaders' property from cattle barons and their tactics, or from disputatious lawyers schooled in obscure clauses in land deeds and probated wills? Will his wife be comfortable socializing with her neighbors and complementing her husband's importance with good taste in home décor and enthusiasm for traveling lecturers and actors?

Crane's "The Blue Hotel" is about the nascent town of Romper, Nebraska. A railroad is coming through, a factory and a schoolhouse have opened, and there are four churches. "Romper'll be a met-tro-pol-is," opined Pat Scully, owner of a hotel painted blue for prominence to travelers. He had provided comfortable living space, good meals, and genial hospitality to Romper's visitors. Crane's story is set in 1875. Scully hosts guests newly arrived and shepherded to his establishment in a blizzard: a salesman from the east, a raw-boned cowboy, and a silent, brooding Swede. The latter is Crane's touchstone. He reiterates all the negative impressions of the Wild West as a pandemonium of thieves, card sharks, killers, bullies, no better than predatory beasts- "wolves." His statement that he expects to be killed provokes especially the congenial host Scully, who takes him to his own rooms, shows him a photo of his daughter "posed against a balustrade of gorgeous decoration," and one of his eldest son, a lawyer and "honored an' rispected gingtleman."

Whiskey softened the Swede's edge. He plays cards with Scully's son Johnnie, but accuses him of cheating. Scully, insulted beyond measure, allows the fight to take place. No longer a guest with "sacred privileges," the Swede is now a poltroon who has insulted the hotel owner's family. "Kill him, Johnnie," shouts the cowboy. The Swede wins the fight and finds a bar in downtown Romper. Here, two businessmen, a district attorney, and a skilled "professional gambler" who only cheats country innocents, never respectable citizens, sit at a table. When the Swede shouts demands that they join him in a drink, and grabs the gambler by the neck to force him to the bar, the gambler slips a knife into the agitated man's gut, killing him instantly.

The easterner concludes that there are multiple guilty parties for a murder. In this one, Johnnie, Scully, the cowboy, and the easterner himself, who saw Johnnie cheat but did not want to stir up an already volatile atmosphere, were coadjutors. Fate inflicts on everyone some guilt for the Swede's death. The reader is trapped too—into despising the crazy, insulting, violent, impulsive Swede, himself the bullying and violent person he thinks westerners are. His sudden murder forces a reader to think about the depths of his/her own contempt for him.

Crane understands that advances of law and order, the presence of representatives of a powerful government and church, and the graces and comforts of the Gilded Age do not prevent well-meaning citizens from violating the bounds of reasonable behavior. Their culture, tolerances, family pride, and social prestige do not insulate them from taking life, as the mad Swede thought would happen from the moment he stepped into The Blue Hotel. Nor does their pride in being citizens privilege them with sensitivity to justice. The gambler gets only three years. After all, he "had a real wife and two real children in a neat cottage in a suburb, and led an exemplary home life."

M'liss, Lassiter, the Outcasts of Poker Flats: Self-Exile From "Home Life"

The heavy weight of a town's right-side-of-the-tracks respectability attempted to inhibit the "uncouth" behavior of the earlier arrivals, who lacked the education, financial resources, tastes in clothing, food, speech, drinking habits, and ways of dealing with enemies, i.e., the habitus, of an incipient "met-tro-pol-is." What they had instead, in addition to "something to do with death," may have been a closer sense of self-reliance, interdependence with people they could trust ("their own kind" rather than distant lawmakers), and a brighter awareness of deep emotional, if anti-social, needs. Two of Bret Harte's most enduring, and endearing, tales concern this. In "M'liss," the young daughter of a hard-luck, alcoholic father is proud of her outcast status. The latter is due to her father's frequenting of "low groggeries, "gambling-hells," and "Dance-houses." He eventually commits suicide; only M'liss can recognize this as a sacrifice to aid her own future development. She boldly asks the town's teacher to educate her. He admires her idiosyncratic sense of superiority to her classmates, her ability to win fights with bullies, and her skill at negotiating the wilderness near Smith's Pocket, which due to gold and quartz deposits boasts "two fancy stores, two hotels, one express-office, and two first families." M'liss reserves her strongest contempt for the school's well-mannered exemplar of a model young lady, sweet and slow-witted Clytemnestra. M'liss fashions a doll resembling her in which she sticks pins.

Her teacher describes M'liss as a "noble savage." When, fearing he is attracted to Clytie, M'liss plans to join a travelling circus, the teacher makes a life-changing decision. He socks the circus impresario and leaves town hand in hand with M'liss. He recognizes her manipulative willfulness is due to her love of "Truth." A social isolate, she has the ability to see beyond good taste, and deference to legal and social authority: no manifestations of civil behavior—"the softness of prosperity," Shakespeare's misanthropic Timon of Athens called it—interest her. M'liss' early years and her stubborn independence are similar to those of Calamity Jane. Her readiness to face down a mountain of opposition is like *Beasts of the Southern Wild's* Hushpuppy. She also had a teacher who, taking over for a dead father, prepared her for dedication to "Truth." There is more than a little of Huck Finn in M'liss. She has the radical self-awareness of Gifford's Sailor and Lula, the will to fulfil tabooed desire of Proulx's Jack Twist, the determination of Compton's Brown Bottle, and the defiant affinity with nature of Offutt's Lige Boatman, the leaving one.

Harte's "The Outcasts of Poker Flats" is about the community's banning of "all improper persons" after recent robberies. Two suspects were hanged. Those banished included two prostitutes, a gambler, an alcoholic thief, and a young couple determined to marry despite all objections. As the outcasts wait out a blizzard in a decrepit hut, they form a self-sacrificing community (except for the thief), far more cohesive than that of Poker Flats, regardless of its newfound "civilization and refinement." In Zane Grey's *Riders of the Purple Sage*, authoritarian distinctions between citizen and outcast reach their nadir. A man in black, a lone gunman named Lassiter with an implacable sense of justice, and a Mormon woman critical of the tyrannical Elders, Jane Withersteen, shut themselves off forever from the evil rectitude of the pious churchmen who steal her land and livestock and plan to reduce her to a baby-producing slave for her "sins." Jane and Lassiter will live in an unreachable, and presumably inescapable Surprise

Valley, with enough natural resources to sustain them indefinitely. Grey ends his Western as an American pastoral, transcendent of obedience to the laws, written and unwritten, of civic authority. Their valley isn't Hushpuppy's "shacko in the backo," or Sailor and Lula's splendid isolation as they drive across the Southwest, or Natty Bumppo's happiness in the company of Chingachgook, The Last of the Mohicans. But each of these very rural habitats ignites enthusiasm for an "old, weird America." "Throw your fist in the air! These are the survivors, those who fight for their joy and their history." That was the anthem of the authors of *Beasts of the Southern Wild.*

Deadwood: From bawdy skits at the Gem to Shakespeare at the Playhouse. Calamity Jane and Wild Bill.

Pete Dexter's marvelous novel *Deadwood* (1986) begins with the fateful year 1876, when Wild Bill Hickok was killed, and ends about 1879, when a terrible fire destroyed the wooden homes, supply stores, saloons, cold water bathhouses, lumber yards, and dance halls. He describes the original pioneers, miners, "whoremen" and their prostitutes, "soft heads," gamblers, firebrand preachers, and shootists. During that time, Deadwood developed from "camp" to city (Figure 9-2). Businesspeople planned for arc lighting and telephone service. Dexter's theatrical pioneers, Mr. and Mrs. Langrishe, were establishing a playhouse to improve "the town's civilities" (Figure 9-3). Solomon Star, whose "talent was money," and his partner, sheriff Seth Bullock, owned the brickworks. Bullock's dour demeanor and steely-eyed stare intimidated any rowdy long-time resident of the camp from raising hell in city limits; the media, encouraged by word of mouth, made him famous as the ideal Western peace officer. Bullock thus became the ideal of the American fighter for law and order.

Wild Bill and his "ilk" were subjects of the newspaper's

crusade to rid the town of rowdies like Bill and his best friend "Colorado Charlie" Utter (see Figure 9-3), a miner, scout, gambler, manager of a house of prostitution, and organizer of wagon trains that brought to town tourists; dry goods retailers; whoremen and their stables; and Chinese suppliers of the needs of the Asian community. The newspaper's action was similar to that in the film *Tombstone* after the O.K. Corral, where the target was Wyatt Earp. He, like Bill, had outlived his usefulness as law, civility, and famous lecturers at the opera house became ascendant and cold-eyed, quick-draw intimidation was only tolerated, if at all, in the saloons and gambling dens on the wrong side of the tracks.

Wild Bill and Charlie, somewhat like Natty Bumppo and Chingachgook, are Dexter's aging protagonists. They are indispensable in the early camp but social isolates in the city. The former has urinary problems and failing eyesight; the latter has leg spasms from being shot twice. Other notables from Dexter's version of the beginnings of the town of Deadwood—shootist Boone May, "whoreman" Al Swearingen, fabulist Calamity Jane, and Hiram, a visionary preacher who had written his own bible about the dark side of God—are all social isolates, past their prime, sick, or dying. But their amorality, energy, indomitable perseverance, reckless courage, and knowledge of the territory had made them representatives of the side of the American character that values and needs what Cawelti specified as "the old lawless American way of life." There is also, at least in in Charlie, Bill, and Bill's widow (emphatically not Calamity Jane), primacy of love and duty: "amigos take care of each other." That contrasts with Mrs. Langrishe. At a posh gathering to announce their playhouse opening, she takes Charlie upstairs for two quickies. When they watch a terrible fire from her bedroom, she remarks that her husband will be furious at the postponement of their posh cultural venture. And she laughs.

The most radical improvement is the rebirth of Deadwood in brick and mortar after the fire. It was set (in Dexter's novel, of course) by Sol Star, who would not say a word about his deed. Star was a misfit with a vision of what it would take to put Deadwood in the vanguard of progress. What Star did was also in revenge for the murder of a Chinese beauty by a local Chinese businessman, probably because Star desired her (the Deadwood fire is an historical event). But it set the stage for the rebuild of the ramshackle camp into a brick-and-stone city, with the prime attraction being Seth Bullock's home. Bullock was praised by Teddy Roosevelt as the model western sheriff. He and Star built Deadwood's first luxury hotel.[89] Bullock had started as a sharp-shooting, stare-down, and quick-witted sheriff in the tradition of Wyatt Earp, but as TR's endorsement indicated, transitioned to the perfect law enforcer for an expanding city protected by the power of its banks and businesses, and eventually by tyrannical George Hearst's mining corporation. The latter organization certainly had something to do with death, not by facing blizzards, Indians, and ravaging animals, but by its monopolistic proclivities, which rebuilt Deadwood in its own image.

---

[89] Of course, Dexter manipulates history to create a coherent work of art. Here are some relevant dates in early Deadwood history: 1875: gold rush in the Black Hills, near Deadwood Gulch, so called due to the number of dead trees there. 1876: dance halls and saloons with gambling and prostitution flourish on Main Street: Charlie Utter organizes a wagon train from Colorado to Deadwood. Wild Bill Hickok, Calamity Jane, and prostitutes and their madams are on board. Wild Bill shot. Seth Bullock and Solomon Star open their hardware store, stocking items needed by prospectors. Deadwood's first clergyman murdered. Town charter written. First telegraph line in operation. Seth Bullock becomes sheriff. 1877: Al Swearingen's Gem Theater opens ("indecent" skits and songs). Homestake Mining Company, under direction of George Hearst, opens, and eventually becomes the most influential gold mining operation in the country. Chinatown section established. Grocery store begins operation. 1878: telephone lines installed. 1879: Opium tax helps fund town and restricts use of the drug but legitimizes opium dens. A fire, started in a bakery, destroys wooden properties, rebuilt in brick within a year. Population changes as many people whose homes are destroyed settle elsewhere. See deadwood.com/history/

A major accomplishment is Dexter's characterization of Calamity Jane as a peerless social isolate. She also is past her prime: corpulent, possibly tubercular, and suffering from a broken leg, not fully healed when she left the hospital. She had to get to Deadwood to attend Wild Bill's funeral, asserting that she was his wife. While there, smallpox broke out. She knew just the concoction that would save most of the sick, and her sanguine nursing demeanor was as important as her medicine. "God gave me the touch to cure and heal, and I best be about my business." That was often followed by her singing "The Battle Hymn of the Republic." Since she openly stated she had the disease herself, no one wanted to be near her. "Once Jane took over smallpox, charity and fear went arm in arm." There were other reasons for wanting her gone from Deadwood. She had the habit of screaming like an eagle; it could be heard from one end of town to another. It scared the tourists. She slept under tables, caged drinks, and told whoppers, made worse by breath so bad it was thought contagious. So the bartenders decided to tell her the chicken pox had passed on to Cheyenne. The citizens there denied it, but after a week of resourceful listening in saloons and in the streets, she found the sufferers, probably punctuating her discovery with a patented eagle war whoop.

Jane's biographical details, if we set aside her boasting, are further evidence of her refusal to embrace behavior patterns and taboos of the military and citizens of Nebraska, Montana, Nevada, the Black Hills, or wherever else she found herself. She had little choice as a child. Her desperately poor parents sent her out to beg, while they spent their time in saloons. Occasionally, she had been a prostitute, or a maid, or whatever else would prevent her from starving. At least three times, she joined the cavalry and infiltrated platoons from which, once discovered to be a woman, she was expelled. One of those discoveries prevented her from being killed at the Little Big Horn. During this time, she proved herself the match for any man in riding, herding, lifting and carrying equipment, drinking, and swearing, and telling tall tales. One of those was having been married to Wild Bill Hickok, and to have had a daughter by him.

On June 8, 1876, that lady prancing down Cheyenne's Main Street in a fancy gown was Calamity Jane. The garment was borrowed; she had just been found not guilty of stealing clothes. In Deadwood, she performed at Swearengen's Gem Saloon—in women's clothes, and came to the rescue of a sister performer whom a customer had cheated by training guns on him and reciting his perfidy. She did treat sufferers from smallpox, and with the same assurance that Dexter describes.[90]

Larry McMurtry's *Buffalo Girls* is centered around a set of letters Calamity, although nearly illiterate, supposedly wrote to Jane Hickok McCormick, who claimed to be the daughter of Wild Bill and Calamity Jane. Thanks to the film *The Plainsman*, to the fact that Calamity is buried next to Hickok, and to the many admirers of Buffalo *Girls*, their love affair has become a western of its own. McMurtry stated to Susan Schaeffer that he is a novelist, not a historian.[91] Her review is aptly entitled "Lonesome Jane." The letters he imagines "your mother, Martha Jane" wrote to "Darling Jane" describe her dismay that, as Bill Cody puts it, "the plains are filling up with towns." She decides to join Cody's British version of his Wild West Show because "lost is lost." Some of her "old pals of the prairie" go too: the mountain men Bartle and Ragg; No Ears, the Indian who knows how to hide from a blizzard in animal dens; Texas Jack Omohundro, the West's best card sharp. They met the Queen; Calamity was too drunk. Her other friends, all characterized by "energy, muscle, will" rather than any city decorum, included Dora DuFrane, a famous madam credited with inventing the term "cat house"; Teddy Blue, who wrote of the "fun" of herding cattle to the

---

[90] Tom Clavin, Wild Bill, The True Story of the American Frontier's First Gunfighter (NY: St Martin's 2019), pp.240-47, 264-66, 291-93.

[91] Susan Fromberg Schaeffer, "Lonesome Jane," *New York Times*, Oct 7, 1990, N Y Times on the Web (search by author and title).

railhead; and Potato Creek Johnny, who found the biggest nugget in the Black Hills (McMurtry acknowledges the many historical figures into his tale). McMurtry's tone is elegiac: "Jane has been the West as long as there has been a West."

Two Southern Noirs with More than a Little to Do with Death

In an elegantly crafted guest appearance in Barry Gifford's *Wild at Heart*, Perdita Durango is rumored to have killed her own child. As a getaway driver, Perdita observes the slapstick death of her boyfriend as he manages to shoot himself in the head while escaping. One would anticipate her career in her own eponymous thriller to be an old-fashioned roller coaster ride between Amarillo and the Gulf of Mexico, with bonus fracases as far west as L.A. It doesn't disappoint. Gifford's ear for down home sardonic humor includes the local name for the Angola prison's electric chair: "Gruesome Gertie," where the rapist killer Bubba Ray Billy ("I am a cold person") gets his. His father, feeling his son deserves to die, sleeps trough the execution. Perdita and her partner Romeo kidnap an attractive young woman, Estelle Satisfy, and her boyfriend, because they are sexually attracted to them: not for ransom, but for their bodies. Perdita tells Estelle that "Your blond pussy's what's keeping you alive...Girls like you got a kind of sickness, and the only way to cure it is to kill it. Always talkin' about what's good, love and that shit, when you're same as me, just no particular piece of trash." She enjoys detaching people from any secure self-image or prideful identity. It's not envy. It's her isolation from and contempt for the illusion of cultural enfranchisement, be it class-, gender-, economic-, or regional-based. She would be a strong representative of a woman of "the lawless wilderness," except that she lives in urban areas from Georgia to Mississippi.

Perdita is not a femme fatale. She does not deceive, does not seduce, and does not operate within a gender role that requires her to gain respect by being glamorously dressed. She has nothing but distain for fads, civility, or the kinds of cultural capital reserved for the elite. That Estelle is comfortable with these conventions explains Perdita's desire to show her she is just like Perdita, under the adorable skin. Because this is stated so matter-of-factly, as a law of nature, Estelle has no comeback, perhaps because she is gagged by her disgust. She does not want to show it and lose this contest, a deadly game. These are fierce opponents, although Estelle's fierceness is submerged in her Southern belle temperament: a product of the moral and aesthetic prerequisites of contemporary living in a decent and peaceful, law-abiding place. That's Gifford's comic genius. He forces one to continually reconsider what is true and the extent to which truth is a matter of one's idiosyncratic perspective. I find in *Beasts of the Southern Wild's* Hushpuppy the perfect nemesis for Perdita Durango: two forces of nature, one, the isolate, an angel of dissolution, the other in her own way fearless, strong-willed all-American female.

The way Perdita Durango and Estelle Satisfy are alike is they have, like everyone else, divergent views of what is valuable and what is of no account. Perdita sees the world as a place to enjoy herself, by exercising complete control over another person's body and conduct, as long as he or she amuses her. She admits she is "trash." Estelle has made herself conventionally attractive by all the generally acceptable standards of feminine beauty in clothes, speech, sweetness of temperament, and a sense of justice, imbued in her by her religious and moral standards. Perdita is not satisfied until she can be her own controlling force. She especially loves belittling folks' illusions of superiority based on class distnctons.

Gifford's objective point of view on the people and events he depicts is perfect for allowing his readers to accept his story with a chuckle soon turned to a gasp. Allusions to mass market popular entertainment take people deep into their own existence. Charles Boyer, Lupe Velez, Ava Gardner, Randolph Scott, "Saint" Henry Fonda, The Red Raiders of Texas Tech, and Russ Meyer (for his

Faster, Pussycat Kill! Kill!) have bit parts, while in the foreground are horrific acts of violence. Perdita's Romeo, a Santeria priest, is a fan of mayhem, sadism, and human sacrifice. He is coldly dispassionate, both to his own fate and those of his victims. When Perdita spots two pre-teens in "tight, short, black skirts, expensive-looking blouses and large gold hoop earrings, she feels for a moment like stabbing them each in the back and chest and throat dozens of times. She imagines their blood running black, dripping down their smooth golden legs. Just as suddenly the feeling passed..." This flash of hatred does not seem like resentment, not only due to its brevity but because it is devoid of envy.

If Barry Gifford reinforces the biblical allusion he makes to Perdita as a nemesis of childbirth, it would be by her continuing career as an irresistible seducer of the willing. The novel ends with her picking up a replacement for Romeo, Shorty Dee. "Here I go," she says. This, as they watch the Holiday Bowl game in Tupelo, Mississippi, birthplace of Elvis. Shorty loves to watch kickoff returns. Gifford dares his reader to make light of his yarn. Don't judge, he seems to be saying, you may get stuck in conventional priorities regarding class, fairness, criminality, and regional, gender, or ethnic viewpoints. Just experience two extremes of the American character write large. Gifford hands over to the reader the chance to produce whatever conclusions s/he likes on good and evil, life and death. Perdita is a killer, maybe even a cannibal. She is anathema to any system of taboos on "fucking and killing." And to any sentimentality or romance, "Always talkin' about what's good, love and that shit." She has something to do with death, something to do with pure ego, and something to do with proud existence as "no particular piece of trash."

In Harry Crews' *A Feast of Snakes*, Joe Lon Mackey yearns for the life of pure feral excitement he had as a high school football star for the Mystic, Georgia "Mystic Rattlers." Now he works for his father supplying the locals with cheap whisky.

He's married to a once-beautiful high school princess worn
down by her chores and her babies' needs. The novel is set in
Mystic during the annual rattlesnake hunt. Joe Lon hangs with
a snake-loving crew, one of whom, a rapist, is the victim of a
painfully hilarious unintentional castration. The group includes
Hard Candy, soon to go to the university as a star majorette.
There's also Berenice, Joe Lon's mistress. She, like Joe Lon, is wild
at heart. He holds her above the snake pit. "All in my blood.
Crawling through my heart." But she has found a new lover.
Boredom is relieved by beer-guzzling, reminiscing about Joe Lon's
gridiron heroics, vicariously experiencing the Vietnam slaughter
on TV (the book was published in 1976), screwing, and fighting.
Only Joe Lon is aware of the effect of decades of viewing vicariously sex and violence. Sometimes, he howls into the night.

When the tourist Poncy arrives at the hunt in a BMW wearing
a Ban-Lon shirt with crossed golf clubs and a golf cap, Joe Lon's
buddies put him through a humiliating initiation that includes
damaging his sleek, expensive car (what did he expect?), forcing
him to dance with Hard Candy while a crowd sneers, and displaying all his squareness in front of the homeboys, girls, and tourists.
He is reduced to an infantile state, unable to control his bowels.
But on the big night, he is sitting in the front row. He thanks
Joe Lon for his rough initiation and gets no reply.

It's important, because Joe is about to do something he was
building up to for years. With that act, he will lose his prerogative
for being part of his community, which is where his loved ones
exist, and where he had once found near ecstasy as an all-time
Mystic Rattler. The epigraph to the novel is from poet Richard
Eberhardt: "If only I could live life at the pitch that is near
madness...violent, vivid, and full of infinite possibility." Mystic
once gave Joe Lon something like that on the football field. He
would have been a college star too, but he was trapped from the
start—he was illiterate. School and university exploited Joe Lon's
athleticism without providing him with this indispensable skill.

Now, he is going to culminate his mystic journey to either

hell or salvation in the snake pit, which is located, remarkably, at the edge of the football field. His sister Beeder watches impassively. She has done nothing since graduation but catatonically watch TV to the puzzlement of her classmates who admired her high school accomplishments. Nothing but watch and wait. A total loner in a dirty nightgown, full of malice. When a friend asks her advice on how to handle an attacker, Beeder's advice is to castrate him. She does, and he bleeds to death.

Beeder's detachment from any of her community's limited options for a normal adulthood makes her very similar to her brother, especially on his last day. He has become a social isolate like his sister, with a nihilistic, wild and lawless, response to the culture from which he self-exiled. It will be a complete rejection of the legitimacy of the community's institutions of law and order. His final act is as obscene as possible to the citizens of a rural town who need their fire-breathing preacher who equates the devil with snakes. Joe Lon shoots the preacher, his own former mistress, and a bystanding snake hunter. Then, "a whole wall of men and women, mouths opened, teeth bared, moved with a single raging voice upon Joe Don." The novel ends with the repressed bitterness of people momentarily so shocked and enraged that they break the chains of law and custom. Pete Dexter notes that the killing of a police officer stimulates something "fundamental that people had felt themselves losing all along." It was "a fracture in history" that incites frenzied response.[92] The result is a communal howl, an explosion of sadomasochistic energy. It has more than a little to do with death.

Joe Lon, his sister, and Hard Candy negate consciousness and rationality by living at the most instinctual, primal, and sensual level. Novelist Michael Perkins explains there is a "terror found at the heart of sensuality [that] helps us escape our individual discontinuous beings and become one with the continuity of

---

[92] Dexter, *The Paperboy* (novel; NY: Random House, 1995), p.5.

existence."[93] The language is similar to Eberhardt's about "life at the pitch that is near madness." It explains the spectators at the snake hunt turning into Aurochs, advancing on Joe Lon as if bent on grotesque feasting. Georges Bataille, in *Story of the Eye*, discusses "all things linked to deep sexuality, such as blood, suffocation, sudden terror, crime, things indefinitely destroying human bliss and honesty." These are the things Crews attributes to his protagonist. They inexorably detach him from Mystic, Georgia's definition of a human being. It is a near perfect embodiment of what Cawelti says are the contending forces of "civilization and wildness."

Crews' novel is a southern gothic, although the extensive passage of time and varied locales are absent. *A Feast of Snakes* is saturated with the protagonist's descent into self-destruction and murder, the brittleness of what once was his stable personality, the undertones of sexual anarchism, and the combination of naturalistic depiction of a community with mythical resonances regarding Eden, madness, and hell. Crews' use of a social isolate as a prime mover of a southern noir is suggestive of the work of other writers such as Flannery O'Connor, Annie Proulx, Denis Johnson, Tom Franklin, Thomas Savage, and Cormac McCarthy.

The Stranger from the Wilderness Helps a Community's Oppressed

James Sallis's Driver emerges out of the dim background of a down-and-out locale to help people contending with menial jobs, shabby housing, poorly funded public schools, and shuttered support services. Proximity to street gangs, gambling venues, and drug dens is as inevitable as it was to the "blighted" areas of post-World War II American cities. These neglected citizens

---

[93] "The Innocence of Evil," in *The Secret Record: Modern Erotic Literature* (NY: Morrow, 1976), p.54.

deserve a strong, independent, and magically skilled savior. Then Driver moves on, not unlike what Raymond Chandler calls a man walking the "mean streets" but "not himself mean." He has brought some justice to a few victims of a community "up on blocks."

Driver is an American archetype, a descendant of Jack Schaefer's Shane, a lone ranger with a car instead of a horse. Sallis writes:

> I came soon to realize that yes, I was writing a contemporary western. No surprise, really, since for many years now I've maintained that virtually all our important writing descends from our frontier literature. Lest there be any doubt, I even ended with Driver riding off into the sunset.[94]

Perhaps in telling his readers that a movie was made of Driver's life, Sallis is comparing him to Harmonica. Perhaps by having Driver fated to kill the man he loved the most, or be killed by him, the author is telling us that his hero's life is contingent on his being face-to-face with death. Probably by having Driver watch a movie about "the self-appointed guardian of a small community" the members of which "never knew what his motivations were," he is thinking of Shane.

I've referred in my introductory paragraphs to this chapter to characters in Westerns, not rural noirs. The latter can be a close cousin to the Western in setting, and sometimes in redemptive and sometimes paralyzing violence, fateful decisions, and closure. Characters are destined to bear a heavy load, often because of early family trauma. Huck Finn's father was a violent alcoholic. Caudill's was tyrannically insistent that his sons labor on his farm. Harmonica was forced to be complicit in his brother's death.

---

[94] James Sallis, Email to me, April 6, 2019. Reproduced with the kind permission of James Sallis.

Driver saw his mother kill his apathetic father at the dinner table. The adult lives of these men were spent as strangers in wide open spaces or underclass neighborhoods. Obsessive and narrowly focused, they asked no quarter and gave none. Neither the rural noir's social isolate or the Western adventurer dwell in shame or regret.

There are more such characters in the Western proper than in other rural noirs. The hero in latter kind of adventure story exists, most remarkably, in stories by Chris Offutt, Denis Johnson, Steph Post, Rusty Barnes, and Tom Franklin. The independence of the Western's lone rider, often a social isolate, from a town's moral consensus is similar to that of the rural noir protagonist's. In many rural noir narratives, characters act as they do because their community denies them the cultural capital required to work within its prerequisites. They cannot access the legal, moral, or financial resources it reserves for people with the "advantages," or the status, that brings them trust and respect. The stranger from the mountain, great plains, or arid southwest helps them free themselves.

Books such as Post's *Lightwood*, Brown's *Dirty Work*, Crews's *Scar Lover*, Johnson's *Jesus' Son*, Heller's *The Painter*, and films such as *Beasts of the Southern Wild* and *Three Billboards Outside Ebbing, Missouri* are, at the novels' endings, breaking free from "twisted sorrow." Brown's, Crews', and Heller's characters, unlike Driver or his prototype Shane, cannot ride into the sunset. The work before them promises redemption in contact with other folks, an American dream with more resonance than just "settling down." Readers have met people such as these characteristically American strivers, protagonists who point forward, to breakouts from the cobwebs of duty, obligation, and piety, when made in bad faith.

***

A Driver on a Harley

James Sallis's *Driver* novels are exemplary of an essentially American dream: a stranger coming from the outside with an outsider's death-defying skills that other people in the community do not have. With them, he can confront and neutralize destructive forces of nature and of human depredation. In Matt Phillips's *Accidental Outlaws* (2017), a lone biker named Packard interjects himself into the lives of people in a Southwestern working-class town. Like some other isolates, Packard has lived within a society's conventions but did not succeed. As an outsider must, he has refined his riding, shooting, and survival skills. With long unkempt hair, and a black vest on his otherwise bare, tattooed torso, he's a death-defying driver on his "black hog with chrome pipes," coming much closer than is healthy to oncoming big rigs, thinking about the "hard wall of force" and then "the other side." He doesn't fear the unknown.

Packard has camped on a canyon rim that allows him a view of the isolated town. From there, he can see a ramshackle tavern in which he had an annoying experience. He was told to leave because he would not agree with the owner, Sketchy's, racist bigotry. Detached from any societal ideal of trust, self-restraint, or justice, Packard burns down Sketchy's place. He realizes the devilishness in doing so. "You do what feels right, and usually that's fine." The 1957 *3:10 to Yuma*'s Ben Wade, Wyatt Earp on the way to the O K Corral, and Denis Johnson's *Jesus Son* think this way. Sketchy creeps up to Packard's tent with a shotgun; inside are his target and Sketchy's former wife, whom Packard has met and dated. Sketchy wants to know why Packard torched his bar. The answer: "A thing worth burning is a thing worth hating." Now comes another impulsive, outlandish act: his wife kills Sketchy. Packard drops her off at her job the next morning. No one misses Sketchy.

But it must be pointed out, especially because Phillips has woven it into his story, that intolerance was an essential component of the belief system that made role models of western men able to conquer cruel enemies and baleful natural forces. In *The Power of the Dog*, Thomas Savage uses Phil as an example of the traits characteristic of the pioneer riders, cattle herders, and trailblazers, and of the social isolate as well: shrewdness, physical strength, rigid standards of manliness, stiff-necked endurance, the equation of leadership with domination, a pitiless indifference to the suffering of animals, and the ability to accommodate oneself to and combat cold, heat, wind, and snow. Engrained in his toughness is his contempt for Jews, Indians, females, and any trace of effeminacy in men. It's a brilliant composite picture of the indominable need for power and the unexamined intransigence in the soul of the western adventurer contending against wild animals, deathly weather, arid river beds, and desert heat with vultures circling overhead. To denigrate such men as emotionally stunted and ignorant of democratic principles is to ignore the character traits they needed for the identity to which they aspired.

Matt Phillips makes clear both the problems of survival in near poverty at the edge of the Great American Desert, and the grit it often takes to do so. Packard's recognition of this is a distant allusion, perhaps, to the 1957 version of the classic Western *3:10 to Yuma* (Figure 9-4). In it, Ben Wade, the leader of a gang of outlaws, admires the determination of Dan Evans, a needy homesteader hired to bring Wade to prison. Evans and Wade live diametrically opposite lives. Yet Wade's tolerances are as broad as his openness to dangerous experiences—as is true of Phillips's Packard, Shane, Dexter's Calamity Jane, Clavin's Wild Bill Hickock, and Sallis's Driver. Wade helps Evans stymie his own gang to allow the homesteader to get on the train with Wade apparently in tow. The penultimate scene shows Wade whistling to his horse to make the kind of daring escape that will once again bring him the thrill of lone conquest. The homesteader will return to his family, amid a golden rain that breaks a withering drought. The rain is reward for truly democratic fellowship, the spur-of-the-moment kind that negates "twisted sorrow," and could only take place "somewhere back in that vast obscurity beyond the city." Stephen Crane, in discussing the struggles of the Nebraska farmer of the 1890s, praises homesteaders like Evans, dedicated to farm, home, livestock, and growing family: "it required the profound and dogged courage of the American peoples who have come into the West to carve farms, railroads, towns, cities, in the heart of a world fortified by enormous distances."[95] Observers like Thomas Berger, Richard Slotkin, James Cawelti, Tom Franklin, Steph Post, Harry Crews, Rusty Barnes, and Denis Johnson would produce incisive emendations to Crane's statement. They would not deny the beauty and strength of his words. Nor would they fail to recognize the hostilities between North and South, pioneers and Native Americans, contenders with wilderness and builders of law and order, that Crane's words imply.

Another such narrative is Ernest Haycock's "A Day in Town."[96] Homesteader Joe Blount, a proudly taciturn, hard-working family man, visits Two Dance to request a bank loan to keep his semi-arid land workable. He can offer no security, but the town banker provides money for a well and windmill. He recognizes Joe as a hard worker with the discipline to deny himself the simple pleasure of tobacco unless and until his wife and children's "hardship and trouble" were relieved. He was a "good risk," and Two Dancer's banker was proud to help.

Ben Wade does what Shane and Driver do to help gritty, resilient, eyes-on-the-prize families make it in America. They both, like diverse wanderers such as Joe Don Looney, Lassiter, Calamity Jane, Harmonica (**Figure 9-5**), and Packard, are indifferent to a life in any social unit they have experienced. But they do help

---

[95] "Nebraska's Bitter Fight for Life," *The Western Writings of Stephen Crane*, ed. and Introduced by Frank Bergon (NY: A Signet Classic , 1979), pp.177.

[96] In *The Western Hall of Fame* ed. Bill Pronzini and Martin Greenberg (NY: Morrow, 1984), pp.159-75.

struggling families and communities with their amoral vitality, endurance, and integrity. They too, like Sweetwater's Jill, *The Searchers'* Indian captive Debbie, and the Bathtub's Hushpuppy and her teacher, "stand up to life and spit in its eye."

Figure 9-1: Charlie Utter, Wild Bill's best friend, erected this memorial after Hickock's murder.
http://www.deadwood.searchroots.com/images/wildbill-gravesite.jpg

Figure 9-2: Deadwood, SD, c.1875. What it looked like when Charlie Utter organized a wagon train to the town, probably with passengers like Bill Hickok. Swearengin's "hurdy-gurdy house" opened at that time, servicing gold prospectors. https://owlcation.com/humanities/Deadwood-South-Dakota-Truth-and-legend

Figure 9-3: The right side of the tracks: opera comes to a western mining town, Central City, Colorado c. 1880. This is the kind of place the first actors in Deadwood envisioned for their Shakespearian presentations, as Dexter envisioned it in his novel, Deadwood. Source: Denver Public Library.
https://westernmininghistory.com/towns/colorado/central-city/

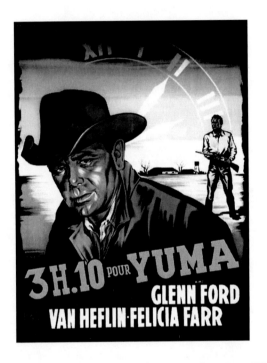

Figure 9-4: In the foreground is Glenn Ford as Ben Wade. Leader of his gang, he nevertheless helped the needy homesteader in the background get his reward for putting Wade on the train to prison, even if it meant double-crossing his gang. The amoral social isolate was savior of a man whose devotion to family he admired. Production Co and Distributor: Columbia Pictures. https://www.movieposterdb.com/310-to-yuma-i50086

Figure 9-5: Charles Bronson as Harmonica in Leone's *Once Upon a Time in the West*, produced and distributed by Paramount Pictures.
https://onceuponatimeinawestern.com/wp-content/uploads/2015/07/Charles-Bronson-as-Harmonica-in-Once-Upon-a-Time-in-the-West-1968-01.jpg

CHAPTER 10

Two Westerns about Freedom in the "Vast Obscurity Beyond the City"

To conclude, I want to first discuss a novel about two diametrically opposite American identities: Native Americans and American pioneers. Then, I want to bring to attention a film based on a book about people made desolate by loss of job, health, and home as a result of investment banking practices—the crash of 2008. In both works, instead of producing a failure story, the writer and filmmaker get beyond twisted sorrow by depicting people who embody what America has made its highest ambition, but is now *all but* impossible to bring about: confident self-respect by and for the unique individual.

Little Big Man (Thomas Berger, 1964): Freedom at the "Center of the World"

This is undoubtedly the best tall tale in American literature. Jack Crabb is 111 years old when he tells how he became a pal of Wild Bill Hickok's, was cold cocked by Wyatt Earp, scouted for George Armstrong Custer, and was the only white survivor at Little Bighorn. Crabb concludes, "Who would ever have believed me? But I am now too old to care. So if you don't, you can go to hell."

Jack, before he attained the honorific Little Big Man, lost his father and mother in an Indian massacre. His father had foolishly offered the Cheyenne liquor, and in a drunken stupor they attacked the wagon train. The Indians, regretting what they did under the influence, returned the next day to make amends. They take Jack and his sister to their camp. His sister escapes after witnessing the way the tribe's women slaughter and cook dogs— "not nice people," she concludes—and rides off on a pony provided in case she did not take to their ways. Caroline becomes a powerful social reformer, a proto-LGBT feminist, and meets Walt Whitman, with whom she has an affair.

Jack stayed to become Little Big Man (LBM), a name given him by his Cheyenne mentor, Old Lodge Skins. He had saved Cheyenne lives while part of a raiding party by killing one of the opposing tribe, shooting three arrows into his back. If he had not, his brother raiders would have been caught, tortured, and killed. The comparison between Jack at the raiding party, and the original Big Man, if not seen through the perspective of the Native American view of heroism, is illogical. But within it, the mythic past lives on in human beings on earth at present, awaiting only the occasion to take their part in an eternal adventure guided by a Great Spirit. Big Man was a mythic figure. An enemy tribe offered him amnesty after all his companions had been killed. He decides "it is a good day to die." He is beheaded after killing many enemies, but his head, raised on a pole, shouts a war cry while his still-agile body pursues the fleeing enemy. Then it lies down among the dead Cheyenne. That feat makes what LBM does seem, however effective, merely a frequent occurrence in warfare, and in his case, survivable. Big Man is superhuman.

From the tribal perspective, the similarity is based on the consonance of the "medicine," or wisdom and virtue, of the white boy with that of Big Man's. To the "enlightened" nineteenth century American, any comparison implies the concept of progression through stages of development, and thus to equate Jack Crabb with a superhuman original is crazy. For a people who believe in an "eternal return" instead of the iron necessity of reaching a modern level of achievement not before possible, the white culture's kind of measurement is part of what makes the Native Americans think of themselves as superior. Thus the Cheyenne term themselves, and only themselves, "human beings." They will not share this distinction with anyone outside their tribe. To Old Lodge Skins, whose wisdom is revered, the Great Father has once again gifted the Cheyenne with a virtuous hero who defies the enemy and insures victory over it. The former Jack Crabb, as the Cheyenne Little Big Man, experiences a freedom from a strictly logical habit of measurement. The Indian acceptance of a young man once part of a wagon train of white pioneers is far more than democratic tolerance of a worthy and useful outsider. It is an act of love, a love returned so full-heatedly to his mentor as to be a mystery to his native country's criteria for inclusion.

It's the mystery of the variety of human identity systems that Thomas Berger evokes. The contrast between the Cheyenne Native Americans and the white pioneers is acute. Berger's protagonist lives as an adult mostly among the whites. He identifies as Jack, until he witnesses Old Lodge Skins singing his death song, attaining a mystic freedom from death. At that moment, he learned what rebirth meant.

If it were not for the army raids on the Indians, LBM might have spent the rest of his life with his tribe. As it was, he is "rescued" by Union troopers, who send him to live with a Missouri clergyman and his beautiful wife, Jack's first crush. Still a teenager, he attends school with much younger kids to catch up on his fundamentals. The Reverend Pendrake is a stentorian preacher and a glutton, but has very fastidious table manners, as befits his profession. Jack remarks that despite his eloquence, he was so intent on the style and precision of his sermons that he did not seem to enjoy his preeminence. It did not bring him freedom from anxiety about maintaining his stature. However, after Jack showed his intelligence, the Reverend took him on a fishing trip and gave him affection he always remembered: it was the "truly kindest thing anybody's done for me, ever." It is especially moving because Jack lost his father in the massacre of the wagon train (his body was affixed to the earth with arrows). He has missed the intimacy of the American nuclear family that he was born into.

The affection that the elegant, perfumed Mrs. Pendrake gave freely is as potent as her husband's. It compares to LBM's loving substitute mother, Buffalo Wallow Woman, "a fine soul," regardless of the tribal practice of eviscerating bodies of opposing tribes' war casualties and boiling fresh-slaughtered dog carcasses. Berger attempts freeing the readers from value-bound comparisons, and prepares them for an ending that invokes the Great Spirit of the Earth. That, in *Little Big Man*, is the ultimate freedom for a Human Being, and that invocation closes the novel. Old Lodge Skins reviews his credentials as a Cheyenne: a warrior, a killer of enemies on a "good day to die," a producer of sons, a dancer at the campfires, and a member of a perfectly coherent social body (Figure 10-1).

The novel's point of view is first person, as recorded by the "man of letters" and collector of Indian artifacts, Ralph Fielding Snell, who serves as Crabb's amanuensis. This character allows the reader to decide which name, LBM or Jack Crabb, best befits the man who tells his story, and the truth of it all. He says in his Epilogue, "I leave the choice in your hands." Larry McMurtry writes that Jack's experience in two worlds "enables [him] to be a kind of trans-Mississippi Zelig; his dual identity allows him, when expedient, to change sides. His duality is particularly useful in the battle scenes."[97] Berger frees his readers to imagine the distant possibility of the same duality in themselves.

Seemingly, LBM allows his Cheyenne identity to evaporate into thin air when he is adopted by the Pendrakes. Much later, he does the same when he gets a glance at Custer's wife Libby.

[97] Introduction to *Little Big Man* (NY: Dial Press Trade Paperbacks, 2014), p.xii.

It is the manners, colorful frills and high-bosomed dresses, gentle eyes, hair the color of the sun, and modest smiles that enamor him: the way the nineteenth century females give an aristocratic aura to the husband's reputation. He also notes, but does not comment on, the sadness in their eyes. Of Mrs. Custer he opines, "I would have killed every Indian on the plains if she had asked me to, or at least if she had been watching." Any Cheyenne would be disgusted at this kind of idealism; only to the Great Spirit would they have dedicated their warrior status.

LBM wanted to kill George Armstrong Custer for the violence of his attacks on the Cheyenne. However, as Jack Crabb, nineteenth century American, he acknowledges the generals' battle drill and his well-crafted persona of a leader of presidential caliber. Custer was his own man, not in any sense a sycophant. He lived, not just flaunted, his ambition. His generals hated him for his self-promotion, which included designing his own uniform. Jack admires the strenuous effort and lonely idealism of the man, alone in his universe in a way his own mentor, Old Lodge Skins, need never find himself in his. Indian leaders are not punished for their success by incurring envy, because they have proven their Great Spirit-given preeminence before their fellow warriors' eyes.

The Indian's nomadic life, the grease and body aromas of the lodges, and the scolding squaws, cannot compare with the nexus of comfort and upward mobility in Denver, since Crabb had discovered an ambition for material security there. He might even run for governor, where perhaps his tribal knowledge would make him a valuable negotiator with the Red Man. But on his return to visit Old Lodge Skins, to warn the Cheyenne to move to safety from the prospectors and troopers, he was "greeted dear as I ever experienced...I knowed [sic] nonetheless that I could never be an Indian again." It points up the dual nature of the man.

The perceptive contrasts Jack makes between Indian and American responses to other people are partial to the Indian. Indians are more "natural" than white men. Indians do not need a persona behind which a fragmented self exists, making difficult any coherent definition of who one is. For the Cheyenne Human Beings, that definition is simply one's place in the tribe. They are free from shame, jealousy, and frustrations that are inherent even in a White Man's proudest achievement, the kind Custer must strive for and then prove again and again. Jack bases these observations on his experience as an American trail guide, mule train driver, businessman, worker on the Transcontinental Railway, and scout for Custer. He has fully experienced both a tribal and a lone individual cultural orientation.

- Americans expect to be deceived by others; Indians assume their fellow tribesmen protect each other. They "can't get away from obligation."
- Pleasure at hearing of others' misfortune is a white man's trait. A tribe's braves see one person's misfortune as an injury to all.
- White men have a pervasive prurient interest in smut. They love dirty stories; the knowledge that they are tabooed as "indecent" is a key element in their enjoyment, as is their deceitful boasting about their conquests. This is one example of the Indian being more "natural" than the White.
- Indians look forward to war, a test of skill and a blessed way to end a warrior's life. Whites hate war and fear dying in battle. To them, a death song is a perversion of human nature, a fatalistic acceptance of defeat.
- The Cheyenne enjoy killing enemies spontaneously. American troopers jeer and curse their victims to enhance their own prowess and prepare for their next success. In the case of Bill Hickok, his killings have earned him national fame. Their long acquaintance ends with Jack's realization that Wild Bill's strut, fine clothes, world-class

gun handling, and dance hall conviviality were all part of a persona in which he had trapped himself. He "never enjoyed anything." "He referred to himself like he was an institution...Wild Bill Hickok, Incorporated." It was another proof than Indians were freer than whites.

The Eternal Return

On one remarkable occasion, Jack discovers in the Cheyenne village the wife and son he lost when the family fled the debts with which Jack had been saddled in Denver. The son is now a robust five years old; the wife is married to a warrior. A delicate negotiation takes place. Jack, assuming his LBM persona once again, claims marriage to the young woman and access to her two sisters. He has sex with each of them. The youngest, soon after that night's intercourse, goes out into the snow and, in the thick darkness, gives birth. She places the child in LBM's arms. Here was an experience gifting him with joy, peace, and freedom. On display is Indian culture's gender stratification, sense of self, patterns of love making, and child rearing; that is, its habitus. A star appears, changing through a rainbow of "marvelous colors." Jack has a sense of all-inclusive power. This is his "medicine."

> *I knew where the center of the world was* [italics in text]. A remarkable feeling, which time turns in a circle, and he who stands at the core has power over everything...Like Old Lodge Skins drawing in them antelope within the little circle of his band, but concentric around them was all other Cheyenne, present and past, living and ghost, for the Mystery is continuous.

The philosopher Mircea Eliade has a name for this: The

Myth of the Eternal Return.[98] In it, there is no history in the sense that Messianic religions conceive of it as a progression through centuries, with a final Armageddon, Judgment, and Heaven or Hell. The earthly world is marvelous because mythological beings that eternally exist can be recognized in it, at its center. That frees human beings from loneliness and imbues the mundane with the divine. "Myths describe...breakthroughs of the sacred (or the 'supernatural') into the World," Eliade states.

Jack ends his epic with the death song of Old Lodge Skins, which occurs when Jack recalls LBM climbing with his mentor above the timber line. It is hard to imagine a more plangent, transcendent moment. As Old Lodge Skins shouts the Cheyenne battle cry, "His blind eyes was [sic] crying with the ferocious fun of it, his old body shaking." "Bold and free," he prayed to the Everywhere Spirit, thanking him for the many days when it was "good for [his enemies] to die," "for the many women [he had] loved," and for one last victory over the white men by the "human beings," "proud and bold and vengeful." He sings into the sudden thunder, there at the center of the world, shedding "tears of joy." LBM builds a scaffold for his true father's body, and "started down the mountain in the fading light." He knew the mysteries of the earth and sky. As Little Big Man, he had abjured, as Old Lodge Skins had, the white men who built railroads, extracted gold and silver from the earth, cultivated the land, killed buffalo, and drove cattle, all the time "hating life."[99]

---

[98] The Myth of the Eternal Return or, Cosmos and History, 1954, rpt Princeton U Press, 1974.

[99] The sequel, published almost forty years later, is entitled *The Return of Little Big Man*. He narrates as the nineteenth century American, Jack Crabb. Jack compares the people who came to the west to "wander" unfavorably to those who came to raise families. He gets a job at a school for Indian boys, interpreting for them the directions the principal gives. He makes sure to substitute for "you must obey" the admonition that the students must learn English or "bring shame to their families." Jack admires Sitting Bull's skill as a "farmer." (His tribe had no choice after federal troops' attacks on their

"Property is Power" vs "Great Wisdom"

Their coveted reward for the strenuous effort was their future plans for keeping and improving upon what they already had. All-important was their property, and their emulation, as far as they could, of those who had it. Property is power. The settlers, especially after the Civil War, were all "Sooners" in that they felt the places they wanted to plant crops, graze animals, build houses, and establish roads were theirs as Americans, even if the federal government had not yet officially proclaimed they could do so.[100] There was no exit from that barreling express. Examples of the power of property are Crabb's deceptive Denver business partners, the railroad tycoon in *Once Upon a Time in the West* who had whole families killed so he could one day see the Pacific from his parlor car, and Custer, avid to get Indians confined to reservations as quickly as seemed possible, and thus clear a path to the White House, the ultimate property, for himself. Mark Twain's, and Robert Coover's, Tom Sawyer is an epitome of this kind of Americanism. Coover has him proposing to kill all the Indians to make way for the Grand Scheme of what God had manifestly ordained, American control of land from coast

---

villages.) A member of Buffalo Bill's Wild West show as it traveled Western Europe, Jack praises Bill's entertainment strategies, noting that the Indians in the show acted out all the qualities that the spectators wanted displayed by "savages." Crabb does deplore the American preplanned murders of Sitting Bull and Crazy Horse, although he accepts Buffalo Bill's explanation for displaying in his Wild West Show Crazy Horse's cabin, without mentioning the disfiguring of the chief's face after his death. As for Wounded Knee, Crabb caustically remarks it was "a satisfactory result for the civilized."

---

[100] Patricia N Limerick, The Legacy of Conquest: The Unbroken Past of the American West (NY: Norton, 1987), p.58.

to coast. Someday, our historians could build a museum to honor the redskins as forbears, opined Huck's pard,

LBM's mentor's joy in his last moments may allude to that of Fennimore Cooper's Chingachgook, the last of the Mohicans, who allowed a fire to consume his seventy-year old body. "He considers this as the happiest moment of his life." We've seen these revelations of "great wisdom," the opposite of the twentieth century "failure story," in such country noirs as Brown's *Dirty Work*, where the limbless Vietnam vet Braiden creates a harmonious world of African tribalism inside his head and smiles at angels. David Joy's *Where All Light Tends to Go* ends with its protagonist choosing a resting place between an afterlife and the North Carolina town which has made him a pariah. In Peter Heller's *The Painter*, a famous artist is offered a new kind of peace, if he is worthy of it, by a man from the Colorado woodlands whose brother he killed. With the same kind of wisdom, the Rastafarian outcasts magically redeem guilt-ridden Pete in Harry Crews' *Scar Lover*, giving him the strength to join the "strangely beautiful" woman who has singled him out for her love.

Chris Offutt's "The Leaving One" (in *Kentucky Straight*) ends with what looks like a direct allusion to the final pages of *Little Big Man's* great wisdom. Vaughn's grandfather, Lige, has been living in the woods since being ostracized from the family for insulting a clergyman. He dresses in buckskins and has learned to survive by observing the animals around him. He takes Vaughn deep in the woods, sings a peon to the "eyes in the woods," and dies. Vaughn finds his way back home by following the direction of a mysterious force, possibly Lige's spirit. Here is the opposite kind of power from that of the white men of America and Europe, who live within a very different *Weltanschauung*. For us, property is restorative power.

Contemporary Native American poet Mark Turcotte, in the autobiographical *The Feathered Heart*, writes of an unnamed spirit's "ancient alien frequency," contrasting it to sirens, radio static, urban signage, and factories. He hears the power of legendary chiefs, "the endless Others," and joins them "dancing toward the rhythm of life" as he had done as a child.

> I'm praying
> to vanish
> Into the gray Gods dancing
> before my eyes.

The Leatherstocking Tales and Little Big Man

Little Big Man, as an epic of the clash of Indian and expanding American cultures, has an antecedent in James Fennimore Cooper's *Leatherstocking Tales* (five novels, published 1823—41). They tell of the courage, woodsman's skills, and moral acuteness of Natty Bumppo, who grew up among the Delaware, and was honored with names such as Deerslayer and Hawkeye. His mentor and spiritual brother is Chingachgook. The name means Big Serpent because of his sagacity in battle. It may also refer to the eternal circle of the Everywhere Spirit, at the sacred center of the natural world. Natty is not as deferential to the Indian vision of the cosmos as is LBM. He was taught about Heaven and Hell by a Moravian minister, slightly similar to Crabb's Reverend Pendrake. He realizes, like LBM, that he could never discard his faith in a Christian universe of progression from a fallen earthly world to a supernal one. Richard Slotkin explains that Indians fetishize the hunt, which "completes the hoop of the world and joins man forever to the god of nature."[101] Christian redemption, in essential contrast, comes through struggle against the "natural" world. It requires baptism and absolution. Natty sees himself as a "man without a cross," meaning that he

---

[101] Regeneration Through Violence: The Mythology of the American Frontier, 1600-1860, p.490-91

has avoided acts of sin such as tribal raids, torture of captives, and feral sexual appetite, including rape, for which tribal people will suffer in Hell if they do not repent before God's throne.

Chingachgook is a more vulnerable and less majestic figure than Old Lodge Skins. He is the last of his race, i.e. the Mohicans; his son has been killed in battle. Heartbroken, he is nevertheless a constant companion of Natty, a hunter who has valued the Native Americans' honesty, pride, and mystic reverence for the game they kill. Natty also has spent a large part of his life in the woods. He kills game without respect for white settlers' legal restrictions. These laws make food less available to those who depend on it and more the property of a privileged class. The aristocratic Judge Marmaduke Temple suspects Natty of being seduced by the pleasures of the hunt. At one point, he has him put in the stocks for lack of commitment to restraining his appetite for the hunt. Natty tells Temple, "One old law," the one that respects a hunter's right to claim a kill as his property, "is worth two new ones." This is fundamental to hunters, be they Indians, mountain men, or trailblazers. Natty, like Daniel Boone, wanted to settle, to cultivate, but with a democratic fairness that a monied aristocracy resists, wishing for an alteration of law that favors themselves. They are avid to control whatever will allow them to maintain their eminence.

When Natty refuses the Temple family's offer to live on their estate, it may be due to his fundamental conception of the conditions that make freedom possible. That belief characterizes a diverse group of proud loners: the misanthropic isolate Boone Caudill; the racist Amos Edwards; mountain man Jim Bridger and the revenant, Hugh Glass; Matt Phillips's Packard (*Accidental Outlaws*); Denis Johnson's *Jesus' Son*; Harry Crews' forlorn, suicidal snake handler Joe Don Looney; certainly Rudolph Wurlitzer's Zebulon (*The Drop Edge of Yonder*); and even Carolyn Chute's Jim Drummond, member of the radical right assassination cult, the eponymous Snow Men. Natty and Chingachgook are social isolates from the dominant culture like them.

Chingachgook's life and the lives of his tribe have a coherent vitality lacking in a nation where so many people center life around an acquisitiveness which makes contact with other people a kind of tentative bargain. *The Last of the Mohicans* contains several examples, such as Hurry Harry and the pirate Hutter, who steal scalps for affluent white collectors of rare curiosities. They are the counterparts of the businessmen who cheat Jack Crabb and leave the enterprises' debts to him, and of the swindler Meriweather, who must "observe the code of my profession, or I cannot live with myself." By code he means a successful deception. Conning others is his religion.

The Pioneers features a tavern scene that makes clear why both Natty and Chingachgook choose to live apart from the town where they find themselves, and in which they are shunned as dirty and inept rustics. After Natty rejects the judge's offer of a comfortable old age as his guest on his estate, the company at the inn entertains itself with a song. At this point a deep and vibrant voice rises. It is Chingachgook, shining forth from "John Mohegan," as he has been derisively named by the townspeople, because his rugged clothes, rustic manners, and drunken stares have disconcerted them. The voice irritates in its unfamiliarity, its volume, its uncouth reverberations. The full force of the Mohican spirituality is before them. Cooper tells us about the "brutal ferocity" his muscles suggest, the tenor of "wild melancholy" in his voice, the alternating "low, quivering" and "elevated" notes, the "vacant countenance" and "wild, bushy hair." The similarity to Old Lodge Skins' war song ("hey hey hey hey") is clear. Natty breaks in to restore his friend to the mundane confinements of the tavern. Chingachgook, the last of his tribe, had been displaying for Americans the habitus of a civilization which lived in the center of the world and worshipped a tangible Great Spirit of the wind and rain. About a century later, and for not much longer, this universe was still alive for Old Lodge Skins, and appreciated by LBM, as it had been for Natty Bumppo.

Nomadland

To conclude with *Nomadland*, the book and film, fits a study that begins with *Beasts of the Southern Wild*. The reason is the threat, the Aurochs. In *Beasts*, they were prehistoric predators. The most technologically sophisticated barriers have not stopped them. That is left to a girl from an isolated rural community who has learned, together with her people, to stand up and stare down. What the Aurochs symbolize is left to the viewer's imagination. In *Nomadland*, the predatory force, which mounted a ferocious strike against the people of America, is the crash of 2008. It was marked by predatory lending, taking advantage of people who never thought they could own a home. The Glass-Steagall Act, enacted after the bank failures of the Depression, had separated investment from commercial banking. The act had prevented using clients' deposits to make investments. It was "partially" repealed in 1999. That was when the investment banks offering mortgages began targeting people who did not have the expertise to spar with the banks' representatives. Nor could they pay for the lawyers who could. When they couldn't pay their escalating mortgage bills, the result was foreclosure, and more property for the investment bankers.

Many well-off Americans, who knew how to manage their way through the financial system, blamed those who defaulted on their mortgages, rather than the investment bankers. Their victims' hatred of the government which had abandoned them grew as they observed that none of the investment bankers, however enriched by their machinations, went to jail. Some homeowners, faced with humiliating eviction and facing repossession, trashed their houses and moved away. No American Dream for them. They had been cheated of their property, after all the promises to be able to point to home ownership as evidence of an American success story. Others adapted creatively, as

Bathsheba taught Hushpuppy to do. "Everything just was, and you had to deal with it," as Sheldon Compton said in his novel *Brown Bottle*. They became "houseless but not homeless," moving into inexpensive vans (as distinguished from pricey RVs). Picking up the pieces after the storm, they drove those vehicles (named Van Halen, The Squeeze Inn, The Manatee, or Swankie Wheels) throughout the parts of West the prairie schooners once navigated.

Chloé Zhao's 2020 film *Nomadland* dramatizes this example of American perseverant ingenuity, using a protagonist with a defiant bullshit detector who, like Harry Crews and his characters, "stands up to life and spits in its face." Which is not a bad description of what Hushpuppy, her father, and her mentor do. "It's better to be poor," declared Daniel Woodrell, "than to be beholden." Houseless but not homeless Americans keep away from consumer culture with its endless pressure to acquire goods, property, status, and "good taste," all of which is touted by celebs as "priceless." "You deserve it." If you can keep it. That warning established itself in the foreground of the average consumer's consciousness. Something else was more significant to a nomadlander: self-sufficiency.

Equality, Personal Initiative, Togetherness: "See You Down the Road"

I'll begin with Jessica Bruder's Nomadland, which The New York Times cited as a "Notable Book" when it appeared in 2017. It is about van dwellers whose nomadic travels took them throughout the vast western part of the country. They took part-time work, learning how to repair their vehicles and appliances on their own, using all their strength to circumvent a system that had driven them off the grid. Like Hushpuppy, they engaged instead with a community of helpers, teachers, and friends who recognize and empathize with other nomads they "see down the road." Mutual help, not contending for control, is the article of faith. Nomadland is therefore like the Bathtub. Everyone is equal. That ideal is what motivated Daniel Boone to found Boonesborough after wealthy landowners closed off hunting grounds. Van-dwelling nomads are a version of the pioneer, a fact brilliantly depicted by both Bruder and Zhao. Their energy, indomitable perseverance, reckless courage, and knowledge of the territory is what is important, and one hopes, quintessentially American: self-reliance in pursuit of freedom.

Bruder, with her own van, interviewing skills, and canny use of social media, gained the trust of the houseless. They told her about what set them on their travels and where they were at present. For Bob Wells, founder of the Rubber Tramp Rendezvous, that ride began with a heavy load. He faced divorce, had two children, and worked low-paying jobs with no safety net. His budget was seriously compromised just by the fuel he needed to get to work. He bought a used truck and despaired at first. Then self-reliance surfaced. He built a bed and a small kitchen in the truck. His water supply came from public places, such as restrooms. A propane-driven heater kept him warm. He parked near a Safeway so that he was first in line for overtime pay if someone called in sick. He was back in control of his life.

This kind of self-conceived response to an Auroch-sized hurdle is like Robert Grainier's in Denis Johnson's *Train Dreams*. After a fire destroyed his home, taking his wife and child, he found the smoking ruin and built a lean-to, bought chickens and fuel, labored part time in exchange for firewood, and built a cabin in the spot where his house had been. It's also like Ree Dolly's perseverance in Woodrell's *Winter's Bone*. Needing proof of her father's death, she braved the fearsome drug dealers for whom he had worked, and who had murdered him for withholding cash from them. She made them see what having to lose her house meant to her and her child. They showed her where her father's body was so she could take fingerprints. Finally, it's also like Kit Carson's daughter in John Keeble's novel *The Appoint-*

ment. She needs to prove herself capable of helping an Oregon-bound wagon train ford a river, recover upended wagons, and sit tight, readying for a fight to the death if a band of Cheyenne decide to attack. Bob Wells came into his own in the same way the three smart and gutsy pragmatists just mentioned do. Rejuvenated, he started "CheapRVLiving.com." Emails from van dwellers with his own level of ingenuity convinced him that houseless living was not just a temporary fix for his country's economic malfeasance but a way of attaining independence from rent or mortgage bondage. What respondents had figured out included how to shower at truck stops, get online by telephone, install solar panels, find wholesome food, repair appliances and cars, and park in areas welcoming to van life. Van dwellers could become a tribe. Bob's Rendezvous confirmed that. It became an annual holiday and hostel, with campfires, songs, lectures, demonstrations, and social mixing that led to friendships and courting. Bruder characterizes Bob as a kind of "evangelist" for a community life. Helping each other solve common problems carried some of the import of Miss Bathsheba's teaching: "You better learn how to survive." As one blogger put it, "I feel that I am camping and do not consider myself homeless. This is a sign of things to come and we will be seeing people living in tents and vehicles everywhere."

Van dwelling is one consequence of the "De-territorialization" mentioned in Chapter 1. This phenomenon connotes the effect on the psyche when someone has to leave a place which can no longer provide opportunity to sustain him or her, as it had done for predecessors. The uprooted lack the dress, vocabulary, income level, leisure activities, and educational status that are marks of urban habitus. The Aurochs, the Beasts of the Southern Wild, in this case come in the form of socioeconomic factors beyond family or town control, such as costs of health care, decaying infrastructure, Big Agriculture's copyrighting of seed, as well as the racketeering of investment banks and their mortgage foreclosures. In his "Trilobites," Breece Pancake's protagonist anticipates the sad awareness of becoming such a stranger: "I'll spend overnight at home. I've got eyes to shut in Michigan—maybe even Germany or China, I don't know yet." Bruder's book shows how houseless denizens such as Swankie, Linda May, or Jen and Ash have found ways to circumvent the loss of home and loved ones.

"A Bigger, More Various, Less Finished Self," Part 1

"Come to the desert or forest and live with your own people who love and care about you." There is a true civility in the phrase "See you down the road." Bruder's insights into some remarkably independent Nomandlanders' joys and ambitions are really the heart of her book:

Chere: Selling her house after the crash for about half of what it was worth before, Chere lives in a Ford van, which she has made into her "mansion." She displays goods at a swap meet so she can park there. Her clothes are packed in plastic bags. At restaurants, she saves part of the meal and the ice water. She can't imagine why anyone would want to live in a "concrete jungle."

Charlene Swankie: Swankie supplied her van with appliances she could use when her engine was running. She explained to whomever asked about the procedure by which one could relieve oneself on cold nights by using a large enough bucket. A fan and solar panel were fastened to her roof. Charlene had kayaked in all fifty states and had a map to prove it. Knowing she had only months to live, she had driven to Alaska, wanting to see wildlife there. When Swankie died, the nomads met to grieve.

Jen and Ash: The pair lives in a camper van. Jen had watched her parents work in a grocery chain with no pension. She often heard her college graduate friends complain about their debt, not being able to find full-time jobs with benefit plans. Those jobs available had been "reclassified" as lower salaried. That was also Ash's problem. To paraphrase the couple, to hell with "disposable jobs for disposable people." Their part-time work at an Amazon warehouse, with free overnight parking, is a feature of van living for many nomads. Categorizing the items could be eye-opening and fun, especially the "adult novelties." Speaking of fun, seeing it in quandaries is something nomads just do. For Jen and Ash, two examples Bruder cites were biking to the "Amazombie" warehouse as the sun rose and holding their feet over a propane heater to watch their sweat evaporate into steam. It's the little things, especially if they are toes, that count.

Linda May: Bruder's treatment of this middle-aged woman is detailed, perhaps because, despite having a past of drug and alcohol abuse, she represents a need for togetherness with and trust of people around her. She has an acute sense of the comfort togetherness brings. When homeless people used the outdoor spigots at her carpet shop and slept on the porch, she gave them job titles so they would not be arrested. When she was a Home Depot cashier, she chatted up customers about their needs so she could redirect them to the best products for their needs. She was a cigarette girl at a gambling venue, and, after that occupation was superseded by vending machines, a cocktail waitress. Despite all this creative, on-the-job effort, no employer had any pension or savings plan for her. She worked, part time of course, in an Amazon warehouse, finding, as did Jen and Ash, that "the best thing about the job was the camaraderie. I made friends everywhere." At sixty, her repetitive, muscle-straining Amazon "CamperForce" experience was bitter but surviving it gave her a sense of self-sufficiency. She moved on to the Rubber Tramp Rendezvous, joining others willing to jostle for a van space on the city limits of dusty, crowded Quartzite, Arizona. The routine included showering at a laundromat, scouting for used goods displayed outside vans and refurbished school buses, and making do with inexpensive comfort food. The reward was the social leveling and the rallies: whatever you have, you're welcome. "Thank goodness for the varied tribes out there that offer so much guidance, advice, stuff, and willing ears," said one RV'er who had been fighting MS but still wanted control of her life. She studied the techniques, skills, and patience needed to function with the useful discards of the consumer class, much like the people of the Bathtub could, and still be positive, as she always had been.

Bruder compares the Quartzite scene with the boom towns of the old west, with "pioneers swarming the site." Sometimes, such places, as in Doctorow's *Welcome to Hard Times*, were hammered to dust by cutthroat competition and betrayal. But Bruder's reference to the van dwellers as present-day resilient pioneers' echoes Griel Marcus's description of "The Old, Weird America" in his book with that title. It features folksongs about heroes who started by recognizing how the wilderness can be lived with and made hospitable. If that wilderness can be compared to the Amazon warehouse, the Safeway and its parking lot, the Planet Fitness and its showers, and the tattered American safety net with its ludicrous Social Security system, then Bruder's comparison is both grim and buoyant at the same time. The Nomadland she delineates is the beginning of something: the kind of humanity that the earth is for.

"A Bigger, More Various, Less Finished Self," Part 2. The Vanguard

Chloé Zhao's film *Nomadland* is a very different experience than Bruder's book.[102] The latter is about people, like the pioneers in their covered wagons, who have gotten where they set out to go, or have at least stood up to their nemesis (or their Aurochs, if

---

[102] I would like to thank Domenic Stansberry, Edgar Award-winning crime novelist, for his poetic and incisive response to my Instagram post on *Nomadland*, March 18, 2021.

you will), and halted its depredation. "After a lifetime of chasing the American Dream, [my people] had come to the conclusion that it was all a big lie," says one of Bruder's interviewees. The book ends with Linda May looking at the clearing in the Arizona desert where she wants to build her Earthship house. Zhao concludes with her heroine Fern visiting, probably for the last time, the house where she and her deceased husband were happy. She is driving across the sand and rock badlands toward the mountain range she loved to stare at from her home's kitchen window. Notably, she's facing west, "somewhere back in that vast obscurity beyond the city, where the dark fields of the republic rolled on under the night" (Fitzgerald, *The Great Gatsby*, Figure 10-2).

Zhao's background colors, i.e., the film's "palette," can be described as "low mist" (the title of one of Ludovico Einaudi's compositions on the soundtrack, from his album *Seven Days Walking*). The soft piano chords imply isolation. It's usually either dawn or dusk. Low lights in the distance might border on the badlands, previously known as "The Great American Desert" (filming was in South Dakota, Arizona, Nevada, Nebraska, and California). There are several night scenes, with neon marking restaurants, bars, or motels. The first episode is at Christmas, with Fern driving to the Amazon CamperForce parking lot. Snow sits on the roadside; one could imagine the mud and ice being a shadowy omen, visible despite the dull light.

The ambience reflects Fern's own state of mind. She cannot bring herself to go to a more comfortable climate, although she would save in heat and gas. She is not yet ready to break the emotional tie to her home in Empire, Nevada. Nor can she trade in her vehicle, which she has dubbed Vanguard, for one in better shape, because she "*lives* in it" (italics mine). She has contrived to elevate her bed and thus create storage space for keepsakes her father and husband gave her. Here we are reminded of Linda May's tattoo: "Is home just a word or is it something you carry within you?" For most van dwellers this is a prideful declaration, but Fern cannot yet abandon the beloved remnants of her past. Linda, Bob, and Swankie have fulfilled their search for a new identity; Fern is still on her way. Although capable of enjoying other people's company, she cannot make satisfaction in camaraderie her endpoint. I've mentioned D. H. Lawrence stating the American need for wandering and discovery as "the sloughing off of the old skin, toward a new youth. It is the myth of America." That image captures the process Fern is undergoing. Other narratives capturing it include Steph Post's *Lightwood*, Peter Heller's *The Painter*, Denis Johnson's *Jesus' Son*, David Joy's *The Line That Held Us* and *Where All Light Tends to Go*, and Harry Crews' *Scar Lover*. All seek, and some find, that "bigger, more various, less finished [solidified] self."

I said earlier the major tenet of the Rubber Trampers is "see you down the road." Zhao makes it the mantra of the heroic and deeply spiritual Bob Wells, founder of the Rendezvous. He did so after his son's suicide because he knows he will see his son again. Helping others cope with low-wage temp jobs and inadequate Social Security, about which congressional legislators have done so little, will bring that mysterious moment closer. It allows him to understand how he can be on this earth when his son is not.

Zhao writes a conversation occurring near the film's end, where Bob is able, for the first time, and in Fern's presence, to speak about the suicide of his son, whom he believes he will see again "somewhere down the road." That homecoming will be a mystic experience, in an otherworldly territory. He founded his Rendezvous to help others cope. He is sure his success will bring that mysterious moment closer. Zhao focused on Wells more than Bruder did to accentuate the contrast between his goal of tribal togetherness and Fern's quest. Her gestures and facial expressions, as well as the sunless, empty road, depict loneliness and continued struggle. She is often alone, washing clothes in a laundromat, exploring giant Sequoias, walking in twilight among buzzing insects, eating in an empty diner, or hastily leaving a parking lot in which she has been forbidden to park. In the film, she quotes two Shakespearian passages to teenagers, one her niece. The first is the "Tomorrow and tomorrow" speech from *MacBeth* (desolation, meaninglessness, one aspect of uprootedness and isolation). Later she recites Sonnet 18, beginning, "Shall I compare thee to a summer's day…So long lives this, and this gives life to thee," with its substitution of a cold artifact (the poem) for the loved one herself. The teenagers to whom Fern is speaking are appreciative, but the quotes are really conversation stoppers to people too young to have faced the problems the nomads have. Fern is searching for another dimension of existence.

Zhao has said of the scene where she is walking among the rocks in the Badlands with David, at their jobs as summer hosts for tourists, that Fern is "exploring and lost at the same time."[103] She's still sloughing off the old skin. The "new youth" is not yet at hand. With her singularly obsessive and narrowly focused determination, she must continue to be a stranger in wide open spaces. When friends and relatives ask if she needs help, she replies she is "good."

Maybe she is not ready to stare into, and stare down, the grief of her husband Bo's death, as Bob has done with the loss of his son. Moved by his confession, she goes back to Empire, knowing Bo and the neighbors are gone. After running her hand over the kitchen counter and looking at the view from the window, she drives on.[104] If this visit is her last, she may have been on the way to extirpating the "twisted sorrow" of homelessness.

---

[103] https://www.nytimes.com/video/movies/100000007612918/nomadland-scene.html?searchResultPosition=6 Google "Nomadland: Anatomy of a Scene"

[104] In January 2011, when US Gypsum closed down the mine due to reduced demand for sheetrock, CNBC reported that the company had installed a chain-link fence around the perimeter of the town, and "its roughly 300 residents were told to pack up and leave."

Bruder's book concludes with Linda's dream that will end her homelessness, the Earthship, about to come true. By contrast, in the last frames of the film, its protagonist is still alone, an aloneness which is noble in its determination. Low-volume, contemplative piano music, generating sympathy, accompanies fadeout.

Fern as Social Isolate: Freedom from the "Big Fear"

Fern has two invitations to end her solitary travels and live in comfort with congenial people. The fact that she does not accept either one indicates her difference from other van dwellers, in that being with good friends and family is a desired result of their mobility. Fern would probably have accepted an invitation to be with Linda May, or Swankie, but does not seek one. One invitation is from taciturn, gentle David ("I like you. You're a good person"). David is not the type to pursue further what looks like indifference. The other offer was from her sister Dolly. Fern tells her she cannot sleep in the room, or in the bed, where she slept growing up. A somewhat darkened family photo shows unsmiling adults. Fern left home "as soon as [she] could," marrying a few months after meeting Bo. She "left a big hole" in Dolly's life. "You were braver and more honest than everybody else. And you could see me when I was hiding from everybody. And sometimes you could see me before I saw myself." Fern replies, "That one's [early departure from the nest] on me."

If the van nomads can be likened to the nineteenth century pioneers, Fern is yet another of that distinctive type of Western adventurer, the social isolate. The Rubber Trampers' camaraderie had made her day but was no more than a nudge driving her forward. The film's closure is like that of Williams's novel *Butcher's Crossing*, where the protagonist, Will Andrews, chooses to leave town, without a clear destination. "It would come to him...He felt behind him the sun slowly rise and harden the air." What motivates Fern is similar to what isolates other country noir isolates. They all stubbornly prioritize an understanding of how they are comfortable behaving. That means discarding a persona, or mask, that projects to the world someone other people can trust, and therefore accept a person as "one of us." The social isolates of the West have in common with Zhao's Fern a need to move beyond the persona of rancher, frontier wife, Indian fighter, homesteader, shootist, gambler, dance hall proprietor or hostess, toward a "new youth." That freedom means a desire to explore yet undefined possibilities, and the belief that the unknown might yield a more fulfilling experience than life as part of a social unit. Such explorers try to use the "dark fields of the Republic" to find themselves. These seekers eschew identifying themselves by the steady job that has become their life, whether they are their own boss, or work as part of a larger entity, such as the real estate business that provides sister Dolly's husband with his family's living. William Gay, in his *Provinces of Night*, has a character observe how "the jobs folks have [are] those curious restorers of order." The job gives them community status, helps give them a political stance, determines the kind of security they want their children to aspire to, and allows them to decide to whom they can offer respect, friendship, or charity. When, at a family party, Fern points out to a real estate agent the hardships of raising mortgage payments, she is stepping out of her place. There is an embarrassed silence.

Jack Crabb had realized white settlers adopt patterns of behavior that could tie them irrevocably to the expectations of people they worked and lived with. Nor could they expect their fellow citizens to admire them without at least a tinge of resentment and envy. It was too bad that the Reverend Pendrake, Wild Bill Hickok "Incorporated," and General Custer could not detach themselves from their personas long enough to enjoy their status. In Fern's case, since she could no longer live in harmony with Bo, she had dedicated herself to fostering the newly emerging self.

Classifying Fern as a social isolate puts her in a diversified company. To review: Natty Bumppo rejected a comfortable life on an admiring aristocrat's estate to live in the woods and blaze trails through them. He died that way, facing west. Russell Banks's Merle, in "The Fisherman," has the same practical skills to refurbish his Bob House that Fern learns in making her Vanguard livable. Both Merle's and Fern's dwellings are free from any hint of stylish trappings. Merle is so alienated from the cash nexus that he throws to the wind the big bills he won in a lottery, allowing his trailer park neighbors to slip and slide on the ice to gather them in. No tyranny of the dollar for him, or for Fern, as she explains when the subject of investment bank mortgages comes up. Merle is fixated on his Bob House tasks, as Fern is on her van, as both places contain what is deeply personal for themselves alone. And Merle would say, along with Fern, "I'm all right." Swankie had said the same when she did not want to be disturbed. Swankie also valued her privacy, almost as much as Merle. She drove to Alaska alone, seeking a new discovery, as Fern is doing, heading toward the Nevada mountains. One hopes Fern is not fated to wander between two worlds. Like *Train Dreams'* protagonist Robert Grainier, she returns to where she and her spouse were happy, not to sentimentalize but to experience for a second time a loss which cannot be put into words, that is, cannot be reasoned with. Like Rudolph Wurlitzer's mountain man Zebulon Shook (*The Drop Edge of Yonder*), she is enigmatic. Zebulon keeps as far as possible from "know-nothing eastern greenhorns honking the arrival of civilization and the dictates of the sabbath." He experiences everything in the way of thievery, murder, imprisonment, gold strikes, and the drunken mayhem of the Mountain Men's Rendezvous with a detachment ("come closer, stay away") like that of Fern: in her van, with David, and when she visits her sister's family. In Zebulon's case, that phrase becomes the only constant personality trait of an enigma who may have ended his days anywhere in the world from the high mountains of Colorado to the Aleutian Islands. Wurlitzer tells us that his death has never been documented. The last photo assumed to depict Zebulon has the face smudged beyond recognition.

While Fern does not rescue anyone, she is similar to Sergio Leone's Harmonica (*Once Upon a Time in America*), Jack Shaefer's Shane, and Huck Finn in that they must continue to ride alone, leaving behind people whom they love and who would be glad to include them in their circle. A weirder analogy would be to Calamity Jane, simply because of Calamity's determination (Figure 10-3). Examples from Dexter's *Deadwood* include unwrapping her broken leg from its hanging splint to exit a hospital, and convincing smallpox victims only she can save them. Her impervious individuality, symbolized by her deafening war whoop, scares hell out of tough cowboys, miners, homesteaders, saloon keepers, and their second-floor women.

The best exemplar of Fern is Ruby Tanner in Chris Offutt's "Back Porch" (in the collection *Appalachia Now*). She's as good an example of an "old, weird American" as are Johnson's Robert Grainier, Banks's fisherman, Franklin's Sketchy, Dexter's Calamity Jane, or Bruder's and Zhao's Swankie Wheels. She fulfills every bit of Harry Crews' assertion that "So far as I can see, nothing good in the world has ever been done by well-rounded people. The good work is done by people with jagged, broken edges, because those edges cut things and leave an imprint, a design…" The amoral, perfected self-possession of the social isolate is key.

Ruby, seventy-six, is returning to her birthplace in the Kentucky Appalachian foothills. The country was much different from New Mexico, where she spent the past half century. "Trees grew bigger, the undergrowth thicker, the shadows very black." Passing through Morehead, she notes the usual "miracle mile": car showrooms, motels, fast food strip malls, trailer parks, dollar stores, and billboards announcing all that working folks settle for. Ruby had not settled. Her folks had been "the wildest of the woods." Her taxi driver had been brought up in this lower middle class, conservative, small city setting. A compliant young man on the job and at home, he mentions how outlandish it is that Ruby, flying in from Arizona, has no luggage. She replies that she has no need for "junk from off." She watches him blush when she tells him that when she was fifty, she learned "the number of men I regretted sleeping with equaled the number of men I wished I'd slept with." Recognizing his shyness, she gives him a gesture he might use to give him the upper hand with his wife: move his finger in and out of his ear and notice the finger feels better than the ear. Ruby has been a sex worker.

Her encouragement probably does not sink in. When they arrive at the homestead, the oldest and most storied in the region, he will not drive across the stream to get to the house. Nor, gallantly, will he let her try to do it. She maces him and wades across the stream. He drives back to Morehead to inform the sheriff, hoping that she is the last of the Tanner clan. "People had been glad when they died off." Ruby, to him, is sheerly outrageous—was she coming on to him? "Go home to your wife," Ruby had told him. And he remembered the finger in the ear gesture. Her loneliness must have grown deeper when she remembered how many times she had said that.

In pain, she wades across the stream. Ruby, cancer-ridden, is coming home to die. In pain, but not in fear. She has stared it down, like Hushpuppy, Woodrell's Ree Dolly, Compton's Brown Bottle, Larry Brown's Walter, John Keeble's Adeline Carson, and even Denis Johnson's Bill Hudson, praying for someone else while walking toward the gas chamber. The closest comparison may be to Swankie, who, like Ruby, sets off on that long-desired journey although terminally ill. Fern and she are almost doubles of each other, as far as staring down The Big Fear is concerned. If Fern had not done so, she would not have pioneered as a Rubber Tramper, working at an Amazon Fulfillment Center and other grueling part-time jobs while meditating on where she might be going, her only assurance being that she was going alone, without even a pet dog for companionship.

No social isolate is susceptible to The Big Fear. They live and die on a plane of existence alien to the practical, rational, community-oriented one. Therefore, when the taxi driver refuses to drive across the stream, Ruby wades it herself. No social isolate would do as Peg does in *He Ran All the Way*, when, although moved by Nick's reaching out for compassion ("Nobody had ever touched her so deeply"), she stabs him out of loyalty to her family. Nor would a person who had learned anything from Pancho, the real protagonist of *Ride the Pink Horse*, do what Sailor did: kill the policeman who offered help if Sailor would trust him. Sailor had remained prisoner of what he learned on the streets: if someone offers trust, flee or fight. The gang is all you have.

The Tanner family is gone, but the land is holy and so is the house—which looks no doubt like those clapboard earth-leaning constructions with unstable brick chimneys on the front covers of country noir paperbacks (Figure 10-4). Offutt's last paragraphs tell of isolation and unity, emptiness and fullness. But now the mystery of what life can be envelopes her, as the trees drip rain. She is not lonely, worried, or sorry. Yesterday is discarded. Her bare feet sink into the loam. Ruby is of that earth, and of the wet weather and the hills themselves. There is uncanny light, faces from Ruby's past, and one at her back that awaits her. The latter is what Vaughn in Offutt's "The Leaving One" senses, directing him the way home. There are vivid elements of Hushpuppy in her, although the latter is young and energetic, and has a place in a coherent loving community. Ruby is alone, dying, and considered an outlier. What they have in common is force of will, and a social isolate's sense of self. Both have learned ways of behaving considered vulgar (Ruby's finger-in-the ear gesture and Hushpuppy's acceptance of the floating dance hall girls as "a heaven of mothers"). Both have a force of will that precludes twisted sorrow.

Ruby skims a stone across the water, as she had done as a child, sitting on the back porch of the now-empty house. She throws her hand in the air. She is who the earth is for. She's ready, as Fern is when she drives toward the mountains after saying her own goodbye to the house where she and Bo lived. Fern is still on her quest. But she, like Ruby, is free from "twisted sorrow." She is all right.

Figure 10-1: Cyrus Edwin Dalin, "Appeal to the Great Spirit."
American Wing, Metropolitan Museum, New York. 1913; cast
ca.1916.

(2020)

Figure 10-2: Final shot of *Nomadland*. Instead of looking through her kitchen window at the mountains beyond, Fern drives toward them. Directed by Chloe Zhao. Distributed by Searchlight Pictures.
https://medium.com/the-partnered-pen/nomadland-the-book-and-movie-e253c4044955

Figure 10-3: Calamity Jane.
https://www.deadwood.com/wp/wp-content/uploads/2017/07/calamity-jane.jpg

Figure 10-4: "The entry to the Appalachian foothills...had a foreboding quality, a warning to travelers that the world beyond was very different."—Chris Offutt, "Back Porch."
https://blueridgecountry.com/downloads/174/download/mounta in-homeplace-.jpg?cb=73871dbb54bffa02daff1c43d0a4ffe9

INDEX

A

B

C

D

E

F

Failure stories, 45, 51–56, 82, 94, 111, 120, 193, 235, 244
Fair Land, Fair Land. *See* Guthrie, A. B.
Fate, Cruel or Benevolent, 64
Faulkner, William, 61, 68, 158
Feathered Heart, The. See Turcotte, Mark
Femme fatale, 66, 104, 105, 112, 217
Fiesta, 95
First Day of Winter. See Pancake, Breece
Fisherman, The. See Banks, Russel
Fitzgerald, F. Scott, 52, 171
   The Great Gatsby, 37, 53, 106, 107, 255
Ford, John, 188
Fracking, 12
Franklin, Tom, 144, 220, 222, 224, 261
   Poachers, 23, 62, 132, 144, 151, 180
Freud, Sigmund, 104, 150
From Roughshod Camp to Gilded Age City, 195–200
From Here To Eternity. See Jones, James
Frontier marshall, 200-210

G

Gifford, Barry, 32, 34, 36, 66, 211, 217–19
   Wild at Heart, 111-14, 141, 217
Give Us a Kiss. See Woodrell,Daniel
Glass, Hugh, 17, 146, 171, 172, 173, 184, 187, 191, 246
Goodis, David, 49, 50, 51, 63, 69, 78
   Of Tender Sin, 153
   Street of No Return, 51, 144
Gothic, 32, 53, 67–69, 86, 112, 142, 144–53, 157–59, 178, 222
Grand Guignol, 79, 153
Great American Desert, 93, 96, 226, 255
Great Gatsby, The. See Fitzgerald, F. Scott

Honored Dead, The. See Pancake, Breece
Horseman, Pass By. See McMurty, Larry
Hot Spot, The. See Williams, Charles
Huck Finn, 103, 108–11, 147, 163, 187–88, 207, 261
Huck Out West. See Coover, Robert
Hud (film), 183
Hughes, Dorothy, 98, 113, 119
    Ride the Pink Horse, 91, 144, 163, 166, 263
Hushpuppy. *See Beasts of the Southern Wild*

I-J

I wish I were / I'm glad I'm not, 66
In the Dry. See Pancake, Breece
Jack Crabb, 235–41, 259
Jackson, Andrew, 186
James-Younger gang, 82, 193
James, Jesse, 17, 20, 32, 81
Jayhawkers, 193
Jen and Ash, 252-54
Jesus' Son. See Johnson, Denis
Johnny Got His Gun. See Trumbo, Dalton
Johnson, Denis, 32, 34, 37, 52-54, 63, 66, 68, 69, 73, 81–85,
98, 131, 222, 225, 262
    Angels, 33, 73-4, 79-80, 141, 148, 197
    Jesus' Son, 54, 148, 195, 224, 246, 256
    Largesse of the Sea Maiden, 65
    Train Dreams, 158-59, 250
Jones, James, 50, 52
    From Here to Eternity, 50
Joy, David, 18, 33, 53, 61, 66, 98, 127
    The Line That Held Us, 256
    Where All Light Tend To Go, 62, 65, 67, 117, 125, 141,
        163, 180, 244, 256

K

Keeble, John, 262
The Appointment, 19, 250
Keene, Day, 60
Kentucky Straight. See Offut, Chris
Kersh, Gerald, 69
Killer Inside Me, The. See Thompson, Jim
Kiss Tomorrow Goodbye. See McCoy, Horace
Kit Carruthers, 182, 186, 191
Kolakowski, Nick, 128, 130, 131

L

Lakota, 108, 110
Lansdale, J. R., 54, 68
Largesse of the Sea Maiden. See Johnson, Denis
Last Danger, The. See Barnes, Rusty
Last of the Mohicans. See Cooper, Fennimore
Latimer, Jonathan, 69
Lawrence, D. H., 53, 142, 144, 169, 180, 184, 256
Sloughing off the old skin, 143
Leatherstocking Tales. See Cooper, Fennimore
LeMay, Alan, 181
The Searchers, 164, 175, 177, 179, 188, 228
Leone, Sergio, 172, 182, 193-95, 261
Lightwood. See Post, Steph
Lincoln, Abraham, 109
Line That Held Us, The. See Joy, David
Lion Books, 78
Little Big Man, 142, 171, 178, 235–42, 244, 245

M

M'liss. See Harte, Bret

Mac Orlan, Pierre, 65, 67
MacDonald, Dwight
 masscult, 76, 77
Malick, Terrance, 180
 Badlands. *See* Badlands (film)
Maltese Falcon, The. *See* Hammett, Dashiell
Manifest Destiny, 135, 186
Martin, Dewey, 188
Masscult. *See* MacDonald, Dwight
Masters, Edgar Lee
 Spoon River Anthology, 134
May, Linda, 252, 253, 255, 258
McCarthy, Cormac, 61, 62, 158, 180, 191, 192, 222
 All the Pretty Horses, 164
 Blood Meridan, 152, 180, 187
 Child of God, 181
 No Country for Old Men, 132
 Outer Dark, 181
McCoy, Horace, 113
 Kiss Tomorrow Goodbye, 81, 84, 111
McDonagh, Martin
 Three Billboards Outside Ebbing Missouri, 54, 63, 131, 156,
  224
McMurty, Larry
 Horseman, Pass By, 183
Methamphetamine (Meth), 13, 17, 118, 129, 180
Methland. *See* Reding, Nick
Misfit, The. *See* O'Connor, Flannery
Miss Bathsheba. *See Beasts of the Southern Wilds*
Mitcham, Robert, 188
Morehead, KY, 261, 262
Mortgages, 130, 207, 248, 251, 259
Mountain Men, 4, 19, 20, 107, 108, 134, 170, 217, 246, 257
My Darkest Prayer. *See* Cosby, S. A.
Myth of the Eternal Return. *See* Eternal Return

N

O

Oxycontin, 12, 13, 21, 118, 130

P

Painter, The. See Heller, Peter
Pancake, Breece, 14, 26–31, 121, 145
    First Day of Winter, 30
    In the Dry, 29-30
    The Honored Dead, 17, 27, 173
    The Salvation of Me, 26
    Time and Again, 36
    Trilobites, 26, 251
    Past All Dishonor. See Cain, James M
Pendrake, Reverend, 237, 245, 259
Perkins, Michael, 69, 221
Phillips, Matt
    Accidental Outlaws, 37, 63, 225, 246
Pioneers, The. See Cooper, Fennimore
Poachers. See Franklin, Tom
Poe, Edgar Allen, 46, 158
Pollock, Donald Ray, 61, 128–29
Polonsky, Abe, 78
Pop 1280. See Thompson, Jim
Post, Steph, 36, 53, 59, 63, 69, 131, 167, 192, 224
    Lightwood, 14, 67, 117, 127, 167, 224, 256
Postman Always Rings Twice, The. See Cain, James M
Poverty, 11, 15, 45, 57, 63, 75, 117, 127, 166, 226
Power of the Dog, The. See Thomas, Savage
Presley, Elvis, 80, 86, 159
Pruitt, Eryk, 18, 58, 192
Punke, Michael
    The Revenant, 171, 187
Purdue Pharma, 12, 13, 21, *See* also Oxycontin

Q-R

S

Willeford, Charles, 64
Williams, Charles, 78, 113, 119
  Hill Girl, 54, 55
  The Hot Spot, 156
Williams, John
  Butcher's Crossing, 37, 54, 170, 258
Winter's Bone. See Woodrell, Daniel
Wister, Owen
  The Virginian, 133-35
Woodrell, Daniel, 3, 6, 31, 54, 59, 67, 120, 131, 135, 167, 192, 193, 249, 262
  Give Us A Kiss, 35, 67
  Joanna Stull, 65, 129, 130
  The Death of Sweet Mister, 36, 120
  The Outlaw Album, 36
  Winter's Bone, 14, 62, 65, 167, 250
Woolrich, Cornell, 51, 69, 78, 95, 113, 153, 158
World War II, 51, 57, 103, 105, 222
Wurlitzer, Rudolph, 54, 184, 260
  The Drop Edge of Yonder, 20, 62, 107, 246

Y-Z

Yeats, William, 7
Zebulon Shook, 108, 184, 246, 260
Zeitlin, Behn, 7, 23, 32, 38
Zhao, Chloe, 250, 254–57, 261
Zozobra, 93–98, 100 (silo)

ACKNOWLEDGMENTS

Grateful thanks to (in no particular order) Kurt Brokaw, Gary Lovisi, Eric Laursen, Mark SaFranco, James Sallis for powerful insights. The following writers discussed their work and the parameters they worked within while getting published: Rusty Barnes, Eric Beetner, Rick Ollerman, Scott Phillips, Eryk Pruitt, Charles Salzberg, as well as Steph Post. Also acknowledged in Chapter 2. I thank the following for allowing me to cite passages in their writing: James Sallis, Email to me, April 6, 2019 (see Chapter 9); Richard Helms for his observation on getting published (see Chapter 2); Domenic Stansberry, for his response to my Instagram post (see Chapter 10).

Photo Credit: Karin Thieme, Edgewater, NJ

JAY A. GERTZMAN has written on the distribution and censorship of erotic literature, the publisher Samuel Roth's unauthorized editions of *Lady Chatterley's Lover* and *Ulysses*, the publishing history of *Chatterley*, and the crime novels of David Goodis. His *Pulp According to David Goodis* was nominated for a 2019 Anthony Award in the category Best Critical or Non-Fiction Work. He has published on Western crime fiction in *Paperback Parade, Mystery Readers Journal, Tough* (website), *Down & Out Books Newsletter,* and Academia.com.

Made in United States
North Haven, CT
20 October 2022